# SOURCES OF KNOWLEDGE

# SOURCES *of* KNOWLEDGE

## On the Concept of a Rational Capacity for Knowledge

ANDREA KERN

●●●●●

*Translated by Daniel Smyth*

▌▌▌

Harvard University Press

*Cambridge, Massachusetts*
*London, England*
2017

An earlier version of this work was originally published as
*Quellen des Wissens: Zum Begriff vernünftiger Erkenntnisfähigkeiten,*
© Suhrkamp Verlag Frankfurt am Main 2006.

First printing

*Library of Congress Cataloging-in-Publication Data*
Names: Kern, Andrea, author.
Title: Sources of knowledge : on the concept of a rational capacity
for knowledge / Andrea Kern; translated by Daniel Smyth.
Other titles: *Quellen des Wissens.* English
Description: Cambridge, Massachusetts: Harvard University Press, 2017. |
"An earlier version of this work was originally published as *Quellen des Wissens:
Zum Begriff vernünftiger Erkenntnisfähigkeiten,* © Suhrkamp Verlag Frankfurt am Main
2006."—Title page verso. | Includes bibliographical references and index.
Identifiers: LCCN 2016015033 | ISBN 9780674416116 (hard cover: alk. paper)
Subjects: LCSH: Knowledge, Theory of. | Reason. | Error.
Classification: LCC BD181 .K3913 2017 | DDC 121/3—dc23
LC record available at https://lccn.loc.gov/2016015033

# Contents

# Introduction

## *"But We Can Always Err!"*

Modern epistemology begins with a line of thought that anyone can apply to herself. If I look back over all the beliefs I have held to be true at some point in my life, I am struck by the fact that a substantial portion of them later proved to be false. Much of what once seemed to me to be true turned out, on closer inspection, to be false. Not everything we take to be true is true. Our taking something to be true is not the same as its being true. Descartes opens his *Meditations* by remarking, "Some years ago I was struck by the large number of falsehoods that I had accepted as true in my childhood, and by the highly doubtful nature of the whole edifice that I had subsequently based on them. I realized that it was necessary, once in the course of my life, to demolish everything completely and start again right from the foundations."[1]

It is essential to the form and self-understanding of epistemology as inaugurated by Descartes that these reflections start from an experience that is available to everyone. Modern epistemology seeks to establish something about knowledge that we ourselves purport to possess. Its claims bear on something that is characteristic of all of us equally. And one of the features that evidently characterizes us as judging beings is that we are liable to err. Sometimes we merely believe we know things,

---

[1] Descartes, *Meditations on First Philosophy*, AT 7:17.

—

1

when in fact we do not know them. By placing the experience of error at the starting point of his investigations, Descartes is not only articulating an essential feature of ourselves, he is simultaneously making the motive of all epistemology explicit. We are seeking to understand how it is possible that creatures who are imperfect in that they can err can nevertheless have knowledge. For this possibility—the possibility of error—which so obviously obtains in our case, raises a question about how knowledge is possible for us. And the answer to this question is not obvious. If it were impossible for our beliefs to be in error, then the question of how we might attain knowledge would not arise. Where there is no space for *false* belief, the question of how knowledge is possible is already settled. Believing something and knowing it would be one and the same thing. When Descartes begins his epistemological reflections by referring to the experience of error, he is not pointing to just any feature of our beliefs; he is pointing to the feature that motivates and initiates his meditations: our imperfection, our fallibility. For that is precisely what our errors reveal: they reveal that we are imperfect, that we are not divine, but finite beings. Indeed, our "errors," according to Descartes, are "the only things that are indicative of some imperfection in [us]."[2] It is on account of this imperfection that it makes sense to raise the question of the possibility of knowledge. An epistemology of infallible creatures would be pointless, because it doesn't even make sense to ask how knowledge is possible for them. For us, however, this is a question whose answer is not immediately clear. We have to undertake an investigation in order to come to understand the possibility of knowledge *for us*. What are the sources of knowledge for creatures who are imperfect in this respect: that they can err?

To say that the experience of error is the motivation for engaging in epistemological reflection is, of course, not to say that everyone is (or should be) moved to undertake such an investigation upon experiencing error. I only mean that it is on account of our cognitive imperfection that the answer to the question of how knowledge is possible for us does not lie ready to hand. Because there is a potential gap between our beliefs and knowledge, there is room for the epistemological question

---

[2] Ibid., 7:56.

to take hold. Moreover, when I say that the experience of error is what motivates epistemology, I am invoking an experience that not only vexes us as philosophers but unsettles us in everyday life. For error is never something we strive for. To say that someone has erred means that she has failed to attain what she was actually aiming for: namely, knowledge. "Error," Descartes says, is "a privation or a lack of some knowledge that somehow ought to be in me."[3] When we err, we have failed in our attempt to acquire knowledge. And this failure is always unsettling—not only in philosophy when we are reflecting on the possibility of knowledge, but whenever we experience error in our everyday lives. Whenever we claim to know something and it then turns out that we were mistaken, our misconception strikes us as something unexpected and surprising. This doesn't mean that we cannot explain our error once it arises and is discovered. But when we err, our error has for us the character of a misadventure, an adversity unexpectedly visited upon us. It is quite different when we are not claiming to know something but merely speculating. I suspect that it will be sunny tomorrow, for instance, because it is sunny today. But if it ends up raining tomorrow, I will not be particularly surprised. In a certain sense, we are already prepared for our speculations to turn out to be false. If I merely suspect that something is so, I'm not ruling out the possibility that my belief is false. But when a belief I have put forward as knowledge proves to be false, I cannot but be surprised. For to claim to know something is to rule out that one's belief is false.

By opening his epistemological reflections with a reference to their underlying motivation, Descartes makes it clear that asking after the sources of our knowledge is something that, in a certain sense, we do quite naturally. Pursuing this question is not some artificial enterprise that contrasts with what we actually do when we claim to know something. When we investigate knowledge, we are attempting to understand something that is an issue for us precisely because we are liable to err. If we were creatures who had never in their lives erred, if everything always ran smoothly with our knowledge claims, then we would have no reason to engage in epistemological reflections.

[3] Ibid., 7:55.

This underlying motive of epistemological inquiry also explains why all reflection on our knowledge, at one point or another, must grapple with skepticism. For the skeptic precisely disputes that the afore-mentioned thoughts can be reconciled. The skeptic sees no way to regard us as creatures who are liable to err and simultaneously as creatures who do know things. The skeptic disputes the idea that philosophical reflection can explain how we can enjoy knowledge despite our falli-bility. For the skeptic, there seem to be only two options: either we have to admit that we are never justified in ascribing knowledge to our-selves, or we must deny that we are susceptible to error.

One reaction to this skeptical problematic, which is surprisingly widespread in epistemology, is that the skeptic is entangled in a pseu-doproblem, because she stipulates a concept of knowledge that does not accord with "our" concept of knowledge. The skeptic thinks that knowledge requires something from us that we could only fulfill if we were infallible. Therefore she must conclude that knowledge and falli-bility are mutually exclusive. But "our" concept of knowledge requires less than what the skeptic thinks it does. "Our" concept of knowledge, instead of excluding fallibility, rather presupposes it. According to this standard reaction, the skeptic mistakenly takes the fact that we are fal-lible to imply that we cannot have knowledge. But this is wrong. Falli-bilism and skepticism are two different things. The skeptic is only skep-tical, so the standard response has it, because she cannot keep the two apart.[4]

This book is motivated by dissatisfaction with this standard response to the problem of skepticism. For this response fails to understand *why* the skeptic cannot keep fallibilism and skepticism apart. The skeptic cannot keep fallibilism and skepticism apart, not because she assumes that knowledge requires something from us that only an infallible being could ever fulfill. Rather, these two ideas coincide for the skeptic, because she cannot see how that which knowledge requires from us could ever be fulfilled by a fallible being. The skeptic identifies falli-bilism with skepticism, not because she simply assumes that knowl-

---

[4] A typical representative of this sort of reaction is Michael Williams; see his *Problems of Knowledge*, esp. 40–42, 219.

edge is possible only for subjects who are infallible, but because she cannot see any way to understand the possibility of knowledge for a subject who is fallible. The identification of fallibilism and skepticism is not the consequence of a concept of knowledge that puts too high a standard on us, but is a manifestation of the difficulty to combine the possibility of knowledge with fallibility. Moreover, if skepticism is a manifestation of the inability to understand fallibility so that it is compatible with the possibility of knowledge, the usual response to skepticism is itself a form of skepticism—albeit one that doesn't recognize itself as what it is. The problem of skepticism, as I will argue, is the problem of our fallibility. Understanding the possibility of knowledge and understanding our fallibility are two sides of the same coin.

Part One of this book develops a preliminary account of the concept of knowledge we seek to understand. What do we mean by the term 'knowledge' when we ask ourselves whether we are capable of possessing knowledge? The answer that has dominated the philosophical tradition since Plato is that knowledge is true and appropriately justified belief.[5] Part One develops this initial account of our concept of knowledge as justified true belief. But this account has a provisional status, for it does not yet show that and how finite beings can enjoy knowledge in this sense—that is, it does not yet show that and how this concept can figure in a characterization of their mental life. Nevertheless, this preliminary elucidation of the concept of knowledge points the way for all our further reflections. However obvious and correct this account may initially appear to us, we will encounter momentous difficulties that can make it seem impossible to hold on to this account. It will take us a while until we will be in a position to appreciate the full import of this account. Only then will we be able to understand not only how knowledge, in this sense, is possible but also what it means to understand the concept of knowledge in this way.

Because the skeptic disputes the idea that we can make sense of the possibility of human knowledge, it appears that we can vindicate our account of knowledge only if we can put our finger on the misunderstanding that forces the skeptic to conclude that, on the basis of this

[5] For Plato's characterization of knowledge, in this connection, see *Theaetetus*.

account, knowledge is impossible to achieve. In the present work, we will confront two of the skeptic's arguments. Part One will address the argument that stands at the center of what is traditionally called ancient skepticism. According to this argument, we cannot enjoy knowledge because any attempt to demonstrate that we know something ineluctably entangles us in an infinite regress of justification. The question, "What grounds or reasons do you have for believing that things are thus and so?" applies to every particular belief we might offer in response to such a quest for justification. And, hence, the quest for justification can never come to an end. Accordingly—so the argument goes—we cannot really know anything.

It will turn out that this regress argument, which the majority of contemporary epistemology accepts as a description of its central problem, rests upon a presupposition that is anything but self-evident. The presupposition is that it is, in principle, impossible for us to possess grounds for the truth of a belief that exclude the possibility of its being false. On the received view, such reasons—let us call them "truth-guaranteeing grounds"—are unavailable to us, in principle. The presupposition is that it is impossible, in principle, to guarantee the truth of a belief by citing, say, what one perceives or what one has learned from someone else. On this presupposition, the claim that one perceives something, or that one has learned something from someone else, can never guarantee the truth of one's belief. Why not? After all, we certainly seem thus to guarantee the truth of our beliefs in ordinary life. Yet the regress argument precludes the very possibility of such truth-guaranteeing grounds.

Part Two will therefore discuss an argument that purports to show that such a guarantee of truth is, in fact, impossible. This is the "argument from illusion," which forms the explicit basis for so-called Cartesian skepticism. It finds its characteristic expression in the thought, "But we can always err!" If it is true that we are fallible, the skeptic argues, then we are, in principle, incapable of believing something for reasons that would guarantee the truth of that belief. Yet if we are cut off, in principle, from truth-guaranteeing grounds, the skeptic argues, then we are, in principle, incapable of having knowledge. There are many angles from which one might think to attack this skeptical doubt in the hopes of refuting it. Yet I will argue that, so long as we accept the argument that our fallibility entails that truth-guaranteeing grounds are unavailable to us, human knowledge is indeed unintelligible. Whether or not we can have knowledge depends, accordingly, upon whether we can defuse this argument.

So what are the presuppositions of the argument? One presupposition, I will show, consists in a particular interpretation of the *nature of grounds* for belief. The presupposition is that a ground for a belief must be independent of the truth of that belief. It will turn out that we must reject this account of grounds for belief. In the fundamental case, a ground for belief is a ground that one cannot have without forming a true belief on its basis and hence, without having knowledge. The proper understanding of the nature of grounds for belief compels us to accept an unsettling insight: namely, that the concept of knowledge is fundamental to an account of what it is to believe something on a ground. But how are we to understand this insight?

Part Three develops a conception of the nature of the human mind and of human knowledge that indicates how this insight is to be understood. What does it mean to claim that the concept of knowledge is fundamental for the concept of a justified belief? It means, as I will show, that the elements into which we broke down the concept of knowledge in Part One are not to be understood as elements of an analytical unity. That is to say, the unity of knowledge cannot be understood as a unity containing elements that are more fundamental than the concept of knowledge itself. The concepts we use to articulate what it means to have knowledge cannot be understood as concepts that we can explain or make sense of without making reference to the very unity whose elements they are. We have to understand the description of knowledge as justified true belief as the articulation of a different sort of unity. So what other sort of unity is at issue here? The central claim of this book is that what we are dealing with here is the *unity of a rational capacity*. The guiding thought that I will develop is that, in order to understand knowledge, we have to recognize that the fundamental use of the concept of knowledge—the use that determines its meaning—consists in the description of a rational capacity for knowledge. The fundamental description of knowledge thus runs as follows: Knowledge is an act that springs from a rational capacity for knowledge.

By placing the concept of a rational capacity at the center of our account of knowledge, we are drawing on a philosophical tradition whose relevance for contemporary epistemology has yet to be fully appreciated. We owe the most significant philosophical reflections on capacities to Aristotle. The philosophical position that explicitly places the concept of a capacity for knowledge at the heart of its considerations—and the position that, more than any other, investigates what it means to have a capacity for knowledge—is undoubtedly due to Kant. Both authors will play a crucial role in our attempt to put the concept of a capacity for knowledge at the center of epistemology. Part Three elaborates the thought that our sources of knowledge are rational capacities for knowledge by, first, unfolding the idea of rational capacities quite generally, and then, correlatively, giving a preliminary account of the idea of capacities for knowledge.

Part Four then develops the teleology of mind that goes hand in hand with the idea of a capacity for knowledge by considering what it means for the concept of knowledge to describe the end or telos of a capacity. We do this first by contrasting our account of knowledge with the one advanced by "virtue epistemology." Virtue epistemology can seem to be guided by an insight similar to the one sketched above—namely, the idea that knowledge constitutes a kind of telos, the realization of which is to be explained by reference to a capacity for knowledge. I will argue that virtue epistemology fails to make knowledge intelligible because it fundamentally misconceives the teleology of rational capacities. It misunderstands the sort of causality that characterizes a capacity for knowledge, for it conceives of the causality characteristic of rational capacities as independent of the telos of the capacity in question. But this undermines the very idea of a rational capacity.

To hold on to the idea of a rational capacity for knowledge, we have to conceive of its mode of causality as one that we will call, following the tradition, "teleological causality." Most of Part Four will be concerned with developing an understanding of the idea of a capacity for knowledge by unfolding the idea of "teleological causality," the most abstract account of which we find in Kant. This account will raise the question of how to understand the very possibility of a capacity for knowledge if we conceive of it as a species of teleological causality. Is such a capacity intelligible? I will suggest a Kantian answer to this question. Kant argues that the only way to account for the possibility of a capacity for knowledge is to conceive of it as a capacity that constitutes itself by "*a priori* knowledge" of its objects. This raises the question of how we shall understand the idea that an empirical subject who is not yet in possession of a capacity for knowledge can ever come to possess it. We will answer this question by developing the relevant notion of "practice" that goes along with the idea of a capacity for knowledge, namely, a practice of acquiring a rational capacity through the exercises of another, competent subject. We will call the relevant acts that constitute such a practice of acquisition acts of learning.

The acts of learning through which one acquires a capacity for knowledge explain one's possession of a capacity for knowledge, not through something that is prior to and, in that sense, more fundamental than a capacity for knowledge. Instead, these acts of learning explain a capacity for knowledge through acts that are already exercises of it, yet exercises of a particular, relational form. For they are exercises that depend on a subject's standing in a particular relation to another subject, namely, a relation of learning. This conclusion vindicates the idea of knowledge as a self-constituting capacity. It is a capacity whose acquisition—thus mediated through the acts of other knowing subjects—can be explained only in terms of acts of learning that already involve the capacity being learned.

The project of epistemology stands or falls with the idea that it makes sense to ask what the sources of knowledge are and to give a general account of them. There is a widespread sense in contemporary philosophy, originally motivated (albeit from quite different directions) by Quine and Austin,[6] that this question does not really make sense. On this account, the project of epistemology is simply not a viable—or even

---

[6] See, *inter alia,* Quine, "Epistemology Naturalized," 75; Austin, *Sense and Sensibilia,* 105.

meaningful—undertaking.[7] When we come to recognize that the sources of knowledge are rational capacities for knowledge, we can see that this must involve a misunderstanding. For if rational capacities for knowledge are the sources of knowledge, this not only means that epistemology is possible; it also tells us what it is to practice epistemology. To practice epistemology is to make one's capacities for knowledge the object of one's knowledge by exercising them, if things go well, in their most articulate and hence most perfect way.

[7] On this point, see Rorty, *Philosophy and the Mirror of Nature,* 155, 163, 317–318. See also Williams, *Problems of Knowledge,* 255.

# PART ONE

## *Knowledge and Reason*

OUR AIM IS TO UNDERSTAND HOW CREATURES OF THE SORT WE humans are can enjoy knowledge. We thus seek an understanding of knowledge that is sufficiently general to explain knowledge as such—and not just how someone can enjoy this or that kind of knowledge. Nevertheless, the idea of different "kinds" of knowledge suggests that we are in possession of principles that enable us to distinguish acts of knowledge not just in terms of their content but in terms of their form. A familiar distinction of this sort is the distinction between empirical and non-empirical knowledge. A first indication that we do indeed have some understanding of this distinction is that we find it very easy to cite examples of these two sorts of knowledge. Examples of empirical knowledge would include my knowledge that the next train to Potsdam departs at 2 P.M., or that it is currently raining, or that a white teacup is on the table before me. Examples of non-empirical knowledge would include, say, my knowledge that the sum of two and two is four, or that in a right triangle the sum of the squares of the two legs is equal to the square of the hypotenuse.

Let us assume for a moment that these examples are genuine, even if we currently lack any more articulated understanding of the principle at work in this distinction beyond the fact that we can adduce such examples. We said above that we seek an understanding of knowledge that makes intelligible to us, in a fully general way, how it is that someone can attain knowledge, regardless of what sort. Yet if knowledge can be subdivided into different kinds, then it would appear that to know something is not to have knowledge in general but rather to have knowledge of a particular kind. So some such particular kind of knowledge should be our starting point here. We will accordingly proceed by inquiring into a quite specific kind of knowledge in order to develop the general understanding of knowledge we aim at. In particular, we will investigate a kind of knowledge that is so deeply rooted in our self-understanding that, however thoroughly philosophical challenges seem to call it into question, we find it impossible to take even the least account of those worries in our ordinary lives. I mean the sort of knowledge we called "empirical." If we have knowledge of any kind, it seems, we have at least

—

13

this sort of knowledge. And if we cannot make sense of this sort of knowledge, it seems, then we cannot make sense of knowledge at all. Yet it is my aim here to show that once we are in a position to understand empirical knowledge, we are in possession of a principle that will allow us to understand other kinds of knowledge as well.

Here in Part One, I will first specify more precisely the concept of knowledge we want to understand. What do we mean by the expression 'knowledge' when we ask ourselves how it is possible for us to have knowledge? The account of the concept of knowledge I will develop in Part One has a preliminary status. For it does not yet show us how it can be a characteristic of our mental life that we occasionally enjoy knowledge in this sense. Nevertheless, this preliminary account will serve as our guiding thread in what follows. For it is my aim to vindicate this account by explaining how knowledge in this sense is possible.

# I

# Finite Knowledge

## 1. Who Are "We"? A Kantian Answer

In the Introduction, I claimed that the motivation behind epistemology arises from the unsettling observation that we can err. Descartes places this observation at the very starting point of his reflections on the nature and sources of our knowledge. He presents our susceptibility to error as something that "struck" him many years prior to his writing. But we cannot simply assume that the actual experience of error is the source of our knowledge that we are liable to err—at least, not if this observation is supposed to represent the starting point of our reflections on the nature and sources of our knowledge. For let us imagine someone who denies that she was ever in error. It is clear that this would pose no objection to Descartes's claim. For Descartes clearly doesn't understand his claim that we are fallible as an empirical observation. Descartes isn't trying to say that observations of himself and others have led him to the conclusion that humans are liable to err. In philosophy, when we say that we are fallible, we are not generalizing from our empirical observation of humans; we are not making the sort of claim that might be confirmed or disconfirmed by further experience of other human beings. Our claim instead specifies the topic of our philosophical reflections. We are indicating which concept of knowledge we seek to elucidate: namely, the concept of finite knowledge as opposed to the concept of infinite knowledge. We are thereby saying that it is a defining characteristic of the sort of knowledge we seek to understand that the relation between the knowing subject and the known content is such as to leave room for the possibility of error. We term this sort of knowledge "finite" in order to distinguish it from infinite knowledge, which does not allow for this possibility.

As Kant characterizes it, infinite knowledge, if there is such a thing, would be infinite in the sense that the knowing subject would not be answerable to the objects of knowledge but instead would bring them into being through having knowledge of them.[1] Infinite knowledge would not be bound by the object of its knowledge but would be the source of what it knows. For this reason, Kant refers to infinite knowledge as "originary" in order to indicate that it is "not dependent on the existence of the object" but instead brings about "even the existence of the object."[2] For an intellect who enjoys such infinite knowledge, what he knows is accordingly not something against which his representations may be measured as true or false. The manner in which the representations of such an intellect relate to their object renders senseless the idea that such representations might be false. An infinite intellect can have true representations only because the objects of his representations are in no way a standard governing those representations but instead are internal to them. The idea of error thus does not apply to such an infinite intellect.

When we say that the sort of knowledge we are investigating is the kind enjoyed by subjects who can err, we therefore specify which concept of knowledge we are investigating—we do not make an empirical claim about our cognitive constitution. Put differently, we specify the kind of subject whose possible knowledge interests us. We are concerned, not with knowledge of an infinite intellect, but rather with the knowledge proper to a finite being that is "dependent" for her existence as

[1] See Kant, *Kritik der reinen Vernunft* [Critique of Pure Reason], B72. (Page references to the *Kritik der reinen Vernunft* use the numbers of the first (A) and second (B) editions; page references to Kant's other writings are given by the page numbers of the appropriate volume of the Academy edition (=AA).
[2] Ibid.

well as her knowledge on the existence of objects.[3] The question is how knowledge is possible for a subject who—unlike an infinite intellect, for whom error is logically impossible—is characterized by her liability to err. It is the knowledge of such a subject that we seek to understand when we seek to understand human knowledge. For humans are finite subjects in just this sense. They depend for both their existence and their knowledge on the existence of objects. If humans are capable of any sort of knowledge at all, they are only capable of finite knowledge— knowledge that allows for the possibility of error.

We seek to understand ourselves as subjects who have beliefs that are such as to be possibly false. As we have seen, this presupposes that the truth or falsity of our beliefs cannot be settled merely on the basis of the fact that we actually do have these beliefs. To understand finite knowledge is to understand acts of a subject that relate to the world as a standard that determines, independently of those acts, whether the latter are true or false. Finite knowledge is, in this sense, *objective* knowledge. Objective knowledge is the prerogative of finite subjects.

If finite knowledge relates to the world as a standard, then our task is to understand something that belongs to the lives of beings capable of judgment. For, if we follow Kant, judgments are precisely those acts of the intellect whose defining feature it is that they can be true or false. Kant arrives at this notion of judgment by first characterizing judgment as a spontaneous act—an act arising from a capacity of "spontaneity."[4] The capacity in question is spontaneous in the sense that it "brings forth representations from itself."[5] For, Kant explains, its exercises consist in the subject's combining representations into a "unity" in accordance with a certain "logical form."[6] This logical form lends a connection of representations the character by which it is suitable to serve as the content of a judgment.[7] A subject who has the capacity "to bring

---

[3] Ibid.

[4] See ibid., B75/A51. For an instructive overview of Kant's various descriptions of the idea of spontaneity, see Pippin, "Kant on the Spontaneity of Mind."

[5] Kant, *Kritik der reinen Vernunft*, B75/A51.

[6] Ibid., B105/A79.

[7] See also ibid., B94–95/A69–70. Note that Kant uses the term 'representation' ['Vorstellung'] in a twofold sense. Sometimes he uses it as a generic expression for various acts

forth representations from itself" is, accordingly, a subject of representations that can be connected with one another in accordance with the logical form that constitutes the unity of a judgment. Following Kant, we can call such representations "conceptual representations." Thus, conceptual representations are characterized by their ability to be conjoined into a unity in accordance with the logical form of a judgment. A subject that has the capacity "to bring forth representations from itself" consequently is a subject of conceptual representations.

Now, for a subject to exercise such a capacity in making a judgment—for example, a judgment she could express by saying "the sun is shining" or "there's apple juice in the refrigerator"—the subject must not only connect representations in the manner that defines the capacity in question, namely, according to the logical form of judgment. The subject must also perform this connection in a particular way. She must connect the relevant representations in such a manner that she *endorses* that connection of representations as *true*. This is what we will understand by a judgment in what follows. To judge is to combine representations into a unity by endorsing that combination of representations as true.

To endorse a conceptual representation as true is to believe it. Some contemporary philosophers have suggested that we should distinguish between judgment and belief, holding that belief is a "standing state" whereas judging is a mental "act."[8] From what we have said so far, however, nothing suggests the need for such a distinction. As we proceed further we will, indeed, need to introduce a distinction between two different logical orders to account for the idea of the act that is our topic, i.e., a judgment that amounts to knowledge. By contrast, the reasons that are usually given for drawing this distinction do not indicate why it is actually necessary. For what one typically wants to capture by the distinction between belief and judgment is the idea that the fact that I believe something does not imply that I am presently reflecting

of consciousness, and sometimes he uses it as a generic expression for the various contents of such conscious acts. But in neither of these senses does Kant mean something like a "mental image" floating before the subject's mind's eye. In both uses of the expression, Kant's aim is to explain what it means to be conscious of something.
[8] See, for example, Shoemaker, "Self-Intimation and Second Order Belief," 36.

on my belief, nor that I am presently focusing my attention on the endorsement that constitutes my belief. Moreover, a belief that something is the case can manifest itself in quite different ways. Someone's belief that the Wannsee is frozen may manifest itself as she is gliding around on it in ice skates, or as she is trying to chip through the surface with a shovel. All this is perfectly true. However, the fact that a certain belief of mine is not presently the focus of my attention does not, as such, imply that it is not a mental act of mine. Nor does the very idea of a mental act exclude the idea of different forms of manifestation. Rather, I will argue that a proper understanding of those phenomena one wants to distinguish by making a distinction between judgment and belief are intelligible only once we have a proper understanding of the nature of the mental act that judging is. Hence, for our purposes, we will not make philosophical use of the distinction between belief and judgment.[9] The very motive for putting philosophical weight on this distinction will start to disappear once we arrive at an understanding of the nature of the act of judging.

We introduced judgment as an act of endorsing a certain connection of representations as true. This entails that such a connection of representations might also be false. Otherwise it would make no sense to speak of a judging subject as endorsing the truth of a particular connection of representations—a connection of the sort that finds expression in the sentence "It's sunny outside." If it were impossible to combine representations in a way that wasn't true, so that the question of truth could not arise in the first place, then it would be impossible to explain judgment in terms of the notion of endorsement. If it is simply foreclosed in advance that a certain combination of representations might be false, then the idea of endorsing its truth has no application. This is precisely the case for an infinite intellect. Thus, it is not only senseless to talk about the possibility of error in reference to an infinite intellect, it is also senseless to talk about such an intellect as endorsing the truth of a particular conceptual representation. In characterizing judgment as consisting in a subject's endorsing a connection of representations as

[9] For an instructive criticism of the distinction between belief and judgment, see Boyle, "Die Spontaneität des Verstandes bei Kant und einigen Neokantianern."

true, we are characterizing it as an act that, as such, resides in the space of truth and falsity.

John McDowell has reformulated the Kantian idea that judgments arise from a self-active faculty in the following way. When Kant says that judgments arise from the capacity "to bring forth representations from itself," according to McDowell, one thing he means is that judgment is an act for which the subject is responsible in the sense that it is an exercise of free cognitive activity. "[J]udging," McDowell writes, "is making up one's mind about something. Making up one's mind is one's own doing, something for which one is responsible. To judge is to engage in free cognitive activity, as opposed to having something merely happen in one's life, outside one's control."[10] McDowell goes on to elucidate the idea of what it is to engage in free cognitive activity through the idea of a particular kind of decision: Judgments—and, correlatively, the beliefs in which they result[11]—are acts in which one makes a decision about what it is true to think about a particular matter.[12] Judgments, on McDowell's reformulation, are thus "brought forth from the subject herself" in the sense that in judging that things are thus and so, the subject makes a particular kind of decision: namely, a decision in which she is guided by the truth as the standard of her decision.

Conceiving judgment in terms of a particular kind of decision is another way of formulating the thought I expressed above when I characterized judgment in terms of an act of combination and endorsement. In judging how things are, the subject's combination of representations is a

[10] McDowell, "Hegel's Idealism as Radicalization of Kant," 71. McDowell's formulation seems to me to build on Stuart Hampshire's characterization of beliefs as those thoughts of a subject that the subject endorses as true: "I make up my mind, and decide, when I formulate my beliefs. [ . . . ] [B]eliefs are those thoughts that I endorse as true. I do not merely find them occurring or lingering: I decide in their favour." See Hampshire's *Freedom of the Individual,* 97f. For an elaboration of this characterization that explicitly builds on Hampshire, see Moran, *Authority and Estrangement,* 113–114.

[11] As already indicated above, the aspects of judgment and belief that concern us in what follows are neutral with respect to a distinction between judging and believing. In this sense, everything we say about judgment applies equally well to belief. This implies, not that there can be no differences between them whatsoever, but instead that we are abstracting from such differences.

[12] McDowell, *Mind and World,* 10, 26, and 60, *inter alia.*

"free cognitive activity," as McDowell puts it, in the sense that it is an activity of combining representations in a manner in which the subject is guided by the truth as the standard of that very activity, which standard she claims to meet.[13]

Because our aim in what follows is to understand finite knowledge, we are interested in understanding something that can only occur in the lives of creatures capable of judgment and, hence, in the lives of creatures who possess concepts. For, according to the above characterization, judgment is an act in which a subject connects particular conceptual representations in a certain way. The idea of a conceptual representation, as I introduced it, is the idea of a representation that is able to be connected with other representations into a unity in accordance with the logical form of a judgment. Thus, the claim that someone capable of judging possesses concepts is not to be understood to suggest that such a subject would have two distinct capacities—a capacity for concepts and a capacity for judgment. The capacity we have in mind when we attribute concepts to someone is essentially actualized in judgment. Kant expresses this thought by saying that "the understanding," which he takes to be responsible for all concepts with respect to their form, "can make no other use of these concepts than that of judging through them."[14] That is to say, having the capacity for concepts and having the capacity for judgment are one and the same capacity. Someone who cannot connect conceptual representations in accordance

---

[13] The idea that judgment can be elucidated through the concept of decision is sometimes misunderstood—as though it meant to claim that judgment is at our command, that it is within the sphere of our will. This accusation is frequently expressed by labeling the present account of judgment and belief "voluntaristic." But that is far from what is meant here. By invoking the idea of decision to characterize judgment, we are by no means saying that one can judge and believe whatever one wants. Quite the contrary. We are instead saying that judgments and beliefs are acts that intrinsically fall within the space of truth and falsity, because they consist in an answer to the question of truth. The concept of decision here is meant to explain what we mean when we say that judging is "answering" or "taking a stance on" the question of truth. Our use of the concept of decision does not contrast with but instead accords with Bernard Williams's critique of voluntaristic conceptions of belief. See Williams, "Deciding to Believe." For a helpful discussion of the confusion behind this critique, see also Boyle, "Active Belief" and "'Making Up Your Mind' and the Activity of Reason."

[14] Kant, *Kritik der reinen Vernunft*, B93/A68.

with the form of judgment does not possess any conceptual representation in the sense that is relevant to our inquiry.

The sort of knowledge that we are investigating is thus knowledge belonging to creatures whose intellect is, as Kant puts it, "discursive" in character.[15] For only creatures that have a discursive intellect can perform acts that one can rightly say are guided by the world as the standard of their truth—i.e., acts of judgment. Creatures that lack the capacity for making judgments about the world lack the capacity to relate to the world as the standard of truth of their acts.[16] Our aim in what follows is to understand the knowledge proper to creatures whose nature is to be "finite thinking creatures."[17] For this is what human beings are: finite thinking creatures.

## 2. Knowledge from the Standpoint of Reason

The aim of this section is to develop a preliminary account of our concept of knowledge. Because the skeptic will be able to accept our account of the concept of knowledge, it is natural to worry that this account isn't a first step toward an understanding of knowledge but rather a first step toward rendering such an understanding impossible. It is my ambition to defend the intelligibility of this conception of knowledge by unpacking what it means to have knowledge according to this conception.

In section 1 of this chapter, we followed Kant in characterizing finite knowledge in terms of an act that intrinsically makes reference to the standard of truth—namely, in terms of an act of judgment. Judging means making a decision about a conceptual representation in which one is guided by the standard of truth. An act whose performance involves the subject submitting herself to a particular standard is, *ipso facto,* a normative act. Moreover, because it is she herself whom the subject

---

[15] See ibid.

[16] Heidegger expresses this by saying that such creatures, who do not have a discursive intellect, are either world-poor [weltarm], like animals and plants, or world-less [weltlos], like stones. See *Die Grundbegriffe der Metaphysik: Welt, Endlichkeit, Einsamkeit,* §46, 284–288.

[17] Kant, *Kritik der reinen Vernunft,* B72.

brings under this standard, such an act is not only normative from some perspective or other: it is normative from the perspective of the subject who performs it. It is a normative act that the subject herself understands as normative. The fact that judgment is a normative act in this sense means that someone who is not in a position to frame a decision in which she is guided by the standard of truth is not in a position to make a judgment or to form a belief. And it means that someone who asserts the truth of her belief is not making a meta-claim about her belief. Rather, she is giving expression to her belief in a somewhat redundant way. To believe that what one believes is true is the same as believing it.

It is for this reason that Austin and others rightly remark that statements of belief in the first-person present tense have a special performative aspect. When someone says, in the first-person present, "I believe that the negotiations to form a coalition for the Berlin administration have stalled," she is doing something by saying so. When we believe that p, we are thereby taking a stance on the question whether p is true—and we are doing so by endorsing the truth of p. Thus, when I say, "I believe the negotiations to form a coalition for the Berlin administration have stalled," I am not simply describing such a stance on the matter, I am publicly performing the act of taking the stance that I describe with those words.[18] I am publicly taking a stance on whether the coalition negotiations for the formation of the administration of Berlin have stalled.[19] Price registers the performative character of first-person present-tense statements of belief by saying that they have a "stand-taking character."[20]

The fact that locutions such as "believe that . . . ," "suspect that . . . ," "think that . . . ," and "know that . . ." have a performative character does

---

[18] See H. H. Price, *Belief,* 30.

[19] Austin accordingly writes, "To suppose that 'I know' is a descriptive phrase, is only one example of the *descriptive fallacy,* so common in philosophy. Even if some language is now purely descriptive, language was not in origin so, and much of it is still not so. Utterance of obvious ritual phrases, in the appropriate circumstances, is not *describing* the action we are doing, but *doing* it." Austin, "Other Minds," 103.

[20] Price, *Belief,* 35. The fact that Price, like Austin, chooses to begin his comprehensive investigation of the nature of belief by emphasizing just this feature is all the more striking in view of the fact that, as we will see, this feature has become practically invisible in a substantial portion of contemporary epistemology.

not, of course, mean that these locutions are performative in the same sense that "promise" and "congratulate" are. When I say, "I promise to do x" (in the appropriate circumstances), I thereby promise to do x. By contrast, when I say (in the appropriate circumstances), "I know that p," this statement does not itself constitute my knowing that p. Though the public expression of a promise is constitutive of the act of promising, this is clearly not the case when it comes to knowledge.[21] That is to say, one need not say that one knows that p in order to know that p. Nor can one who doesn't know that p make it the case that she knows that p by saying that she does. The performative character of such locutions, unlike performative locutions in the full sense of the term, does not consist in their signifying actions that one can perform only by using them in an utterance. Instead it consists in the fact that someone who uses such a locution in an utterance can thereby perform the very action that the locution signifies in a public manner.

With this in mind, let us consider the "standard analysis" of the concept of knowledge.[22] On the standard analysis, someone knows that p if and only if (1) she believes that p, (2) it is true that p, and (3) her belief that p is sufficiently justified. In its initial form, the standard analysis says nothing more than that these three conditions are necessary and sufficient for the truth of the claim "she knows that p." In what follows, we will unfold the internal connection between these three conditions.

Consider condition (1), which requires that the subject believe the proposition in question. What the belief condition makes explicit is that only an act or state that involves taking a stance on the truth of some matter can count as knowledge. Of course, not all of our beliefs amount to knowledge. But whenever we do know that something is the case, we also believe that it is.[23] So what is the difference between someone's

---

[21] On this distinction, see also Vendler, "Telling the Facts," 220–221. It would be a misunderstanding to cite this important distinction as grounds for rejecting Austin's view that propositional attitude concepts also have a performative character. The important point is to develop an adequate understanding of the performative character Austin rightly identifies.

[22] Regarding a "standard analysis," see Williams, *Problems of Knowledge*, 15–17.

[23] The fact that ordinary language sometimes separates the concept of knowledge from that of belief—e.g., when I say, "I don't believe p, I know it"—does not show that

merely believing something and her knowing something? A first pass at an explanation might be: Someone who knows that things are thus and so is certain that things are as she believes them to be. One cannot say, "I know that the Berlin coalition negotiations have stalled, but I'm not certain." Yet someone who merely believes something need not be certain. I can very well say, "I believe that Amsterdam lies farther south than Hamburg, but I'm not certain." This seems to suggest that the distinction between knowledge and belief can be characterized in terms of a difference in one's degree of certainty. In that case, we would say: When I know something, I perform an act of endorsing a conceptual content that has just the same form as the act I perform when I merely believe something, or opine something, or suppose something. The difference between these acts lies solely in the fact that the act of knowing involves a maximal degree of certainty in the truth of what I believe. Knowledge, on this account, lies on the far end of a scale with different gradients of certainty, the other end of which might be occupied by mere supposition, say.

But let us imagine someone who says she is totally certain that it will rain tomorrow. And let us suppose that, the next day, it does not in fact rain. Her claim that she was completely certain is not thereby falsified. She may well have been completely certain, even though what she believed with such certainty was false. We might imagine her saying, "Although I was completely certain, it turned out I was mistaken." The case is altogether different for someone who had claimed to know that it would rain tomorrow. When it fails to rain the next day, she must correct herself and say, "I only thought that I knew it would rain, but I didn't really know." Her prior claim to know is falsified by what happens in a way the other person's claim to be certain is not. This difference shows that the distinction between knowing something and merely believing it cannot be explained in terms of degrees of certainty. It is surely correct that someone who knows something is also certain of the truth of her belief.

knowledge does not entail belief. It instead shows that knowledge is belief with a special status: namely, the status implied in the making of an assertion. To say "I believe that p" is to register some reservation about the assertion that p. On this point, see Wittgenstein's *On Certainty*, §424.

But the distinction between such claims as "I believe that p," "I suppose that p," and "I am absolutely certain that p," on the one hand, and the claim "I know that p" is not a psychological distinction. It is a logical distinction. This logical distinction rests on the fact that the concept of knowledge—unlike the concepts of the other propositional attitudes just mentioned—does not simply describe a relation between a subject and a statement—it describes a relation between a subject and a fact. Wittgenstein expresses this by saying, "'I know' has a primitive meaning similar to and related to the meaning of 'I see'. [ . . . ] 'I know' is supposed to express a relation, not between me and the sense of a proposition (as with 'I believe') but between me and a fact. So that the fact is taken up into my consciousness."[24]

We might reformulate this by saying that the concept of knowledge, in contrast to such concepts as belief, opinion, supposition, being absolutely certain, etc., has a factive sense. Someone who knows something holds a propositional attitude that implies the fact described by the propositional content of that attitude. If someone says she knows it is raining, this implies that it is indeed raining. And precisely the same thing holds when I ascribe knowledge to someone else. Someone who ascribes knowledge to herself or to someone else is, by taking that stance, jumping to a different logical level from the one relevant to ascriptions of belief, opinion, certainty, etc.[25] Thus, while it is logically possible to believe something that is false and even to be certain that it is true, it is logically impossible to know something false.[26]

---

[24] Ibid., §90.

[25] Accordingly, Austin writes, "saying 'I know'," in contrast to saying 'I believe' or saying 'I am quite sure', "is taking a new plunge." See "Other Minds," 99.

[26] It is, of course, important in this context not to confuse two distinct issues. Because the concept of knowledge is factive, anyone who uses that concept in an utterance is using it factively. But this does not mean that, because the concept was used factively, we may infer that things are as such a factive use would suggest they are. Wittgenstein spins out a dialogue that centers around this confusion even further: "But doesn't my utterance 'I know, etc.' enable me to infer 'it is so'? Indeed, and from the proposition 'He knows that there is a hand there' it also follows 'there is a hand there'. But it doesn't follow from his utterance 'I know . . .' that he knows" (On Certainty, §13). The confusion that Wittgenstein is discussing here is possible precisely because the concept of knowledge has a factive sense (see also §20).

We can thus describe the position of someone who knows something through the following conditional principle: *If one knows something, one cannot be wrong about it.*[27] To say that the concept of knowledge has a factive sense and to say that someone who knows something falls under this conditional principle are two ways of saying the same thing. What one is saying is that the concept of knowledge describes a relation between a subject and a propositional content that implies the truth of that content. The standard analysis of the concept of knowledge expresses this factive sense of the concept of knowledge by supplementing the belief condition with a further condition: the condition of truth.

On the standard analysis, the concept of knowledge additionally demands that one knows what one believes only when one has a sufficient justification for that belief. Why is that? Usually the justification condition on knowledge is motivated by the thought that, when I know something, the truth of my belief is not simply a matter of luck or chance. Imagine, for example, a contestant on a quiz show who is asked which of the following rivers is the longest: the Danube, the Rhine, or the Elbe. Our contestant has no idea which rivers these are. She doesn't know where they are, she hasn't heard their names before, and she hasn't the faintest idea how long they are. Obviously she wants to get the question right, but she has no way to decide on an answer apart from guessing. So she guesses the Danube and she's correct. But even though her response was *correct,* it would be absurd to say that she knew the answer. Someone who just has a lucky guess doesn't have knowledge. Someone who knows something not only has a true belief, she has a belief whose truth is not a matter of luck or chance. The concept of knowledge cannot be reduced to the concept of true belief because it contains the idea of a particular explanation of that belief that renders its truth non-accidental.

---

[27] See also McDowell, "Knowledge by Hearsay," 420, where he calls this principle a "truism." Compare Austin, "Other Minds," 98; Peacocke, *Thoughts: An Essay on Content,* 135; Audi, *Epistemology,* 292. Peacocke and Audi maintain that this principle can be defended only in an "externalist" fashion. The status and the significance of this principle will become increasingly central for us as the discussion progresses. Indeed, it will turn out to be the pivotal point around which the discussion with the skeptic turns. At this point we simply want to introduce the notion.

This is the point of the third condition on knowledge. Now, on the standard analysis, the explanatory element in the concept of knowledge is to be understood in terms of the idea of justification. Let us get clear about why.

A justification is a particular form of explanation. To justify a particular act means, in general, that one explains one's act by presenting it as fulfilling or nearly fulfilling a normative standard. Accordingly, one can only justify acts that make some reference to a normative standard. For we make reference to such a normative standard when we explain an act in such a way as to justify it. Now we said above that it is a characteristic of beliefs to make reference to the standard of truth. Moreover, they make reference to that standard not simply from some perspective or other but from the perspective of the subject who holds the belief. Belief is accordingly something, the occurrence of which, in the fundamental case, is explained by invoking the form of explanation that we have characterized as justification. That is, a form of explanation in which one renders the *explanandum* intelligible by representing it as realizing, or nearly realizing, a particular norm—in this case, the norm of truth. When we characterize beliefs as acts in which the subject is guided by the standard of truth, this means that a belief is something that, in the fundamental case, is explained by reference to the norm of truth, not just from some perspective or other but from the perspective of the subject herself. The fact that someone has a belief means, in the fundamental case, that she is in possession of something that represents her belief as an act that realizes the norm of truth, or at least as one that nearly does so. From now on, let's call this "something" a reason or a ground for belief. We can accordingly describe beliefs as acts whose performance consists in being performed "for a reason." An act whose performance consists in being performed for a reason, in this sense, is, *eo ipso,* such that the subject herself can justify it—namely, by the subject presenting precisely the reason for which she performed the act in question.

On this account, a belief is something that is typically explained by a ground or reason for its truth—one that the subject herself can adduce. McDowell has formulated the idea of an intrinsic connection between belief and justification in a quite general form as follows:

[T]he concepts of the propositional attitudes have their proper home in explanations of a special sort: explanations in which things are made intelligible by being revealed to be, or to approximate to being, as they rationally ought to be. This is to be contrasted with a style of explanation in which one makes things intelligible by representing their coming into being as a particular instance of how things generally tend to happen.[28]

As applied to the concept of belief, the thought here is that it is constitutive of a belief to be the object of a form of explanation that has two characteristics. First, it is a normative explanation, i.e., that one explains the occurrence of a belief by making reference to the norm of truth—that is, by representing it as an act that realizes, or nearly realizes, that norm. Second, it is a self-conscious explanation in the sense that it is available to the believing subject herself. It is an explanation for which the *explanandum* is not present unless the subject could herself produce the relevant explanation.

This puts us in a position to answer the question we raised above—about how exactly we should understand the explanatory element in the concept of knowledge. If the concept of knowledge contains the concept of belief, it follows that it contains the concept of such a normative, self-conscious explanation of belief. The justification condition invoked in the standard analysis of the concept of knowledge gives expression to just this interconnection.

But what must the character of such a justification be? To examine this, let us imagine that we have some apparatus and that we know, in some unproblematic way, that it generates outcome A in ninety-nine out of a hundred cases and otherwise outcome B. Perhaps we're dealing with a roulette wheel with ninety-nine red pockets and one black pocket. Now say we're obliged to predict on which color field the wheel will stop on the next spin. Obviously, we're going to predict red. So let us suppose we make this prediction and then spin the wheel and the outcome is indeed red. Did our prediction have the status of knowledge? Did we know that the outcome would be red? Of course not. Because, for all we knew, the outcome might have been black.[29] Thus, our belief that

---

[28] McDowell, "Functionalism and Anomalous Monism," 328–329.
[29] See also McDowell, "Knowledge by Hearsay," 422.

the outcome would be red is only accidentally true. Nothing depends here on how high the probability is. Even if we alter the situation so that the probability of red is even higher, this does not change the fact that we would not be able to know that the outcome would be red. We still would not be in a position to know the outcome in advance precisely because, for all we knew, the possibility of an alternative outcome would still remain in such a situation. Even if there is just a single black field among a million red ones, one cannot hazard the logical leap of saying that one knows the outcome will be red.

If we admit that the concept of knowledge cannot be reduced to its factive sense—namely, because it also contains the idea of a particular form of explanation of belief—it follows that the only form of explanation that is compatible with the factive character of knowledge is a mode of justification of a very special sort. The mode of justification appropriate to the concept of knowledge must be one that is incompatible with the falsity of the belief in question. Alternatively, we might say that the only mode of justification that is compatible with the factive character of knowledge is one in which the truth of the belief is *guaranteed* or *established,* or any other equivalent formulation that indicates that the justification in question rules out the falsity of the relevant belief. We can accordingly say that someone who knows something has a ground for her belief that guarantees its truth.[30] When I say that I know that p, I am thereby saying that my grounds for the truth of p guarantee the truth of p. Wittgenstein accordingly expresses the connection between knowledge and justification as follows: "One says 'I know' when one is ready to give compelling grounds. 'I know' relates to a possibility of demonstrating the truth."[31] The logical distinction between someone's knowing something and her merely believing it rests on the fact that, in the first case, the subject has a justification that guarantees the truth of her belief, whereas, in the second case, she has a justification that accomplishes less. For her justification, in the second case, is compatible with the falsity of her belief. The right way to understand the standard

---

[30] On this point, see also Austin, "Other Minds," 100–101, as well as Tugendhat, *Vorlesungen zur Einführung in die sprachanalytische Philosophie,* 254–255.

[31] Wittgenstein, *On Certainty,* §243.

analysis of the concept of knowledge with which we initially began is thus: *Someone knows something just in case (if and only if) she believes something on a ground that guarantees its truth.*

In what follows, we must seek to understand this concept of knowledge in such a way that it is no mystery how finite creatures, such as we humans are, can have knowledge.

### 3. The Dogma: Justification without Truth

The account of the concept of knowledge we just developed will serve as our guiding thread in what follows. The lynchpin of this account of the concept of knowledge lies in how it construes the relation between the justification requirement and the truth requirement—namely, by maintaining that a belief with the sort of justification required for knowledge is *eo ipso* a true belief and, hence, constitutes knowledge of the matter in question. By possessing the sort of justification for belief that is proper to knowledge, one fulfills not only a necessary but a sufficient condition for knowledge. Now as it happens, most contemporary epistemological accounts not only fail to take issue with this account, they typically don't even provide reasons for not taking it into consideration. On the vast majority of prevailing accounts, justification is taken to be a necessary but insufficient condition for knowledge. That is to say, they understand the justification condition in the standard analysis as a requirement that can be fulfilled without the justified belief in question being true. "The logical independence of truth and justification," as William Alston observes, "is a staple of the epistemological literature."[32]

---

[32] Alston, "Concepts of Epistemic Justification," 70. Alston takes the roots of this unchallenged premise of epistemological discussions to lie in an "internalist" conception of justification. His claim is that the conditional principle of knowledge cannot be defended internalistically, from which he infers that we need an externalist conception of justification (71–72). Our understanding of beliefs as spontaneous acts subject to a normative standard, by contrast, presupposes that the sort of justification that is relevant for knowledge is something a knowing subject doesn't simply happen to have, for it is constitutive of this sort of justification that it can itself be provided by the subject. We will return to this point.

In what follows I will refer to the idea that truth and justification are, in this sense, independent of one another as the "dogma of epistemology." A significant portion of the literature on epistemology, as we shall see over the course of our investigation, is guided by the thought that we cannot give up this dogma. Yet I will show that the epistemological dogma is based on the very skeptical doubt that it is meant to resolve. My claim will thus be that this response to the skeptical doubt is nothing other than a reformulation of the skeptical doubt. In order to bring this connection between skepticism and the epistemological dogma into view, I'll first proceed negatively, by showing how Robert Fogelin's attempt to give up the dogma fails.[33] By reflecting on what goes wrong with Fogelin's position, it will become apparent that one cannot give up the dogma without first understanding the skeptical problem that motivates it. Fogelin's proposal is illuminating because he is one of the few authors who identifies this dogma as a false presupposition of so-called Gettier cases.[34] The whole of epistemology following Gettier's 1963 essay, "Is Justified True Belief Knowledge?," has been framed by this presupposition.[35] The aim of Gettier's essay was to show by counterexample that knowledge cannot be understood as justified true belief, because there are cases where someone has a belief that is true and justified but that nevertheless fails to amount to knowledge. In providing these examples, Gettier is thus presupposing the following two premises:

(1) The justification condition on knowledge is a necessary condition for knowledge but not a sufficient one. Thus, someone can have a belief that is justified in the relevant sense, even though it is false.

(2) If a subject S justifiably believes that p, and p implies q, and S infers q from p, then S is justified in believing that q.

---

[33] Fogelin, *Pyrrhonian Reflections on Knowledge and Justification.*

[34] Other rare exceptions include Almeder, "Truth and Evidence" and "On Seeing the Truth: A Reply," as well as Dretske, "Conclusive Reasons." I will return to Dretske in discussing skeptical doubt in Chapter IV, section 3.

[35] Gettier, "Is Justified True Belief Knowledge?" For an overview of the ensuing (and often philosophically obscure) discussion of Gettier's essay, see Shope, *The Analysis of Knowing: A Decade of Research.*

Since the appearance of Gettier's article, the bulk of the literature has attacked the second of these premises, in order to rescue the analysis of knowledge as justified true belief from the threat of Gettier cases.[36] Fogelin recognizes that it is only possible to solve the Gettier problem if we call into question the first premise—i.e., the premise we have called the dogma of epistemology. Fogelin begins by asking why Gettier—as well as everyone who has subsequently engaged with the Gettier problem, whether implicitly or explicitly—believes that a person can have a justified belief that is false. Neither Gettier nor anyone else has ever seemed to think it necessary to defend this premise. Fogelin reconstructs the following implicit rationale: If we were going to dispute this premise, then we would seem to be obliged to claim that someone's belief is justified only if his ground for it entails its truth. This claim would have the consequence that so-called inductive grounds could never provide a justification sufficient for knowledge—at least, not if we take such grounds to fail to imply the truth of the belief in question.[37] Fogelin shares with the advocates of the dogma that we must admit such "inductive grounds" if we do not want to foreclose from the very outset the possibility of something like empirical knowledge. For if there is such a thing as knowledge of empirical facts, according to Fogelin, it cannot arise from deductive grounds. Yet if it does not arise from deductive grounds, Fogelin takes it to follow that the only way we can make room for empirical facts in the realm of the knowable is by admitting inductive grounds. Fogelin's strategy is accordingly to find a position that enables us to give up the dogma—premise (1) above—while simultaneously admitting inductive grounds.

Fogelin arrives at his position in two steps. His first step is to suggest that we must distinguish between two senses of the concept of justification: a deontological sense and an epistemic sense. When we say that someone has a justified belief in the deontological sense, what

---

[36] Another reaction has been to simply give up on the justification condition for knowledge rather than trying to modify it. This would, of course, mean abandoning as unsalvageable the traditional analysis of knowledge. This is, for example, Ansgar Beckermann's conclusion in "Wissen und wahre Meinung."

[37] See Fogelin, *Pyrrhonian Reflections,* 16.

we mean to say is that he has formed his belief in an "epistemically responsible" manner—i.e., that he didn't simply guess but applied an "inductive procedure."[38] Nor did he pursue "a dubious inductive procedure—for example, he did not consult bird entrails."[39] In the deontological sense of justification, someone can have a justified belief without having knowledge of the matter in question.

Alongside the deontological sense of the concept of justification, according to Fogelin, there is also a second, epistemic sense. To say that a claim is justified in the epistemic sense is not to make an evaluative statement about the epistemic behavior of the subject; it is to make an evaluative claim about the quality of grounds on the basis of which the subject has formed a certain belief. In particular, it is to evaluate whether the grounds in question establish the truth of the belief.

According to Fogelin, the justification condition for knowledge on the standard analysis must be understood to contain both components. The first demands that the subject form her belief in a responsible manner. The second demands that the grounds on the basis of which the subject believes what she does establish the truth of her belief. The standard analysis of the concept of knowledge should thus be understood to claim that "S knows that p if and only if S justifiably came to believe that P on grounds that establish the truth of P."[40]

This twofold characterization of the justification condition, Fogelin wants to argue, enables us to save the traditional analysis of the concept of knowledge from the threat of Gettier cases. For, according to Fogelin, the protagonists in Gettier cases are justified only in the deontological sense but not in the epistemic sense. The Gettier problem, on this account, rests on a failure to distinguish these two senses of the concept of justification and to think that the justification condition for knowledge can be met by a belief that is justified only in the deontological sense.

---

[38] Ibid., 18. For a similar terminological distinction, see also Alston's "Concepts of Epistemic Justification," which has since become standard.

[39] Fogelin, *Pyrrhonian Reflections,* 18.

[40] Ibid., 28.

Now what does it mean, on Fogelin's account, for a subject to have grounds that establish the truth of her belief? The essence of Fogelin's position lies in its second step. And it is only in light of the latter step that the import of his distinction between two senses of the concept of justification becomes clear. For in this second step, Fogelin explains what it means to have grounds that establish the truth of a belief. His central insight here is that the idea of truth-establishing grounds is fundamental to the idea of epistemically responsible behavior. In order to understand what it is to behave in an epistemically responsible manner, we have to appeal to the idea of truth-establishing grounds. At the same time, however, we are not in a position to understand what such grounds are by providing a further analysis. From the first-person perspective, therefore, the idea of grounds that guarantee the truth of one's belief and the idea of behaving in an epistemically responsible manner are one and the same. For, according to Fogelin, a subject cannot be behaving in an epistemically responsible way if she forms her belief on the basis of grounds that, from her own perspective, do not establish the truth of her belief. By contrast, when it comes to other people, we can of course describe cases in which a person acts in an epistemically responsible manner even though the grounds on which her belief rests do not establish its truth. According to Fogelin, such cases are possible precisely when someone comes to her belief through an inference that is inductive rather than deductive. So what is Fogelin's account of this distinction?

Fogelin characterizes the distinction between deductive and inductive inference as follows. While the addition of further premises can never turn a valid deductive argument into an invalid one, the addition of further premises can transform a strong inductive argument into a weak one. In the case of a deductive argument, additional information may well lead us to revise our view of some of our premises and ultimately oblige us to admit that an argument we initially thought was sound is, in truth, not sound. In such a case we would be forced to admit that we were proceeding in an epistemically irresponsible manner in basing our belief on (what turned out to be) an unsound argument. When it comes to inductive arguments, however, things are quite different. When additional information is brought to bear on an inductive argument, that may lead us to revise our sense of how strong that argument is, even if it does not lead us to revise our view about the truth of any of the initial premises.[41]

It is precisely this feature of inductive inferences—namely, the fact that their strength depends on what information the subject has access to—that Fogelin thinks leads to Gettier cases. Because the strength of an inductive inference is information-dependent, a belief founded on an inductive inference can be formed in an epistemically responsible way even though it rests on a ground that does not establish its truth. Given the information the subject had, it might well have been epistemically responsible for her to believe that her ground established the truth of p, even though we, who possess more relevant information, can see that her ground does not establish the truth of p, despite the fact that all of the premises on which she bases her inference are true. For Fogelin, it is the fact that we have access to information that is not available to the protagonists of Gettier cases—it is this "information mismatch"—that explains such cases.[42] In all these cases, we can rightly say that the protagonist has inferred her belief in an epistemically responsible manner and, moreover, that she based that inference exclusively on true premises, and yet nevertheless maintain that her belief is not suitably justified for it to count as knowledge. For we have more information—information that puts us in a position to "know" that the protagonist's belief is justified deontologically but not epistemically.[43]

## 4. The Puzzle: Truth-Guaranteeing Grounds

Fogelin wants to say that the idea of a justification that is incompatible with the falsehood of the belief in question—i.e., the idea of a truth-guaranteeing justification—is an essential component of our concept of

---

[41] This distinction is sometimes marked by saying that deductive inferences are monotonic, whereas inductive inferences are non-monotonic. The idea that inductive inferences are non-monotonic is supposed to register that the strength of inductive inferences is information-dependent: their strength varies depending on what information the subject has access to. See, for example, Williams, *Problems of Knowledge*, 44–47.

[42] Fogelin, *Pyrrhonian Reflections*, 23.

[43] On this point, see Williams's comment on Fogelin's position in *Problems of Knowledge*, 51.

knowledge. We appeal to this idea whenever we ascribe knowledge to ourselves or to others. At the same time, however, Fogelin believes that a positive understanding of what a truth-guaranteeing justification would be is, in principle, unavailable from the first-person perspective. That is the price he thinks we must pay in order to reject the epistemological dogma.[44] But this is a misunderstanding. So long as we do not understand what it means to have a truth-guaranteeing justification for a belief, we cannot understand what it is to know something. To see this, let's consider Fogelin's position more closely.

According to Fogelin, a subject who makes a knowledge claim thereby assumes that she has a ground for her belief that guarantees its truth. In the case of empirical beliefs, these grounds are supposed to be inductive grounds, which are characterized by the fact that they do not entail the truth of the belief in question, as deductive grounds do. What is the status of this assumption about the quality of her grounds in the case of inductive grounds? Is it possible for the subject to ever know that she has an inductive ground for her belief that guarantees its truth? Let's ask how the subject could justify her assumption about the quality of her inductive grounds. In the case of inductive grounds, one way to justify that assumption is ruled out from the outset: she cannot justify her assumption about the quality of her ground by pointing to the truth of her belief. For an inductive ground is precisely defined to be a ground that does not entail the truth of one's belief. Thus, the only way to justify her assumption about the quality of her inductive grounds is to have inductive grounds for it. Yet whether the subject knows something through inductive grounds depends on whether those inductive grounds guarantee the truth of the relevant belief. And because that is something the subject can know only through further inductive grounds, we end up in a regress of explaining a subject's empirical knowledge.

The analysis of empirical knowledge in terms of a ground that does not entail the truth of the belief in question, and a subject's belief about

---

[44] In the present discussion, Fogelin's position serves as an exemplar for a host of views. It is representative of the sort of socially oriented approach that underlies Robert Brandom's *Making It Explicit,* as well as Albrecht Wellmer's "Der Streit um die Wahrheit—Pragmatismus ohne regulative Ideen."

the truth-establishing quality of that ground, on any level of its explanation, cannot provide an answer for the question of whether the subject's belief about the truth-establishing quality of her ground is true and, hence, whether her belief based on that ground is true. For any answer to that question will be faced with the same question. Whether or not one has a ground that guarantees the truth of a particular empirical belief is, according to Fogelin, not something that one can know: it is something one can only assume. Thus, for Fogelin, every empirical knowledge claim must ultimately be viewed as resting on an assumption—the assumption that one's ground guarantees the truth of one's belief. And on this account, it is, in principle, impossible for the subject who makes this assumption to know whether it is really true.

This consequence brings Fogelin's position to ruin. For the mere assumption that the ground for one's belief is truth-guaranteeing cannot transform a belief that itself has the status of a mere assumption into one that has some more noble epistemic status. If, in the absence of such an assumption regarding the truth-guaranteeing character of its grounds, a belief does not amount to knowledge, then the addition of a mere assumption about the character of those grounds will not improve that belief's epistemic status one jot. For the epistemic status of a belief cannot be stronger than the weakest premise on which it is based. As things stand, on Fogelin's account, our beliefs about the world rest on nothing more than the mere assumption that we have an epistemic justification for them. Yet beliefs that rest on the assumption that one has an epistemic justification for them do not have the status of knowledge. They are rather beliefs we *assume* to have this status. But that is not what we wanted to understand. What we wanted to understand was what it means to know something—not what it means to assume that one knows something.

Fogelin's genuine insight is that we have to find a way to reject the epistemological dogma on which Gettier cases trade—the dogma according to which a subject can justify her belief in the manner requisite for knowledge even though that belief is false. Fogelin's error stems from his failure to see what it actually takes to reject this dogma. We must explain what it means for a subject to believe something on the basis of a ground that establishes the truth of that belief.

# II

# Finite Justification

## 1. Agrippa's Trilemma

In Chapter I we discussed how one might abandon the epistemological dogma by distinguishing between two senses of the concept of justification. What we learned was that the price for doing so is that we were unable to explain what it means to know something and had to limit ourselves to explaining what it means to assume that one knows something. This is too high a price to pay to give up the dogma. For it amounts to nothing other than making the skeptic's doubt about the possibility of knowledge a premise in our account of knowledge. It is telling that Fogelin himself confesses such skepticism in claiming that there is no philosophical solution to one of the oldest skeptical problems of all—namely, "Agrippa's Trilemma."[45] Fogelin believes "the Agrippan problem" cannot be resolved by a theory of epistemic justification and that it is, in that sense, "unanswerable."[46] In what follows, I will show that we must regard the epistemological dogma, which Fogelin rightly thinks we must reject, as an attempt to avoid the skepticism we seem to fall

[45] Compare Williams, *Unnatural Doubts: Epistemological Realism and the Basis of Scepticism*, 60–68.
[46] Fogelin, *Pyrrhonian Reflections*, 119.

---

into without the dogma. Yet because Fogelin does not see that the dogma is itself a response to skeptical doubt, he cannot see that his way of giving up the dogma cannot solve the problem to which the dogma responds. For his proposed solution simply recapitulates the problem that it was the principal motive of the dogma to avoid.

Agrippa's trilemma characterizes a pattern of skeptical argumentation that is as simple as it is contagious. We might follow Sextus Empiricus in describing that pattern as follows.[47] Let us suppose that we claim to know something. And suppose further that someone asks us what grounds we have for our knowledge claim. That is, suppose we are asked for a ground that not only explains why we believe what we believe but also explains why our belief amounts to knowledge. And suppose we respond by supplying some such purported ground. It is clear that any belief we provide as our ground can explain why our initial belief amounts to knowledge only if it, too, counts as knowledge. Thus, in order for the belief that we adduce as a ground for our challenged belief to be able to explain why the latter has the status of knowledge, we must have a ground that explains, in turn, why the former belief, which we are invoking as a ground, is itself something that we know. But that means that the task of providing grounds continues infinitely. For the demand for justification recurs at every level where we provide a belief as ground for another belief. And that means that whenever we claim to know something, we can respond to the ongoing demand for grounds only in one of the following three ways:

(1) By refusing at some point to provide a further ground—i.e., by making a dogmatic assertion or presupposition. (The trope of presupposition)

(2) By repeating at some point something that we already said at a previous point in the chain—i.e., by moving in a circle. (The trope of circularity)

(3) By continuing to search for something new to say—i.e., by falling into an infinite regress. (The trope of infinity)

[47] Compare Sextus Empiricus, *Outlines of Pyrrhonism,* 95. Another source of this ancient skeptical argument can be found in Diogenes Laertius, *Lives of the Philosophers* IX, 79–88. For other textual sources of these ancient tropes, see Julia Annas and Jonathan Barnes, eds., *The Modes of Skepticism,* 19–30.

On Sextus's presentation of Agrippa's trilemma, anyone who claims to know something is in a situation that can be fully described by applying these three "tropes," which collectively force us to retract our judgment about the topic in question. They constitute a trilemma because all three possibilities are equally unsatisfactory. For they represent nothing other than three possible ways our justification might fail. That is the problem that Agrippa's trilemma poses: whenever we attempt to justify or ground our claims to knowledge, we are confronted with a choice between these three ways in which our justification is bound to fail. For we must either accomplish the impossible by running through an infinite chain of justifications, or we must satisfy ourselves with one of the other two options—namely, we must either ground our belief in an ungrounded assumption, or move in a circle and adduce as a ground the very belief for which we are seeking a ground.

Agrippa's trilemma presents us with a problem that we cannot ignore if we want to understand how finite creatures can enjoy knowledge. It must, therefore, be part of any account of knowledge to provide a solution to this problem.[48] Any epistemology that, from the very outset, regards Agrippa's trilemma as insoluble is a nonstarter.

Ancient authors tend to present Agrippa's trilemma in connection with (at least) one further trope that is supposed to lead to suspension of belief—namely, the trope of conflict. This trope is based on the idea that we humans have different views about a variety of things. This might tempt one to short-circuit the trilemma—one might think that the trilemma is valid only in cases where two subjects actually disagree. Whenever two subjects are in disagreement about something, their insistent reciprocal objections and demands for further justification may bring about the situation in which each is forced to choose between the trilemma's three options. But the extent of Agrippa's trilemma would remain limited. If that were the case, the only thing the trilemma would show is that such differences of opinion can never be settled. But to restrict the trilemma to cases of actual disagreement would be to misunderstand its point. The trilemma is independent of any actual

[48] Compare Fogelin, *Pyrrhonian Reflections,* 121: "A theory of epistemic justification, as I understand it, is an attempt to solve the Agrippa problem."

disagreement between subjects. The trilemma instead aims to describe the situation in which we each find ourselves whenever we claim to know anything—regardless of whether another person comes along to challenge our claim by demanding an explicit justification.[49] If one wanted to restrict the trilemma to cases in which there is an actual conflict of opinion, one would represent justification as "a purely dialectical exercise," as Michael Williams puts it.[50] In that case, one would justify one's belief only if and only because another belief called it into question. But this would misunderstand the role of justification from the very outset. For the role of the concept of justification, as we saw above, is not to describe an act that might or might not be conjoined with one's act of believing. It instead describes a constitutive element of this very act of belief. In justifying one's belief, one isn't providing some external addition to the belief—something that makes sense only when someone else calls one's belief into question. In justifying one's belief about how things are, one is instead engaging in an activity that is a constitutive element of what it means to have a belief. This does not imply that one, in fact, has a justification of each and every belief one holds. But it does imply that, in the fundamental case, to have a belief is to be in a mental state that one would not be in if one did not have a ground for the truth of one's belief. Believing something means subjecting oneself to the demand that one provide grounds for the truth of one's belief.

What Agrippa's trilemma claims is that, in principle, there is no justification that can guarantee the truth of a belief. Hence it is, in principle, impossible to make a knowledge claim. That is the result the skeptic comes to. And the discovery of Agrippa's trilemma is a first way in which one might arrive at this result.

## 2. Two Answers to Agrippa's Trilemma

There are two possible ways of answering Agrippa's trilemma. The first is to dispute whether it is a genuine trilemma and to attempt to

---

[49] On this point, see also Williams, *Problems of Knowledge,* 64–66.
[50] Ibid., 65.

make do with one of the three options. Because the infinite regress of justifications clearly cannot be a real option, only the other two options remain. As we saw above, Fogelin's strategy is to make do with the "trope of presupposition." Another strategy would be to accept the "trope of circularity." That is the path taken by classical coherence theories.[51] BonJour, for example, explicitly justifies his epistemology through an "argument by elimination," in which he compares the trilemma's various options and attempts to progressively determine which is the least unacceptable.[52] That is to say, BonJour takes Agrippa's trilemma to exhaust the options for developing a theory of epistemic justification.[53] The conclusion BonJour comes to is that circularity is the best of the three options and that we can understand knowledge in accordance with a coherence theory of justification. BonJour characterizes the latter by saying that the fundamental unit of justification is not a single belief but a finite closed system of beliefs that cohere together. Hence, a single belief can only ever be justified in a derivative manner—namely, by demonstrating that it forms part of a coherent system of beliefs. On the coherence theory of justification, Agrippa's three options thus do not represent a genuine trilemma. That theory instead maintains that the "trope of circularity" can be understood in a way that enables us to make sense of the possibility of knowledge.

---

[51] For contemporary defenses of coherentism, see *inter alia* Davidson, "A Coherence Theory of Truth and Knowledge," or BonJour, *The Structure of Empirical Knowledge.* It is worth noting that BonJour has now renounced the version of coherentism his book so vociferously defends. He now defends a position that he himself calls "foundationalism." See BonJour, "The Dialectic of Foundationalism and Coherentism."

[52] BonJour, *The Structure of Empirical Knowledge,* 88. BonJour's thesis is that the regress problem is the central problem of every theory of knowledge. He accordingly holds that every theory of knowledge essentially consists in developing a distinctive answer to this problem. See BonJour, "Can Empirical Knowledge Have a Foundation?"

[53] There is, *prima facie,* a fourth option on BonJour's account—namely, the idea that the regress comes to an end because we arrive at an empirical belief whose degree of justification "is not inferentially dependent on other empirical beliefs and thus raises no further issues of empirical justification" (*The Structure of Empirical Knowledge,* 21). But according to BonJour this is only an apparent option, because he believes he can show that no such empirical beliefs are possible (32).

The second way of responding to Agrippa's trilemma is more radical. Whereas the first response tries to find a solution within the trilemma, the second maintains that Agrippa's trilemma would be a genuine skeptical trilemma only if its three options truly exhausted the spectrum of alternatives. That is to say, the second response holds that we can resolve the Agrippan problematic only by viewing it as a *reductio ad absurdum* of one of its presuppositions. This is what the skeptical force of Agrippa's trilemma consists in. It is a trilemma that we can only resolve if we can undermine it—even though it appears *prima facie* unavoidable, given that its explicit steps rely only on beliefs that we accept. For the explicit steps of Agrippa's trilemma only presuppose that a belief must be justified in order to have the status of knowledge and that no belief that lacks the status of knowledge can serve as a reason for a belief and thereby bestow such status on it. In light of what we have said about knowledge thus far, we must accede to these claims. For a subject who attempts to justify her belief by another belief that does not itself have the status of knowledge has failed to adduce a reason that guarantees the truth of the belief in question. And that means that the trilemma cannot be resolved from within. We can escape the skeptical force of Agrippa's trilemma only if we are in a position to identify an implicit presupposition of the trilemma that we can show we are not committed to.

So what presuppositions does the trilemma rely on? Well, one of its presuppositions is that the only possible way to justify a particular belief is to provide a second belief from which we can infer the truth of the first. For only then will the demand for justification necessarily recur, because what we have provided as a justification is the same sort of thing as what it is supposed to justify. If we accept the present presupposition that adducing further beliefs is the only way a belief can be justified, then Agrippa's trilemma follows and it is, in principle, impossible to base a belief on a ground that guarantees its truth.[54]

---

[54] Every coherence theory must proceed from the idea that this presupposition is indisputable. See also Davidson's unquestioning formulation of this premise: "All that

We can see this by recalling the general form that justification takes when we justify one belief with another belief. When we provide one belief as justification for another, we are proceeding on the basis of a certain claim, q, that represents the content of the justifying belief, and inferring from this claim the truth of another claim, p, that represents the content of the belief to be justified. The deep insight at the core of Agrippa's trilemma is that if we accept that only beliefs can serve as grounds for beliefs, we will never be in a position to justify any such inference. The trilemma thus rests on the premise that beliefs can only be grounded in other beliefs. It accordingly cannot hold the following two claims apart:

(1) Beliefs are explained by grounds for their truth.
(2) Only beliefs can serve as grounds for beliefs.

Assuming we accept the first claim, it must be possible to dispute the second if a solution to Agrippa's trilemma is indeed possible. On the other hand, if one cannot hold these two claims apart, then it is clear that there can only be two kinds of justification: viz., deductive and inductive. On this presupposition, therefore, the only way to render empirical knowledge intelligible is to understand it as the result of inductive justification.

If we look back on our previous discussion with this result in view, we can understand why Fogelin's position is couched exclusively in terms of these forms of justification. For Fogelin's claim is, as we have seen, that we can make sense of empirical knowledge only if we abandon the dogma of epistemology in a way that enables us to allow for inductive grounds for knowledge. Thus, one can entertain the idea that one has to make room for inductive grounds in order to understand empirical knowledge only if one unquestioningly accepts the premise that Agrippa's trilemma depends on. Only the presupposition that beliefs can only be justified by beliefs would compel us to think that empirical knowledge has to be understood as the result of inductive justification.

counts as evidence or justification for a belief must come from the same totality of belief to which it belongs." See "A Coherence Theory of Truth and Knowledge," 153.

And then we have to admit that it is impossible to understand how one can ever have a truth-guaranteeing ground for an empirical belief. Yet, without such an account, we cannot understand how empirical knowledge is possible.

## 3. The Category of a Truth-Guaranteeing Ground

The concept of a truth-guaranteeing ground is our topic and our riddle. We have seen that and why this concept is essential to any account of knowledge. But whether we can make sense of such a concept is, as yet, unclear. Up to this point all we have seen is how this concept is not to be understood. We cannot make sense of this concept so long as we hold that only beliefs can serve as grounds for beliefs. This riddle—about whether and how it is possible to render this concept intelligible—will occupy us for the entire length of this book. The result of our reflections up to this point has been that we have to make room for the concept of a kind of reason for beliefs that are not beliefs.

At this point, our formal account of the sort of justification that is requisite for knowledge runs as follows. The particular type of justification that is requisite for knowledge is one that answers the question "why do you believe that p?" in such a way that the question of p's truth no longer remains open. We have termed this a truth-guaranteeing justification. We might accordingly call the question that such a justification settles the doxastic why-question. A why-question asks for an explanation. The doxastic why-question asks for a special form of explanation: namely, one whose very form exhibits the thing it explains as an act of belief.[55] And an explanation that exhibits its object as an act of belief, we argued, is one that makes the occurrence of that belief intelligible by revealing it to be true (or likely to be true). The fact that answering this sort of why-question consists in giving grounds in favor of the truth of one's belief means that the sort of explanation we are interested

[55] On this point, see also Rödl, *Self-Consciousness,* 87–88. Accordingly, Rödl calls this form of explanation "belief explanation."

in here—namely, one in terms of which its object is intelligible as an act of belief—has a specifically normative sense.

This point is sometimes expressed by saying that the doxastic why-question asks not for the "causes" of a given belief but for "reasons." Yet this characterization of the distinctive form of explanation that is our topic is correct only if one restricts the notion of a cause to the particular form of explanation that renders things intelligible, as McDowell puts it, "by representing their coming into being as a particular instance of how things generally tend to happen."[56] That is to say, this contrast between reasons and causes is cogent only if one identifies the very idea of a cause with the distinctive application of that notion in the sorts of explanations that are paradigmatic of the natural sciences.

But then one has simply built the relevant distinction between these types of explanation into the concept of cause. And in so doing, one is ruling out from the very start that reasons can themselves be causes of belief. But why should we do this? What reason do we have to restrict the concept of cause to a particular form of explanation? This restriction is not only not self-evident, it is also in danger of being misunderstood. For it suggests that answering the doxastic why-question by citing reasons for the relevant belief does not, of itself, amount to a complete explanation of that belief. Such a restriction suggests that explanations from the standpoint of reason can never be complete explanations, because it presupposes from the outset that they do not address what caused the belief. Yet in what sense is my explanation incomplete when I explain why I believe that it is raining outside by saying, "Because I see that it is"? One of the central conclusions of our investigation will be that such an answer is complete in every sense that is applicable to beliefs if the subject's answer does in fact cite the very reason or ground for which she believes that it is raining. When I cite my perception as the ground for which I hold my belief, it simply isn't the case that I am providing a less than complete explanation because I have cited only a ground and not a cause. I have indeed provided a complete explanation of my belief, precisely because in giving such an explanation I cite the

---

[56] McDowell, "Functionalism and Anomalous Monism," 328.

ground I have for believing what I do as that which is effective in my formation of this belief, and in that sense, as its cause.[57]

Thus, in order to capture the distinction that this contrast is meant to express, what we have to keep apart are not grounds and causes but two different types of explanation. Then we are free to say that justification is indeed a form of causal explanation. When I cite the ground for my belief, I am giving a specific causal explanation of why I believe what I believe. Moreover, my explanation makes it clear why this belief is to be endorsed from the standpoint of reason, since the grounds I am adducing are grounds for the truth of my belief.

We said above that the sort of justification that is requisite for knowledge is one that answers the doxastic why-question in a way that settles the truth of the belief in question. This means that not just any answer to the doxastic why-question will suffice for knowledge. There must be ways to answer the doxastic why-question that do not settle the truth of the belief in question. Otherwise we would be ruling out in advance that someone could have a justified belief that nevertheless lacked the status of knowledge. We would thereby exclude those modes of belief that we typically characterize as mere opinion, speculation, assumption, hypothesis, etc. If we do not want to rule out these modes of belief in advance—and it will become clear in due course why and in what sense they belong to any proper account of finite knowledge—then we must distinguish between two sorts of answer to the doxastic why-question. We must distinguish between answers that guarantee the truth of the relevant belief and those that do not guarantee its truth but accomplish something less. While the first sort of answer is sufficient for knowledge, because it forecloses the possibility that the belief is false, the latter is insufficient, because it precisely does not foreclose this possibility.

Agrippa's trilemma maintains that it is impossible for us to justify our beliefs in a way that is sufficient for knowledge. In response we

---

[57] A representative formulation of this thought in relation to explanations of action can be found in Davidson, "Actions, Reasons, Causes." See also Anscombe, *Intention*, §§ 5–19, as well as her "The Causation of Action" and "Memory, Experience, and Causation." See also Strawson, "Causation and Explanation." I will explore the full significance of this thought in more detail in the course of this inquiry.

suggested that the trilemma should be understood as a *reductio* of one of its presuppositions. The presupposition we identified as problematic was the idea that the only thing that can serve as a ground for a belief is another belief. For only then is it not only possible but also necessary to repeat the question that initially called for a ground and apply that question to the ground itself. And if every ground is such as to invite the same question with which we began—viz., "why believe p?"—then there is no way to answer this question that forecloses the possibility that p is false.

We therefore conclude that this premise must be false—it cannot be the case that the only way to justify a belief is to cite another belief from which the first can be inferred. There must be answers to the doxastic why-question that settle the truth of the belief in question. A necessary condition on any such answer is, as we saw, that it is not in turn susceptible to yet another reapplication of the doxastic why-question. For otherwise the truth of the belief in question is left up in the air.[58]

Let us reflect on the status of our foregoing considerations. At this point we have claimed neither that we do have truth-guaranteeing grounds nor how we might make sense of them. We have claimed only that the category of truth-guaranteeing grounds is necessary if the concept of knowledge is to be intelligible. We have been led by purely conceptual considerations to assert the necessity of the category of truth-guaranteeing grounds for any adequate account of knowledge. The grounds that belong to this category must exhibit the following two characteristics:

---

[58] It is along these same lines that I understand Wittgenstein when he writes: "Reasoning which leads to an endless regress is not to be abandoned because we cannot thus arrive at its goal but because here there is no goal; so that it makes no sense to say, 'we cannot arrive at it.' We easily think that we must traverse the regress a few levels and then abandon it in despair, as it were. Whereas its lack of a goal [...] is discernable from its point of departure" (*Zettel*, §693). If a ground and what it grounds are identical in kind, then it is already evident from the "point of departure" of this line of thought that no ground will be able to settle the question that it is supposed to answer.

(1) Such grounds must guarantee the truth of what they are grounds for.

And a necessary condition of (1) is:

(2) Such grounds must not be subject to reapplications of the doxastic why-question.

Let us imagine for a moment that there actually are grounds that belong to this category. If there are such grounds, this means that there are grounds that are different in kind from what they are grounds for. What must such a ground be like? For the sake of contrast, let us recall the form our justifications take when we justify one belief by another. Imagine I answer the question "Why do you believe p?" by saying, "Because I believe q," and the question "Why do you believe q?" by saying, "Because I believe r," and the question "Why do you believe r?" by saying, "Because I believe s." What I am doing in this series of answers is changing the content of my propositional attitudes—I ground p with q, q with r, and r with s—while holding constant the nexus between the respective content and myself. Each time, the nexus is specifically that of belief, even as the content varies. And it is for precisely this reason that the very same question that is posed of the content p can also be posed of the content q, etc.

It follows that there can be truth-guaranteeing grounds only if there are mental acts that we can cite in response to the question "Why do you believe p?" and that do not adduce a different content from the one that is to be grounded but instead exhibit a different sort of nexus with this content—namely, one that answers the doxastic why-question in a way that forecloses the possibility that the content, to which we stand in such a relation, is false.

## 4. Are We Familiar with Grounds Belonging to This Category?

The foregoing considerations show that we need truth-guaranteeing grounds if we are to understand how knowledge is possible for us. They do not, however, show that such grounds are actually available to us. Now one might suppose that the skeptical trilemma holds just in case we cannot establish, on the basis of purely conceptual considerations, that we have grounds belonging to this category. But this inference is not sound. For how could conceptual considerations ever show that we have grounds that belong to a certain category? Conceptual considerations can only show us that we must necessarily have such grounds but not that we actually do enjoy them. At this point, conceptual considerations cannot bring us any further. We must turn and address this question to ourselves. We must ask ourselves: Are we ourselves familiar with such grounds? Can we find expressions we employ that at least seem to describe grounds that meet the characterization above? Because we ordinarily describe ourselves as knowledgeable, we might expect to find such expressions. And indeed, there are such expressions that we are all familiar with. Consider, for example, expressions such as, "perceive (see, hear, smell, taste, feel, etc.) that . . ." or "remember that . . . ," or "learn from so-and-so that . . . ," or "prove that . . . ." These expressions at least seem to signify a nexus to a propositional content that falls under the category of a truth-guaranteeing ground. When someone responds to the question "Why do you believe p?" by saying, "Because I see that p," she is bringing into play not some new content to ground her belief but instead a new nexus to the content in question. In particular, she is bringing to bear a nexus that answers the doxastic why-question in such a way as to foreclose the possibility that the content, to which she stands in such a relation, is false.

As things stand, we can formulate this thought so that it expresses something that should not be controversial. When someone sees that p, she has a ground for her belief that p that guarantees the truth of that belief. That she has such a truth-guaranteeing ground is due to the fact that there is a deployment of the phrase "S sees that p" in which 'sees' is a factive expression. It would be inconsistent with the use of this expression for someone to see that p when p is not the case. If p is not the case, one can at most have a visual experience that p—but one cannot see that p. The same holds for the other expressions mentioned above. Let us call any position designated by such an expression—". . . perceive that . . . ," ". . . learn from so-and-so that . . . ," ". . . prove that . . . ,"

"...remember that...," etc.—a "guaranteeing" epistemic position.[59] Someone who occupies a position that satisfies one of these expressions has a ground for her belief that guarantees its truth. Thus, when someone grounds her belief by citing a position designated by one of these expressions, she is thereby adducing a truth-guaranteeing ground for her belief, to which the doxastic why-question is no longer applicable. One can sensibly ask, "Why do you believe that there is a teacup over there?" But one cannot in the same sense ask, "Why do you see that there is a teacup over there?" In particular, one cannot pose this question in the sense that aims to determine whether the propositional content in question is true.

I said that these formulations should not be controversial. Now, in philosophy, when we put forward a formulation that we think should be uncontroversial—e.g., when we note that saying that someone perceives that p implies that p—we are not attempting to give a philosophical analysis of the relevant expression or, accordingly, of the phenomenon it describes.[60] All we are doing is fixing the object of our analysis. Such formulations thus aim to do nothing more than to specify the sense of the

---

[59] McDowell makes a similar point in "Knowledge and the Internal," 397–398. For the relevant terminology, see also Blackburn, "Knowledge, Truth and Reliability," 176–177.

[60] This misunderstanding of the role of self-evident claims in philosophy finds expression, for example, in Austin's critique of the analysis of perceptual verbs offered by Ayer and Price, among others. According to Ayer and Price, perceptual verbs have a twofold use in ordinary language—one factive, the other non-factive. Ayer's thesis is that the epistemologically fundamental use of such verbs is non-factive (see *The Foundations of Empirical Knowledge,* 20). Now, Austin believes he can criticize Ayer's position by arguing that he is mistaken about our use of perceptual verbs. For as they are ordinarily employed, Austin maintains, perceptual verbs have just one sense—namely, a factive one (see *Sense and Sensibilia,* 91f). Yet Austin's attempt to refute Ayer's claim that our perceptual verbs have a twofold use is irrelevant to the epistemological question. For the crucial point, from an epistemological perspective, is how we are to understand the factive use of these verbs—e.g., in saying that someone sees that p. In order to dispute Ayer's epistemological claim that the fundamental use of perceptual verbs is non-factive, it is not sufficient to show that it is incorrect, in ordinary discourse, to apply perceptual verbs to cases of hallucination, etc. Moreover, such a demonstration is not even necessary. We can see this by considering how Anscombe attempts to resolve the dispute. Anscombe claims, *contra* Austin, that one can very well say that Hamlet saw his departed father or that Macbeth saw a dagger when none was before his eyes. Yet Anscombe also maintains, *contra* Ayer, that it is a mistake to

aforementioned expressions that we want to give an account of. Our task now is to understand these expressions and, thereby, the phenomena we describe when we use them in the specified sense.

Let us briefly review where our reflections have brought us in regard to our skeptical problematic. We have shown that Agrippa's trilemma, considered in itself, does not formulate a skeptical problem, because it presupposes what a skeptical argument was meant to show—namely, that it is impossible to justify a belief by a mental act that guarantees its truth. Agrippa's trilemma must rule out from the very start the idea that someone might justify her belief by saying "because I see (or saw) that p" or by saying "because I learned from my neighbor that p." Consequently, Agrippa's trilemma expresses a skeptical problem only once we come up with a compelling argument showing that these grounds—i.e., grounds that, in light of our ordinary self-understanding, seem to fall under the aforementioned category—cannot in fact fall under that category, despite any appearances to the contrary.

## 5. The Role of Perceptual Grounds

Up to this point we have argued as though we had to abandon the presupposition that beliefs can only be justified by other beliefs because the epistemological problem that Agrippa's trilemma confronts us with would otherwise be insoluble. Yet this is not the deepest reason that compels us to reject this presupposition. We have to give up the trilemma's presupposition not because we will otherwise be unable to solve the epistemological problem but because we will otherwise be unable to understand how we can so much as perform acts of the sort that the trilemma claims can never be adequately justified so as to count as knowledge: namely, beliefs that have objective content in the sense that their truth is dependent on how things are in the world. This is how we first introduced the concept of finite knowledge: in terms of beliefs for

infer from this that the direct objects of perception cannot be material objects but must be sense data. See Anscombe, "The Intentionality of Sensation."

which the world constitutes the standard that determines, independently of those acts, whether the latter are true or false.

Now the trilemma presupposes that it is at least conceivable that we can perform such acts. For in order to claim that it is impossible for us to justify our beliefs about the world in such a way as to rule out the possibility that they are false, one must presuppose that we can at least have beliefs that have objective content in the above sense. So let us ask whether this presupposition can be fulfilled even as we simultaneously uphold the trilemma's other presupposition that only beliefs can serve as grounds for beliefs.

Let us suppose that beliefs are the only mental acts that a subject can adduce as grounds for doing what one does when one forms a belief—namely, deciding to endorse a particular conceptual content as true. This would mean that the sole mental acts through which someone can normatively explain why she believes what she believes would have a conceptual content that resulted from a decision on the part of the subject about the truth of that content. Thus, if beliefs are the only candidates to cite in a normative explanation of beliefs, this means that nothing that might guide the subject in forming a belief is such as to reflect that the truth of her belief is *dependent* on how things are in the world. Rather, on this supposition, everything that might guide the subject in forming a belief instead depends on a decision on the part of the subject. This means that nothing capable of guiding the subject in fulfilling the standard of truth, to which she subjects herself in forming a belief, involves the thought (either for the subject or for anyone else) that meeting this standard *depends* on how things stand in the world.

Yet if this is the case, it becomes unintelligible how a subject can so much as perform mental acts whose truth she understands to be dependent on how things are in the world. The idea of a belief whose truth the subject understands to be dependent on how things are in the world dissolves. Yet, if one cannot understand the possibility of such a belief, then the question of how to account for a belief's status as knowledge cannot even arise. And if that is so, then there is no problem for the trilemma to formulate.

In order for it to be intelligible that a subject can have beliefs in the sense of acts with objective content whose truth or falsity she understands to be dependent on how things stand in the world, there must be grounds for beliefs that do not result from the subject's decision about the truth of their conceptual content but instead depend on how things stand in the world. In order for a subject to have beliefs whose truth she understands to be dependent on the world, she must possess grounds that reflect precisely this dependence. She must have grounds that, in Kantian parlance, are characterized by "receptivity."[61] Moreover, in the present case, the receptivity of such grounds must be such that they enable a subject to endorse the truth of a conceptual representation of how things are in the world. There must accordingly be mental acts that spring from a faculty to, as Kant puts it, "receive representations" from the objects that are represented.[62]

Now, our faculty of sensibility is defined to be receptive in this sense. It consists in the ability "to receive representations through the manner in which we are affected by objects."[63] Thus, in order to account for mental acts that are not dependent on a subject's making a decision about the truth of their content, we need to think of ourselves as sensible beings that have the ability to receive representations through being affected by objects in a particular manner. A subject who has a ground for her belief that involves her ability to receive representations through being affected by objects in a particular manner would be in a mental state that is not the result of a decision on her part but that instead is given to the subject by the object's affecting her. She would be in a mental state that, unlike a judgment, neither consists in nor rests on a deed on the part of the subject but is rather suffered by the subject on account of the object. Such a ground for belief would thus reflect her understanding of her belief as an act whose truth is dependent on how things stand in the world.

We have been reflecting on how it is possible to form beliefs whose content is objective in the sense that their truth depends on how things are in the world. But what do these reflections show us? They show us that the fundamental case of justifying a belief about the world must

---

[61] Kant, *Kritik der reinen Vernunft*, A19/B33.
[62] Ibid.
[63] Ibid.

contain a mental act that exhibits a receptive nexus between the subject of the act and a particular content.[64] For we are able to explain how
a subject can have beliefs whose truth is dependent on how things
are in the world only if there are mental acts that exhibit a nexus between a subject and a particular content that is receptive as well as
justificatory.

In what follows, we will call beliefs that can be traced back to such a
receptive ground "empirical beliefs" and we shall likewise term any
acts of knowledge corresponding to such beliefs "empirical knowledge."
A few of the expressions we listed above as ostensibly designating
mental acts that fall under the category of truth-guaranteeing grounds
seem to belong to the class of expressions that describe just such a receptive nexus. In particular, the expressions "perceive that p" and
"learn from so-and-so that p" seem to describe nexus that are both justifying and receptive. For when someone perceives something, she has
a particular sensory experience. The fact that a subject has a particular
sensory experience means that she enjoys a mental state that differs
from a belief insofar as her being in that state does not, as such, imply
that she has decided to endorse a particular conceptual content. This is
readily apparent from the fact that one continues to have the sensory
experience that a stick submerged in water is bent even when one has
come to know that it is straight. It is, of course, true that one can make a
decision about whether one should open one's eyes, or whether one
should turn on the light in order to see better, or whether one should
look very carefully or only fleetingly. But once one has decided all these
things and opened one's eyes and sees what is open to view, what one perceptually experiences is not the result of a decision regarding the truth of
the relevant content. Rather, it is something one receives through an impact that things make on one's senses.

It is similar when one learns from so-and-so that p. When one learns
from so-and-so that p, this entails that one has heard so-and-so saying

[64] It follows that the idea of a receptive nexus is necessary if we are to make any sense of
the idea of an inferential justification of empirical beliefs—i.e., if we are to make
sense of the idea of grounding an empirical belief by deriving it from some other empirical belief. For otherwise there would be no beliefs with an empirical content from
which we might derive the truth of another empirical content.

that p. Having heard so-and-so saying that p does not, as such, imply that one has decided to endorse what one has heard from her. Here, too, it is clearly true that one can decide whether one should put oneself in a position to hear so-and-so saying something to oneself, in the present situation, or otherwise deliberate about whom one should give the opportunity to tell one something. But once one has decided these things, and put oneself in a position to hear so-and-so saying that p, and learns from her what she enables one to learn, what one hears so-and-so saying is not dependent on one's decision to endorse the truth of what one hears so-and-so saying.

Agrippa's trilemma rests on the premise that the only mental acts that can justify beliefs are other beliefs. If this premise is correct, then our considerations suggest that the trilemma articulates a skeptical problem that runs even deeper than we initially thought. For then the problem it poses is not merely epistemological but transcendental in the sense that it makes it unintelligible how our beliefs can have the kind of content they at least purport to have, namely objective content whose truth is dependent on how things are in the world. That is, it makes it unintelligible how we can form empirical beliefs that so much as purport to be about objects in the world around us.[65]

Agrippa's trilemma offers no argument to the effect that the premise on which it rests is actually true. Indeed, we have found expressions in our ordinary modes of speech and thought that ostensibly provide examples of mental acts belonging to the category of receptive truth-guaranteeing grounds. The expressions "perceive that p" and "learn from so-and-so that p" seem to describe mental acts that instantiate nexus that are both justificatory and receptive. The skeptical force of Agrippa's trilemma thus depends on the availability of considerations demonstrating that these expressions, which we use in our ordinary thinking to identify nexus that are both justificatory and receptive, cannot, in fact, denote any such instances.

---

[65] No one disputes that Agrippa's trilemma aims to demonstrate the impossibility of justifying empirical beliefs. See BonJour, *The Structure of Empirical Knowledge,* 21; see also Fogelin, *Pyrrhonian Reflections,* 116.

In what follows, we will restrict our investigation to the question of how we are to understand perceptual knowledge. We will begin, in Part Two, by considering an argument that purports to show that the expression "perceive that p" cannot designate an instance of such a receptive and justificatory nexus. The import of our investigation, however, reaches far beyond the case of perceptual knowledge. The case of perceptual knowledge is exemplary for us insofar as working out how perceptual knowledge is to be understood will bring to light an account of the nature of knowledge in general. Thus, we will approach the question of whether there are grounds belonging to the category that we have demonstrated is necessary to any explanation of knowledge by giving an account of perceptual knowledge. But it will become apparent that our considerations will apply equally well to the case of knowledge by hearsay.

# PART TWO

*The Primacy of Knowledge*

THE FORM OF ANCIENT SKEPTICISM THAT FINDS EXPRESSION IN Agrippa's trilemma maintains that it is impossible to adduce a ground for a belief that guarantees its truth. The question why someone believes something can never be answered in such a way as to rule out the possibility of the belief's being false. The ancient skeptics concluded from this that we are obliged to suspend judgment about all things where truth or falsity is at issue.[1] Now, in Part One we saw that Agrippa's trilemma is unavoidable only if the ostensible solution that we identified proves impossible. That is, if it turns out to be impossible to understand someone who perceives something (or learns something from someone else) as possessing a truth-guaranteeing reason for belief. Agrippa's trilemma itself offers no argument against this solution. It simply presupposes that such a solution is impossible. In this part I will show what argument this form of ancient skepticism must take for granted here. It is precisely the same argument that provides the explicit motivation and support for Cartesian skepticism.[2]

If it is true that ancient and modern skepticism are connected in the way that I will maintain, then one can no longer accept without some qualification Hegel's view that ancient skepticism is superior to modern skepticism. Ancient skepticism, as Hegel understands it, takes up a "purely negative attitude."[3] Ancient skepticism "holds back altogether

[1] The ancient skeptics prove to be quite consistent on this point, because they saw very clearly that their argument against the possibility of knowledge was at the same time an argument against the possibility of beliefs with objective content. We will address this point explicitly in Chapter V, section 3. But our claim that the skeptic is quite consistent in perceiving a connection between challenging the possibility of knowledge and challenging the possibility of belief does not yet address the practical question of whether one can take this consistency seriously in the sense of bringing one's life practices into "consistency" with one's theoretical views. On the latter point, see Burnyeat, "Can the Skeptic Live His Skepticism?"

[2] Here I am parting ways with Michael Williams, who takes ancient and Cartesian skepticism to constitute two fundamentally different forms of skepticism. See Williams, *Unnatural Doubts: Epistemological Realism and the Basis of Scepticism*, 47–88. See also his *Problems of Knowledge*, 61–62.

[3] Hegel, "Verhältnis des Skeptizismus zur Philosophie, Darstellung seiner verschiedenen Modifikationen, und Vergleichung des neuesten mit dem alten," 67.

—

from expressing any certainty and any being"[4] in order to thereby resist "against the dogmatism of ordinary consciousness."[5] By contrast, in Hegel's view, the hallmark of modern skepticism is that "ordinary consciousness, with its whole range of facts, has an indubitable certainty."[6] For this reason, Hegel thinks that modern skepticism is nothing more than a form of dogmatism and thus without much "merit."[7]

This reading of the relation between ancient and modern skepticism overlooks the fact that ancient skepticism must implicitly presuppose the cogency of the very argument that lies at the center of modern skepticism. My aim in what follows is, first, to unfold this skeptical argument and then to discuss a family of general strategies I call "positions of moderation," which characterizes how most of contemporary epistemology reacts to this skeptical problem. It is characteristic of these positions that they regard the skeptical argument as valid but are nevertheless convinced they can make knowledge intelligible. However, this conviction is, as we shall soon see, without foundation.

[4] Ibid., 66.
[5] Ibid., 68.
[6] Ibid.
[7] Ibid., 69. Accordingly, Hegel also refers to the modern variant as "dogmatic skepticism."

## III

# Doubting Knowledge

## 1. Objectivity and the Possibility of Error

Skeptical considerations about knowledge aim to show that we cannot understand how it is possible for finite creatures to have knowledge. If epistemology consists in explaining how knowledge is possible, then skepticism is the view that all epistemology is doomed to fail. But epistemology only has to confront these skeptical lines of thought if we grant a certain assumption: we must assume that skeptical doubt about the possibility of knowledge results from a line of philosophical reasoning that is compelling for everyone who rationally reflects on the nature of knowledge.[8] The skeptic has to understand her doubt to result from considerations that are, as Hume puts it, "necessitated by reasoning."[9] "[S]keptical doubt," Hume writes, "arises naturally from a profound and intense reflection on those subjects."[10] The skeptic's claims are, as she understands them, nothing more than "the obvious dictates of reason."[11]

---

[8] Cavell emphasizes this point repeatedly in *The Claim of Reason,* 130–144. It is important to appreciate this point in order to understand why skepticism is a serious problem and not just an intellectual puzzle.

[9] See Hume, *An Enquiry concerning Human Understanding,* 152.

[10] Hume, *A Treatise of Human Nature,* 219.

[11] Hume, *An Enquiry Concerning Human Understanding,* 152.

---

We can see the same point at work in the opening of Descartes's *Meditations,* when the meditator, after having observed that his senses are prone to err about objects that are too small or too far away, is not immediately willing to draw the conclusion that it would be appropriate to doubt all objects of the senses whatsoever, including the apparent fact that he is currently sitting in a dressing gown in front of the fire with a paper in his hand, etc.[12] Rather, he objects that only an "insane" person would conclude from such occasional errors that the senses are universally dubious; and it would hardly do to set such ravings up "as an example for [oneself]."[13] If skeptical doubt rested on such an unreasonable inference, it would literally not have a leg to stand on. Accordingly, it would no longer represent a challenge to epistemology nor to anyone's ordinary sense of herself as a knower.

It was for this reason that we said that a serious skeptical problem would arise only (and precisely) when we encounter a compelling argument challenging the idea that someone who perceives something should be understood as standing in a nexus with a content that is both receptive and justificatory. I will call such an argument "genuinely" skeptical. I employ this term not only because this is an implicit presupposition of Agrippa's trilemma but also because, as will emerge, the bulk of contemporary epistemology—quite unintentionally—will reveal itself to be deeply skeptical, insofar as it uncritically accepts the validity of such an argument.

In Part One we asked whether there are locutions we employ that appear to describe mental acts that not only fall under the category of a truth-guaranteeing ground but are also receptive. We hit upon the locutions "perceives that..." and "learned from so-and-so that..." as purported descriptions of such mental acts. Such locutions appear to describe a nexus that is at once justificatory and receptive. For there is a particular employment of these locutions in which they have a factive sense. Let us concentrate on perception in what follows. The skeptic wants to argue that it is impossible for finite subjects to ever use such locutions in a factive sense. The argument that is supposed to show this is the

---

[12] Descartes, *Meditations,* AT 7:18.
[13] Ibid., 7:18f.

traditional "argument from illusion," as it has come to be known. I prefer to call it the "argument from the possibility of error" in order to emphasize its underlying motive. For the chief motivation of this argument is to account for a conceptual necessity arising from the fact that the concept of knowledge at issue here is a concept of finite knowledge. This means that what we are trying to comprehend is a concept of knowledge that is to be elucidated in terms of judgments whose characteristic feature is that they can be true or false. For the concept of finite knowledge—as opposed to that of infinite knowledge—pertains to acts whose contents are objective in the sense that they refer to the world as something on which the truth of these acts depends. The possibility of error constitutes one aspect of the objectivity of the contents of finite knowledge. Finite knowledge is objective knowledge. Objective knowledge is fallible knowledge.

The chief motivation of the skeptical argument, then, is to do justice to and find a place for this possibility of error in its account of knowledge. The argument is supposed to show that, in order to account for the possibility of error, we are compelled to reject the idea that the sense of a statement of the form "S perceives that p" consists in describing a truth-guaranteeing ground. The argument is based on the following sorts of considerations.

A subject who perceives how things are has a perceptual experience that things are thus and so. And on the basis of this perceptual experience, the subject believes that things are thus and so. Yet it must be possible for the subject to be mistaken. And when a subject errs in this way, we have a case in which the subject has a perceptual experience that things are thus and so without its actually being the case that things are thus and so. Moreover, this experience must be phenomenally indistinguishable, from the subject's point of view, from a case in which things actually are as her experience presents them to be. If it is to be possible for a subject to err, then we must allow for such phenomenally indistinguishable cases. For let us imagine that the subject can phenomenally distinguish both kinds of cases—e.g., because she has access to a differentiating criterion of some sort. If the subject were to employ some such differentiating criterion that enabled her to distinguish those cases in which she has the experience that things are thus and so when things are not as she experiences them to be, on the one hand, from the cases in which she had that experience and things are as she experiences them to be, on the other, then it would be impossible, in principle, for her to err on the basis of a perceptual experience. So if we want to make room for error, we must allow for such cases. And to allow for such cases, we must give a particular description of the mental basis on which perceptual beliefs are formed. In particular, we must hold that when a subject believes that things are thus and so because she actually perceives how things are, she is relying on a mental basis that is compatible with her belief being false. To make room for the possibility of error, we have to maintain that the best possible mental basis that a subject can have for a perceptual belief is one in which she has a perceptual experience that she can equally well have in both a case where she actually perceives how things are and in a case where it merely appears to her as if things were thus and so without things actually being thus and so.[14]

So the argument goes. I claimed above that the argument from the possibility of error constitutes the explicit basis of modern skepticism. But this should by no means be taken to suggest that this argument finds its first formulation in Descartes. It was, indeed, a thoroughly familiar argument in ancient philosophy. Plato presents it as a well-known line of reasoning in the *Theaetetus*,[15] where Socrates introduces it as an "objection" that he assumes Theaetetus has "often heard before."[16] And Aristotle likewise discusses the argument as a familiar line of thought in his *Metaphysics*.[17] What I mean to claim is rather that it is only in

---

[14] On generalizations of this argument—not only to other forms of knowledge but also to an understanding of the concept of action—see Dancy, "Arguments from Illusion"; Williamson, *Knowledge and Its Limits*, 54–60; Stout, *Things That Happen because They Should*, 23–28.

[15] Plato, *Theaetetus*, 157e.

[16] Ibid. 158b.

[17] See *Metaphysics*, bk. Gamma (IV), 1009–1010. For an excellent discussion of this argument in Aristotle, see Anthony Kenny, "The Argument from Illusion in Aristotle's *Metaphysics*."

modern skepticism—starting with Descartes—that this argument is deployed as the fundamental basis of skeptical doubt.

Descartes famously formulates the skeptical argument as it applies to perceptual knowledge. It sometimes happens, Descartes claims, that one imagines things while asleep—e.g., that one is sitting by the fire in a dressing gown—when one is, in fact, lying undressed in bed. If we reflect on such occasions "more carefully," we must, according to the meditator, "plainly see that there are no sure signs by means of which being awake can be distinguished from being asleep."[18] This lack of "sure signs" to distinguish sleep from wakefulness is supposed to mean that there are cases in which we do not actually perceive anything—namely, because we are dreaming—but that we nevertheless cannot distinguish through any phenomenal criterion from other cases in which we do indeed perceive things. Yet if we cannot differentiate between such cases by means of any phenomenal criterion, this means, on Descartes's view, that we must admit—not in a way that is "flippant or ill-considered" but in a way that "is based on powerful and well thought-out reasons"—that it is inexplicable how we could ever know anything through our senses.[19] For if it is possible for a subject to be in a state where she perceives nothing and which she cannot phenomenally distinguish from cases in which she does perceive something, this means that a subject's best possible mental basis for a perceptual belief is that it *appears* to her as if things were thus and so. But this means that she can never have a basis for a perceptual belief that excludes the possibility of its being false.

The cases Descartes invokes in formulating his skeptical argument are ones in which the subject is either dreaming or being manipulated by a malicious demon. One might object at this point that it is unreasonable to appeal to such cases in order to arrive at a philosophically adequate description of the basis for our beliefs. For, as I claimed above, the skeptical argument carries weight for us only if—and insofar as—it relies on considerations that are reasonable. One would like to know

[18] *Meditations,* AT 7:19.
[19] Ibid., 7:21–22.

how on earth reflection on such outlandish cases—e.g., cases in which we are being manipulated by a malicious demon, or are just brains in vats—is supposed to help us understand what it means to have finite knowledge. To arrive at an adequate description of our knowledge, so the objection goes, we must rather take our orientation from cases drawn from ordinary life.

This objection rests on a misunderstanding, however. One misses the point of the argument from the possibility of error if one takes it to depend on our envisaging particular outlandish but possible ways to err. The argument aspires to do nothing more (and nothing less) than to keep hold of a possibility—namely, the possibility of error, quite generally. The skeptic then considers exemplary cases of purported knowledge and maintains that, in order to account for the objectivity of our knowledge, we must make room for a further class of non-veridical cases that are, for the subject concerned, indistinguishable from cases in which she actually has knowledge.[20] The point of the so-called skeptical hypotheses (the dream hypothesis, the malicious demon hypothesis, etc.) is not to confront us with particular possibilities, such as the possibility that we may be dreaming, or that a malicious demon may be manipulating us. Their point is rather to give a vivid example of a kind of case—a case that, were it to obtain, would prevent us from being able to acquire knowledge on the basis of a perceptual experience and a case whose possibility we have to make room for in our description of the basis of our beliefs.

Thus, one gets things wrong from the very outset if one thinks one can resist the skeptical challenge to our knowledge by searching for an argument that will rule out these so-called skeptical hypotheses *a priori*—e.g., by arguing that the hypothesis that we are all brains in vats must be false.[21] The skeptic's doubt is not fueled by the idea that we

---

[20] On the significance of "best cases" for the discussion of skepticism, see Cavell, *The Claim of Reason*, 133–135; Williams, *Unnatural Doubts*, 135–139.

[21] The *locus classicus* for such a view is, of course, Putnam's *Reason, Truth and History*, 1–21. In this connection, see also Brueckner, "Semantic Answers to Skepticism" and "Brains in a Vat." Davidson's position in "A Coherence Theory of Truth and Knowledge" likewise relies on this misunderstanding in a crucial place. Davidson holds that the skeptical problem consists in the thought that each and every one of our beliefs

cannot disprove the obtaining of completely "unreal," far-fetched circumstances—e.g., that a malicious demon is manipulating us. The scenario in which a malicious demon is manipulating us is a vivid example of a limitless supply of possible circumstances that we have to take into consideration in epistemology if we are to make room for the possibility of error.

For the same reason, one cannot resist this skeptical line of argumentation, as Austin attempts to do, by accusing it of some form of the following fallacy. According to Austin, the skeptic makes an illicit move from the fact we sometimes do err (or are otherwise unable to determine how things stand) to the idea that we are always and everywhere deprived of the possibility of knowledge.[22] But the skeptical argument in no way depends on an inference from some cases to all cases—neither from the fact that there are some cases in which we have indeed erred, nor from the fact that there are some cases in which it is possible for us to err. The argument from the possibility of error instead establishes a philosophical description of the basis for our beliefs in light of which it is supposed to be so much as possible for us to err. The skeptic's doubt rests on the thought that as soon as we admit this possibility, we have to conclude that the grounding nexus between a subject and a particular content must, in every situation, be weaker than would be necessary to guarantee the truth of a belief about the world. The skeptic's claim that there is no case in which we can have knowledge does not, therefore, rest on a generalization from a particular case to all cases.[23] It is rather that everything that holds in the case the skeptic describes

---

could be false. Thus, in order to show that his own position is non-skeptical, Davidson thinks he only has to show that the idea that the totality of our beliefs might be false is ultimately incoherent on account of the internal connection between meaning and belief. The idea of such global falsehood does not express a thought, as the conception of the omniscient interpreter is supposed to show. Yet this is not the skeptical problem. The skeptical problem is that we cannot know of any particular belief whether it is true. On this point, see Brueckner, "The Omniscient Interpreter Rides Again," and Craig, "Davidson and the Sceptic: The Thumbnail Version."

[22] Austin, "Other Minds," 88.

[23] As Cavell formulates the point in his critique of Austin, the skeptic's inference is trivial, not fallacious. See Cavell, *The Claim of Reason*, 134–136.

also holds for every other case precisely because such a case is exemplary of all cases.

## 2. The Paradox of Knowledge

So what is the consequence of the argument from the possibility of error? The skeptic concludes that the concept of finite knowledge leads us into an aporia. For it forces us to conjoin two characterizations of knowledge that exclude one another: namely, its liability to error, on the one hand, and its being based on truth-guaranteeing grounds, on the other. The concept of finite knowledge thus involves a paradox that assumes an exemplary form, as it is applied to perceptual knowledge. The paradox of knowledge—as applied to perceptual knowledge—consists in the incompatibility of the following two claims:

(1) Perceptual knowledge must be grounded in perceptual experiences that guarantee the truth of the judgments they ground; for knowledge is factive.

(2) Perceptual knowledge must be grounded in perceptual experiences that are compatible with the falsehood of the judgments they ground; for knowledge is liable to error.

Affirming the first claim, in which, according to the skeptic, one acknowledges the factive character of knowledge, precludes one from affirming the second claim, in which, according to the skeptic, one acknowledges the fallibility of knowledge. And affirming the second precludes one from affirming the first. According to the skeptic, the aporia is insoluble. The concept of finite knowledge is intrinsically paradoxical.

According to the considerations we elaborated in Part One, we are committed to saying that the skeptic gets this much right: if it is a consequence of acknowledging the fallibility of judgments grounded in perceptual experiences that we cannot make sense of the idea of perceptual experiences that guarantee the truth of the judgments they ground, then the concept of finite knowledge is ultimately unintelligible.

## 3. Is Philosophy Necessarily Skeptical?

I've said that I take the argument from the possibility of error to constitute the deepest skeptical argument against the possibility of knowledge. All other kinds of skeptical argument must ultimately fall back
on this argument. Contemporary epistemology has recently enter-
tained the idea—advanced by Barry Stroud—that skeptical doubt does
not arise from a particular philosophical argument but is instead an
unavoidable concomitant of any attempt to understand knowledge in a
philosophical manner.[24] If our interpretation of the roots of skepticism
is correct, then Stroud's contention must be false. And that means it
must be possible to show that Stroud's description of what a philosophical understanding amounts to already presupposes that the argument
from the possibility of error is cogent. That is, he must understand the
cogency of this argument to constitute a mark of any philosophical posture. This is precisely what I will attempt to show in what follows. The
possibility of making sense of finite knowledge, we can therefore conclude, stands or falls with the possibility of resisting the above skeptical argument.

Stroud characterizes the nature of philosophical reflection as follows:

What we seek in the philosophical theory of knowledge is an account
that is completely general in several respects. We want to understand

---

[24] Two other philosophical arguments for skepticism have emerged. One concerns the
principle of epistemic closure and the other concerns the concept of objectivity that
we use to characterize the status of the contents of our judgments. The latter argument can be found, for example, in Nagel, *The View from Nowhere,* chaps. 5 and 6, as
well as in Williams, *Descartes: The Project of Pure Inquiry,* 32–71, esp. 64–67. Yet both
these lines of thought are flawed because, as I aim to show in what follows, they either
presuppose the argument from error or they are not capable of formulating a doubt
that can have rational force for us. The claim that the principle of epistemic closure is
the premise of skeptical doubt will concern us in Chapter IV, section 3. That the concept of objectivity cannot, as such, ground any form of skeptical doubt—as Williams
and Nagel take it to—I show in my paper "Einsicht ohne Täuschung: McDowells
hermeneutische Konzeption von Erkenntnis." See also McDowell's criticism of this idea
in "Aesthetic Value, Objectivity, and the Fabric of the World." We will come back to the
notion of objectivity at the end of our inquiry in Chapter X, section 3.

how any knowledge at all is possible—how anything we currently accept amounts to knowledge. Or less ambitiously, we want to understand with complete generality how we come to know anything in a certain specified domain.[25]

Let us assume that the realm that we are seeking to understand is knowledge of the world that sensibly affects us. Stroud deploys the idea of "complete generality" to characterize the kind of understanding we aim at. We seek to understand with "complete generality" how we come to have knowledge of the world that sensibly affects us. Yet at first blush this idea is rather indeterminate and open to many interpretations. One might understand it to mean that, in philosophy, we seek to understand with "complete generality" in the sense that we seek an understanding of the sources and the nature of our knowledge. This entails, among other things, that we aspire to understand the nature of the sort of grounds that we have for such knowledge. The idea that such an understanding is general would then mean that it holds independently of what the particular content of our knowledge may happen to be. The only relevant condition is that the knowledge in question is knowledge of the sensible world—whether its content happens to be that there is a chair yonder or that it is raining outside or whatever. We are not seeking to understand the constitution of the specific ground we have for a particular belief but instead how grounds in general are constituted.

Yet this is not how Stroud understands the expression "complete generality." He instead takes it to mean "an assessment of all our knowledge of the world at once, [which] takes the form of a judgment on that knowledge from what looks like a detached external position."[26] According to Stroud, aspiring to a general understanding means attempting to assess our knowledge from an external standpoint. That is supposed to involve answering the question whether the grounds that we allege to be grounds for knowledge, from an internal standpoint, are actually grounds on the basis of which one can enjoy knowledge of the world. And we are meant to settle this question without already

[25] Stroud, "Understanding Human Knowledge in General," 32.
[26] Stroud, *The Significance of Philosophical Scepticism*, 209.

presupposing that the grounds in question are knowledge-enabling. Now, the only way one can answer this question is by attempting to trace back our knowledge of the world to grounds that we would still have access to if it turned out, in the course of our investigation, that we didn't have knowledge of the world after all. That is to say, the only way one can actually pursue this question is by claiming that the fundamental mental acts on which our knowledge of the world is based are characterized by the fact that we could engage in them even if we had no knowledge of the world. Stroud's idea is accordingly that our pursuit of a philosophical understanding of our knowledge of the world is an attempt to ground our knowledge of the world in mental acts that would still be possible even if we had no such knowledge.

Viewed in this way, this is nothing more than a claim about the order of philosophical justification. On this account, what we seek to do in philosophy is find a legitimating explanation of our knowledge of the world in terms of something that doesn't already imply that we actually have knowledge of the world. This means, as Michael Williams describes the project of traditional epistemology, that in philosophy we seek an account of our knowledge of the world that "traces our knowledge of the world to something that is *ours,* and that is *knowledge,* but not *knowledge of the world.*"[27]

Let us assume for a moment that this is a coherent project. What would then follow about the order of justification from an "internal standpoint"? The answer is simple: nothing. If the idea that we have to explain our knowledge of the world by reference to grounds that do not already presuppose that we have knowledge of the world is itself grounded in nothing more than a "methodological constraint"[28] that

---

[27] Williams, *Unnatural Doubts,* 92. For this characterization of the "traditional epistemological project," see also his "Epistemological Realism and the Basis of Scepticism." Williams believes that this represents the strongest justification of skeptical doubt. For that reason he believes that the argument from the possibility of error leads "merely" to fallibilism, not to skepticism. See Williams, *Problems of Knowledge,* 61. I will argue at length below that this characterization of the root of skepticism is wrong.

[28] This is how Williams understands Stroud's characterization of the epistemological project in *Unnatural Doubts,* 57–58, 90–92, 103–104, 113–115. See also Stroud, "Understanding Human Knowledge Philosophically."

we place upon ourselves while philosophizing—and if the result of the reflections that are subject to such a constraint is that they make knowledge of the world unintelligible—then the only well-founded doubt that can arise at this point is not a doubt about our knowledge of the world but rather one concerning such a methodological constraint. Defenders of such a methodological constraint will want to object at this point that the constraint is no artificial invention but instead describes what we are seeking when we aim to give a satisfying philosophical explanation of our knowledge of the world. But let us imagine for a moment that someone executed a philosophical project in which she showed, among other things, that it is impossible to perform mental acts that are subject to such a constraint unless one actually has knowledge of the world. Imagine, that is, that our philosophical reflections lead us to recognize that the methodological constraint that Stroud touts as the hallmark of philosophical explanations turns out to be incoherent. We would thereby have shown that we must instead account for our knowledge in a manner that violates such a constraint. What then? Stroud says that, in such a case, we would not have arrived at a satisfactory explanation of knowledge: "[I]f we did come to see how and why the epistemological enterprise is not fully valid, or perhaps not even fully coherent," we should not, according to Stroud, then believe that "we would then possess a satisfactory explanation of how human knowledge in general is possible. We would have seen, at best, that we cannot have such a thing. And that too, I believe, would leave us dissatisfied."[29]

According to Stroud, we would then find ourselves in the following situation. We would, indeed, understand how we could have knowledge of the world, but we would not have the sort of understanding we had sought. But why is this? The mere fact that an understanding of our knowledge of the world is supposed to be completely general by no means entails that a satisfying understanding must satisfy this method-

[29] Stroud, "Understanding Human Knowledge in General," 49. Compare also Stroud's skepticism about transcendental arguments in his articles "Transcendental Arguments," "Kantian Argument, Conceptual Capacities, and Invulnerability," and "Kant and Skepticism." For my critique of Stroud's understanding of the Kantian position and its relation to skepticism, see Kern, "Philosophie und Skepsis: Hume—Kant—Cavell," esp. 28–35.

ological constraint. Least of all if this methodological constraint should turn out to be incoherent. Skeptical doubt about our knowledge of the world can arise only if we can derive the idea that our beliefs must be grounded on nothing more epistemically ambitious than mental acts that are compatible with the falsity of those beliefs from an indisputable feature of human knowledge—not just from some methodological philosophical doctrine. And that is precisely what the argument from the possibility of error seeks to demonstrate. Thus, Stroud's claim that such an understanding is a fundamental characteristic of any philosophical inquiry into our knowledge of the world must uncritically presuppose the cogency of this argument.

Stroud wants to say that an explanation in the absence of this methodological doctrine cannot be satisfying for us. But why not? What it means for a philosophical explanation to be satisfying is, doubtless, difficult to say. And there is probably no general account to be had here. But to claim in advance that no explanation that violates Stroud's methodological constraint could ever be satisfying is to stick one's head in the sand, while maintaining that nothing can be done to ever pull it out again. And that hardly seems like a position to which reason can compel us.

# The Dilemma of Epistemology

## 1. The General Redemptive Strategy: Less Is More!

There are essentially two philosophical strategies for countering skeptical doubt: One can prosecute either a transcendental critique or a diagnostic critique. By a transcendental critique I mean a paradigmatically Kantian strategy of proving something in roughly the following manner.[30] A transcendental critique of the skeptic's position aims to show that, in formulating her argument, the skeptic must appeal to a premise to which she is not entitled—and one to which she can be entitled only if she grants the reality of precisely the thing that her argument is meant to show is impossible. A transcendental critique thus refutes skepticism in the sense that it reveals the skeptic's position to

---

[30] I am not here concerned with the question of what status this argument has in Kant—i.e., whether or not it is central to his overall argument. And, obviously, I do not intend the above characterization of a transcendental argument to provide a comprehensive account of the precise nature of transcendental arguments in general. For an overview of the relevant discussion, see Stern's excellent book, *Transcendental Arguments and Scepticism: Answering the Question of Justification*. I take the characterization provided above—to the extent that transcendental arguments are deployed against the skeptic—to be quite minimal. The point of such an argument in relation to the skeptical problematic is easy to understand when it is considered in comparison to the diagnostic strategy. And it is with this contrast that I am solely concerned.

---

be self-undermining. It reveals it to be a position that no one could reasonably adopt.

The general problem in any transcendental refutation of skeptical
doubt—e.g., as it bears on empirical knowledge—lies in the fact that it
can only ever show that one cannot rationally dispute or deny the actuality of such knowledge. It does not, however, show how what the
skeptic doubts is, in fact, possible. Such a transcendental critique does
not itself show how finite beings can have empirical knowledge. Hence,
no transcendental refutation of the skeptic is entirely satisfactory when
it is pursued as a self-sufficient enterprise.[31] The fundamental question
in the debate with the skeptic, therefore, cannot be whether it is possible to refute the skeptic. It must instead be whether we are capable of
explaining the nature of knowledge in such a way as to deprive skeptical doubt of its point of attack.

A diagnostic critique circumvents this problem from the very outset.
By a diagnostic critique, I mean a form of debate with the skeptic that
refutes her by diagnosing a presupposition of skeptical doubt and
attempting to show that such a presupposition is not genuinely compulsory. According to a diagnostic critique of skepticism, the skeptic's reflections on the nature of knowledge rest upon a premise that we can
abandon. What this premise is varies from diagnosis to diagnosis. But if
we give up this premise, the argument goes, then it becomes intelligible
how finite thinking creatures can have knowledge. In contrast to a transcendental critique, in a diagnostic critique the refutation of the skeptic
and the demonstration of a non-skeptical understanding of knowledge
come together. The refutation of the skeptic is achieved precisely by
means of an alternative account of the nature of knowledge—one that
claims to be non-skeptical.[32]

---

[31] In "Varieties of Skepticism," Conant accordingly distinguishes between Cartesian
   skepticism, which asks whether knowledge is actual, and Kantian skepticism, which
   asks whether such a thing as knowledge is so much as possible. And it is clear that so-
   called Cartesian skepticism cannot be answered simply by indicating that knowledge
   is possible, unless this demonstration itself contains an explanation of what it means
   to answer the question of the actuality of knowledge.

[32] Williams characterizes the form of diagnostic critique that he helped make prominent as follows: "The idea is to put skeptical doubts in a wholly new light: to make

In what follows we will discuss two varieties of a diagnostic response to skepticism, both of which rest on the same diagnostic thought. It will be easy to see that this thought underlies the bulk of the positions in contemporary epistemology. We will term the positions characterized by this thought "positions of moderation." It will become apparent that neither of these responses actually disarms skeptical doubt. For both responses are united in thinking that it is possible to formulate a non-skeptical position that accepts the argument from the possibility of error rather than repudiating it. So in what follows we will be concerned, not with particular individual positions, but rather with a structure of argumentation that is common to quite different positions. This will enable us to abstract from all other—often quite radical—differences between these positions. The only difference that we will need to take note of is the contrast between the "internalist" and "externalist" variants of this position.

As we have seen, the problem we are confronted with is that the concept of knowledge appears to be paradoxical. For we have to combine two features of knowledge that appear to be mutually exclusive: its factive character and its fallibility. Applied to the case of empirical knowledge, it means that in order to account for the first feature, we must claim that empirical knowledge must be based on perceptual experiences that give a subject truth-guaranteeing grounds. To account for the second feature, we must claim that empirical knowledge is based on perceptual experiences that are compatible with the judgment's being false. The general strategy pursued by what I have called "posi-

---

them appear, not as natural doubts, but as an unwanted consequence of dispensable theoretical ideas" (*Unnatural Doubts*, 318). Wright has objected that a diagnostic critique can never suffice as a refutation of the skeptic. In order to refute the skeptic, according to Wright, one must show that her position is false—not just that it is not compulsory. See Wright, "Facts and Certainty," 461. Yet it is a mistake to apply this demand to the skeptical position. For there is an asymmetry between a philosophical position that leads to skeptical doubt and a position in which such doubt has no place. As we saw at the beginning of Part Two, the skeptic cannot understand the doubt to which she is driven as a merely possible doubt. She must understand it as truly unavoidable. Wittgenstein formulates this asymmetry as follows: "In philosophy, one must always ask oneself: how must one view this problem so that it is solvable?" (*Remarks on Color*, II, §11, 16). See also Michael Williams, *Problems of Knowledge*, 146–147.

tions of moderation" in epistemology is to seek to dissolve the paradox of knowledge by taking issue with the first claim. On this view, the first claim does not articulate a condition of knowledge. Grounds need not be truth-guaranteeing in order to serve as grounds for knowledge. We can make sense of knowledge, so the thought goes, without the idea of a truth-guaranteeing ground. I will argue that this is wrong. It is impossible to make sense of knowledge in terms of the concept of a ground that is anything less than truth-guaranteeing.

To this end, let us first consider the general sort of diagnosis that is characteristic of these positions. Once we have the general outlines of this diagnosis in view, we will then be in a position to see what particular shapes it assumes in each of its two versions—viz., externalism and internalism. Positions of moderation reformulate the skeptic's argument in the following way:

(1)  In order to know something, I need a ground that rules out any circumstance in which it would be false to believe what I believe.

(2)  Yet I can never have a ground that rules out every circumstance in which it would be false to believe what I believe.

(3)  Therefore, I can never know anything.

If we reformulate the skeptic's argument along these lines, then the diagnosis common to all positions of moderation is that the skeptical trouble ultimately stems from premise (1): the idea that someone who knows something must have a foundation for her belief that rules out each and every circumstance in which it would be false to believe what she does. The strategy of moderation is to argue that we need not accept this premise. The idea is that the skeptic misunderstands the concept of knowledge because she simply demands too much of the ground on which the subject must base her belief in order to know something. A more reasonable formulation of the justification condition for knowledge ought rather to be that a belief is sufficiently justified and thus counts as knowledge just in case a subject can justify it in a manner that rules out all the relevant circumstances in which it would be false to hold that belief.

This general diagnostic critique of the skeptic's doubt—the upshot of which is to relax the justification condition on knowledge—finds expression in two distinct variants. The two variants differ in how they describe the nature of those factors that determine whether or not a circumstance is "relevant." The internalist variant characterizes these factors exclusively in terms of so-called internal factors, i.e., ones that belong to the subject's consciousness. The externalist variant, by contrast, characterizes the factors that determine relevance (also) through so-called external factors, i.e., ones that do not belong to the subject's consciousness.[33]

## 2. The Internalist Variant

Positions of moderation are characterized by the thought that a knowledgeable subject need rule out, not all the circumstances that are incompatible with the truth of her belief, but only the relevant ones. On the internalist variant of this view, what makes a circumstance relevant—and thus a possibility that the subject must foreclose—is to be understood as a function of the grounds that the subject has for believing that such a circumstance obtains. A prime example of this strategy can be found in the work of J. L. Austin, which has been recently revived by numerous authors in the contemporary epistemology literature. On the internalist view, the relevance or irrelevance of a certain circumstance—one that would render my belief false, were it to obtain, and that, accordingly, would have to be ruled out by the ground on which I base my belief, if I am to have knowledge—depends on whether I have reason to assume that the circumstance might obtain. The internalist version of the justification condition on knowledge can thus be described as follows: A subject has a justification sufficient for knowledge

---

[33] The distinction I am drawing between internalist and externalist variant is meant to capture the paradigmatic features of each family of views—i.e., it is meant to shed light on the general principle that characterizes each version of the variant as such. The point of the argument that we are developing is that nothing hangs on which of these variants one pursues.

just in case she bases her belief on a ground that rules out every circumstance that would falsify her belief and that she has reason to assume might obtain. No other circumstances need to be ruled out.

Austin elucidates this characterization of the justification condition on
knowledge with the following example. Let us imagine that I claim there
is a goldfinch in the garden. In order for my claim to enjoy the status of
knowledge, according to Austin, I must be in a position to answer the
question "Why do you believe there is a goldfinch in the garden?" in a
manner that rules out the possibility that it is really a sparrow, thrush, or
blackbird. I must accordingly be able to provide features that rule out
such possible alternative identifications of the object in question. If I do
indeed adduce such features in order to justify my claim, then, according
to Austin, I have produced "justification enough" for knowledge. And, as
he puts it: "Enough is enough: it doesn't mean everything. Enough means
enough to show that (within reason, and for present intents and purposes)
it 'can't' be anything else, there is no room for an alternative, competing,
description of it. It does *not* mean, for example, enough to show it isn't a
*stuffed* goldfinch."[34]

According to Austin, the fact that my basis for belief is sufficient for
knowledge does *not* mean that it rules out that the object of my assertion is not as I claim it to be. I claim that there is a goldfinch over there.
But the basis that I must have for this claim in order for it to enjoy the
status of knowledge still leaves it open whether it really is a goldfinch
over there or only a goldfinch decoy. My basis for asserting that it is a
goldfinch need not rule out the possibility that it might only be a stuffed
goldfinch. I would have to rule out such a circumstance only if it were
relevant. And it would only be relevant if I had reason to assume that it
might obtain. The upshot of the internalist variant of the position of
moderation is thus contained in the following claim: "[T]he doubt or
question 'But is it a *real* one?' has always (*must* have) a special basis,
there must be some 'reason for suggesting' that it isn't real."[35]

[34] Austin, "Other Minds," 84.
[35] Ibid., 87.

The internalist variant of the position of moderation describes the acquisition of knowledge as a process governed by something that we might call an "epistemic rule." Let us call it the "rule of reasonable doubt." This rule regulates the acquisition of knowledge in the sense that following it is a necessary condition for a subject's counting as knowledgeable.[36] This is occasionally expressed by saying that the justification of knowledge claims has a "default and challenge" structure: a knowledge claim is something that one must only justify if one has reason to doubt the truth of the belief in question.[37] So long as the subject has no reason to doubt her belief, her knowledge claim enjoys the status of a "default entitlement." That is to say, the subject is entitled to her knowledge claim simply by default and not by the fact that she has a truth-guaranteeing ground for her belief.

Austin, as a paradigmatic representative of the internalist variant of the position of moderation, wants to say that none of the situations that classical epistemology envisions in order to get clear about the possibility of knowledge involves any reason to suspect that a circumstance obtains that would falsify the belief in question. In all these situations where classical epistemology would plant the seeds of skeptical doubt—for Descartes as he sits by the fire and touches the paper in his hands, for Price as he beholds his tomato, for me as I stare at my white teacup, etc.—there is no reason to deprive belief of its default status as knowledge. Now the classical epistemologist would maintain that, in order to have knowledge, we really do need a basis for belief that is capable of ruling out such a falsifying circumstance. But to Austin, such a view is "silly"—indeed, simply "outrageous."[38] Similarly, Putnam says that the

---

[36] A characteristic formulation of this epistemic rule as applied to knowledge by hearsay can be found in Price. Price describes the "policy for forming beliefs" as applied to knowledge by hearsay as follows: "accept what you are told, unless you have specific reasons for doubting it" (*Belief,* 127).

[37] See, *inter alia,* Williams, *Problems of Knowledge,* esp. 150–158; Brandom, *Making It Explicit,* 176–184, 204–206, 238–342. Willaschek also advances a version of the internalist strategy of moderation, building upon Austin and Williams. See Willaschek, *Der mentale Zugang zur Welt,* 182–205.

[38] Austin, "Other Minds," 84. On this point, see also Cavell, *The Claim of Reason,* 52.

criteria that the skeptic levies against ordinary knowledge claims are straightforwardly "absurd."[39]

Stanley Cavell has formulated the following objection to this aspect of Austin's position: in demanding that our suspicions regarding the circumstances we are obliged to rule out must be motivated or well-founded, Austin's view is precisely incapable of achieving what it means to achieve—namely, a refutation of (or answer to) skeptical doubt. Such a position of moderation cannot address the skeptic's doubt precisely because the question whether we have reason to suspect that a particular falsifying circumstance might obtain is precisely what is up for debate. Austin takes himself to know that, in the situation envisioned by classical epistemology, there is no reason to think that such a circumstance might obtain. At this point Cavell raises the question of how, then, we know what Austin here takes himself to know. Moreover, how do we know what would even count as such a reason for suspicion? "How do we know what would count as 'a reason to think so'?"[40]

Yet Cavell's objection to Austin is not meant to dispute Austin's view that we do indeed know such things. Quite the contrary: "anybody who can speak knows these things."[41] Cavell's objection is rather to be understood methodologically. If advocates of a position of moderation contend that there is no reason to suspect that falsifying circumstances obtain in the sort of situation that classical epistemology investigates, then the evidence in favor of this contention must be the sort that any competent speaker of the relevant language would be able to recognize. It cannot be the private opinion of the epistemologist that there is no reason to suggest that such a circumstance obtains. For the proponent of a strategy of moderation needs to maintain that, in the cases in question, *no one* has reason for such a suspicion. Yet that is precisely what the skeptic disputes. Thus, the problem with this strategy, according to Cavell, is that it presents a methodological dilemma of the following form. Either no one whatsoever would challenge the claim that "there is no reason here for suspecting that a falsifying circumstance obtains." But then there would

[39] Putnam, "Skepticism," 256–257.
[40] Cavell, *The Claim of Reason,* 56.
[41] Ibid., 51.

be no skeptic, and the claim would be addressed to no one. Or, on the other hand, there might indeed be someone who disputes that claim. And then the claim is false. "If the epistemologist does not *accept* such a statement as 'There is no reason to ask', *that* fact must count as evidence that the statement is false."[42]

In the course of what follows, we will see that the methodological dilemma facing positions of moderation is not the deepest problem with them. For this methodological problem bears only on its internalist variant. The externalist variant does not face such a problem, because what makes a falsifying circumstance relevant, on the externalist view, does not (or does not have to) involve reference to the grounds that are available to the thinking subject. The deepest problem with this position, as we shall see, is one that afflicts both its variants. But let us first consider the externalist variant in its own right.

### 3. The Externalist Variant

According to the externalist variant of the strategy for moderating the justification condition, whether a falsifying circumstance is relevant (and hence needs to be ruled out) does not depend on whether the subject has reason to believe that that circumstance could obtain. Rather, the relevance of falsifying circumstances depends on factors that may lie outside the subject's consciousness. That is the unifying thought shared by authors such as Goldman, Dretske, and Lewis. One of Dretske's examples, on the basis of which he develops his criticism of the skeptical problematic, runs as follows. I go with my son to the zoo, look at various zebras and explain to him that what he's looking at are zebras. I take myself to know that these are zebras. They look like zebras. They are in a pen bearing a placard that says "Zebras." And we are, after all, in a zoo. Yet I then pause to reflect: A zebra is not a mule. Nor is it a mule that has been cleverly disguised to look like a zebra. According to Dretske, however, I do not know (in the circumstances we're imagining) that

---

[42] Ibid., 57.

what I have identified to my son as zebras are not, in fact, cleverly disguised mules. Now what follows from this? In Dretske's view, the skeptic
will conclude from the fact that we do not know that the animals we
identified are not cleverly disguised mules that we likewise do not
know that they are zebras.[43] Dretske wants to claim that the skeptic's
inference here is fallacious. For it is valid only on the assumption that
someone knows something only if the basis for her belief forecloses all
circumstances in which that belief would be false. Yet we can challenge
this assumption. Someone can know something so long as the basis for
her belief rules out all the circumstances that constitute relevant alternatives to her belief. In the context of the present example, this means
just the same thing for Dretske as it did for Austin: namely, that the
basis one has for believing that there are zebras in the pen must indeed
establish that the animals are correctly identified—i.e., one must rule
out that they are gazelles, lions, or antelope. But one need not rule out
such alternative scenarios according to which they are cleverly disguised mules.

The first step of Dretske's suggestion for solving the skeptical problem
is thus quite the same as Austin's. When someone knows something,
according to Dretske, there is a series of propositions that are "necessary
consequences"[44] of the proposition that is the content of her knowledge
claim. We must sort these consequences into two classes: those that the
subject must indeed know to be true (in order for her belief to count as
knowledge), and those that she need not know to be true, but which instead have the status of "presuppositions." The idea here is that some of
the "necessary consequences" of the proposition that someone knows
to be true must be understood, not as themselves part of the asserted
content of what is known, but instead as presuppositions for those
knowledge claims. This will then enable us to understand how one can
know, in the circumstances described above, that the animals in the pen
are zebras. Some of the consequences of a statement, Dretske writes, "although their truth is entailed by the truth of the statement, are not part

[43] Dretske, "Epistemic Operators," 1015–1017.
[44] Ibid., 1007.

of what is *operated on* when we operate on the statement with one of our epistemic operators."[45]

We can thus join the skeptic in saying that, any time someone knows something, there is a series of propositions whose truth is entailed by the truth of the known proposition. Yet we can simultaneously maintain, against the skeptic, that one need not know all these further propositions to be true in order to enjoy the knowledge in question. Let's briefly consider another example. Let's imagine a subject who judges, on the basis of her visual experience, that a particular wall is red. According to Dretske, the proposition "the current light conditions are normal" belongs to the class of propositions whose truth is entailed by her perceptual knowledge that the wall is red but that the subject need not actually know to be true in order to enjoy the knowledge that the wall is red. For if her judgment that the wall is red is true, then this entails that it is not a white wall that has been cleverly lit to appear red. Yet according to Dretske, the subject cannot know, on the basis of a perceptual experience of a red wall, that the wall is not white but cleverly lit to appear red. If the wall were white but cleverly lit to look red, she would have precisely the same perceptual experience. So her perceptual experience cannot rule out that the wall isn't white but cleverly lit to look red. On Dretske's view, this leaves us with just one way to understand how a subject can know that the wall is red on the basis of her perceptual experience: we have to challenge the claim that someone can know something only if her experiential basis for believing it rules out alternative situations involving, say, abnormal lighting conditions. We must reject the idea that someone must know that the lighting conditions are normal in order to know that the wall is red on the basis of her perceptual

---

[45] Ibid., 1014. Compare this strategy to the one Alvin Goldman pursues in his incisive essay, "Discrimination and Perceptual Knowledge," which initially considers situations similar to those above—in his case the trouble is with facades of barns—as objections to a purely causal account of perceptual knowledge, but which anticipates a solution closely analogous to Dretske's. Paradigmatic developments of this externalist position or moderation can be found in Stine, "Skepticism, Relevant Alternatives, and Deductive Closure"; DeRose, "Solving the Skeptical Problem"; and Yourgau, "Knowledge and Relevant Alternatives."

experience. The claim "the current lighting conditions are normal" has the status of a presupposition that the knowing subject need not know.

The systematic upshot of Dretske's response to the skeptical problematic is that we must sort the statements whose truth is entailed by the truth of the known statement into those that the subject must know and those that she need not know. But what is our basis for making this distinction? The externalist approach faces a systematic problem at this point, which does not arise for the internalist. For the externalist does not have any criterion for making this distinction. And in the absence of such a criterion, the distinction appears quite arbitrary. The internalist variant of the strategy for moderating the justification condition does possess such a criterion. It distinguishes relevant from irrelevant circumstances in accordance with the internalist epistemic rule: an alternative scenario is relevant and must accordingly be ruled out by the knowing subject just in case the subject has reason to suspect that it might obtain. To make a principled distinction between relevant and irrelevant circumstances, the externalist must likewise formulate some such epistemic rule.

It is hardly surprising that different externalist epistemologists have hit upon different epistemic rules. Yet the ways in which these various proposals differ have no bearing on the general question of whether formulating such a rule (or several rules) can provide an answer to the skeptical problematic. David Lewis has rendered the structure of this conception of knowledge completely perspicuous by listing and defending all the rules that the externalist literature employs in elucidating the concept of knowledge.[46] We will discuss only one of these rules—namely, the one that stands at the center of all externalist theories of knowledge and that bears immediately on the skeptical problematic. This is the "rule of reliability." The rule of reliability states that, in nearly all cases, we are right to ignore the possibility that the "causal processes"[47] responsible for the empirical content of our beliefs—e.g., our acts of perceiving—may not function as they usually function. According to the rule of reliability, we are permitted in nearly all contexts to presuppose

---

[46] See Lewis, "Elusive Knowledge," 225.
[47] Ibid.

that these "causal processes" run their course in the way they normally do—i.e., in a way that leads to the formation of a true belief.

The possibilities that the externalist rule of reliability permits us to ignore, in most contexts, are the very same possibilities that the internalist variant of the strategy of moderation takes aim at in its own (and only) epistemic rule: namely, possibilities such as that we are hallucinating, or looking at a decoy or imitation, or seeing double. What is decisive for the skeptical problematic is that the rule of reliability does not state that we can ignore these possibilities of an aberration in the "causal processes" that influence the formation of our belief in *all* contexts. No, we can legitimately ignore these possibilities only in *most* contexts. In particular, we are entitled to ignore these possibilities only in those contexts in which they do not obtain. That is to say, I am permitted to ignore the possibility that I am hallucinating only when I am not hallucinating, and so on.

Thus, with reference to the possibility of error—say, because I am hallucinating—the externalist strategy of moderation maintains something like the following. The externalist agrees with the skeptic in claiming that we can never rule out such a possibility of error: "Of course it is possible to hallucinate—even to hallucinate in such a way that all my perceptual experiences [ . . . ] would be just as they actually are. That possibility never can be eliminated."[48] The only thing we can do is to "ignore" such a possibility.[49] And this is precisely where the externalist parts ways with the skeptic, in claiming that we are genuinely entitled to "ignore" this possibility in a variety of contexts—namely, in precisely those contexts where the possibility is not actualized.

This conception of knowledge is externalist because it denies that the justification that is sufficient for knowledge can and must be available to the subject of that knowledge *qua* being its subject. The question whether a subject is sufficiently justified to believe what she believes, i.e., whether a subject can legitimately ignore the possibility of error in a particular context, is not treated as a question whose answer can and must be given by the believing subject herself, as it is according to the

---

[48] Ibid., 229.
[49] Ibid.

internalist strategy. Rather, it is treated as a question whose answer is dependent on the truth of the relevant belief. And because the truth of a belief is treated as something for which the subject herself cannot, in principle, adduce a ground that *guarantees* it, the question whether her belief is sufficiently justified, cannot, in principle, be answered by the believing subject herself.[50] For, the subject herself can only address this question—viz., whether her belief is true and hence whether it properly ignores a particular possibility of error—in such a way that she cannot rule out the possibility that her answer might be false. "That possibility never can be eliminated."

Thus, according to the externalist strategy, the question whether one's belief is actually knowledge is one whose answer must, in principle, outstrip the consciousness of the believing subject. We can have knowledge, the suggestion goes, only at the cost of giving up the idea that knowledge is an intrinsically self-conscious mental act, i.e., one that one cannot but perform self-consciously. For that would precisely exclude the possibility that one could know how things are in the world and yet fail to know that one knows how things are.

## 4. The Paradox Returns

Both variants of the position of moderation we have described concede the following thought: a subject in a particular situation is, in principle, incapable of ruling out all the alternative scenarios in which it would be false to believe some particular content. Positions of moderation unquestioningly presuppose this idea. They do not argue for it. That is to say, they presuppose the cogency of the argument that claims to establish precisely this conclusion—namely, the argument from the possibility of error. For according to this argument, we cannot grant that a

[50] There is, quite obviously, a wide variety of possible versions of externalism—including some that would hold that the relevance or irrelevance of a certain possibility is *also* dependent on cognitive factors. That is the sort of externalism elaborated in the work of David Lewis, Michael Williams, and Robert Fogelin. See Lewis, "Elusive Knowledge," 230; Williams, *Unnatural Doubts,* 350–359; Fogelin, *Pyrrhonian Reflections,* 83–84.

subject is capable of ruling out all possible falsifying circumstances without denying the possibility of error. Rather, we must claim that the best possible perceptual basis that is available to the subject must be such that it is compatible with the belief's being false.

The skeptic concludes from this argument that the concept of knowledge is inherently paradoxical. But in the eyes of the epistemologist of moderation, this involves a misunderstanding. For the supposed paradox, in the epistemologist's view, depends on the idea that the concept of knowledge can be meaningfully employed only if it is understood to entail that someone knows something only when the basis for her belief establishes what no basis could possibly establish: namely, that all the circumstances in which the belief in question would be false fail to obtain. And this is a claim we can dispute, according to proponents of a position of moderation. We can retreat to a less demanding justification condition on knowledge. The first variant of this strategy weakens the justification condition by formulating an internalist epistemic rule: the rule of reasonable doubt. The second variant of the strategy of moderation weakens the justification condition by externalizing its fulfillment in such a way that it is no longer part of the subject's consciousness.

Advocates of both variants believe that we can resolve the paradox of knowledge by challenging its first claim—namely, the claim that a subject has knowledge only if she has a truth-guaranteeing ground for her belief that she can adduce to justify her belief. In what follows, I will show that this strategy of moderation is wrongheaded. By challenging the first claim of the paradox, one doesn't escape from it, one simply charts a different way into it.

According to the internalist variant of this strategy, one can have a ground that is sufficient for knowledge even in a case in which what one believes is false. For it does not follow from the fact that we have no ground for believing that the goldfinch is stuffed that it is not, in fact, stuffed. Even if we have done everything that, on this account, we must do for our own part in order to secure a basis for believing what we do that is sufficient for knowledge, we nevertheless base our belief on a ground that is compatible with things being otherwise than we believe them to be. For it is a feature of every basis for belief, according to the first premise of the paradox that it cannot rule out that things are otherwise than we take them to be on that basis. Even the best possible ground we could have for a belief would still be compatible with the falsity of the belief it supports. But if that is so, it follows that the truth of our beliefs, on this account, is a matter of luck in the sense that even when we have the best possible basis for our beliefs, they may or may not be true.

The internalist strategy of moderation thus suggests that, in order to understand knowledge, we have to accept the view that we described in Part One as the dogma of epistemology. That dogma consists in the idea that someone can have a justification sufficient for knowledge even though her belief is false. When we first encountered the epistemological dogma in Part One, I claimed that we would understand its significance only once we understood it as a reaction to the skeptical problematic. We are now in a position to see just where the dogma of epistemology intercedes in the skeptical picture. The skeptic claims that if no perceptual experience is capable of guaranteeing the truth of a belief, I can never attain knowledge through it. The dogma of epistemology is an objection that is aimed not at the antecedent of this conditional but at the conditional itself. The thought is that we can avoid this inference if we can dissolve the connection between the justification condition and the truth condition on knowledge that the skeptic asserts. We have to realize that a justification sufficient for knowledge cannot require that the subject rule out the possibility that the belief she thus justifies may be false.

The externalist variant of the strategy of moderation, by contrast, thinks that the justification condition for knowledge and the truth condition for knowledge must be interconnected. The price he thinks he has to pay for this is to deny the self-conscious character of justification. The idea of a justification sufficient for knowledge, in his eyes, is not the idea of a ground that must be available to the subject such that she can adduce it to justify her belief, knowing it to be sufficient. Rather, the question whether a subject's ground is sufficient for knowledge is a question whose answer must be dependent on, among other things, whether things are as the subject believes them to be. However, that is a question whose answer is not available to the subject, on this account, for that would require that a ground for belief be available to the subject that rules out the possibility of her belief's being false. And because that is impossible, according to this account, we cannot require that a justification sufficient for knowledge must be such as to be available to the subject.

Thus, the internalist and externalist strategies represent two complementary ways of moderating the justification condition for knowledge. The internalist insists on the self-conscious character of justification. This seems to force him to deny the inner connection between the justification condition for knowledge and the truth condition. According to him, one can fulfill the justification condition without the belief's being true. By contrast, the externalist wants to hold on to the inner connection between the justification condition for knowledge and the truth condition. According to him, one cannot fulfill the justification condition without having a true belief. This seems to force him to give up the self-conscious character of the justification condition for knowledge. The consequence of both strategies is the same. The outcome is that, for every subject, it is, in principle, an open question whether a belief she forms on the basis of a sensory experience is true. From the perspective of the subject, the grounds she may have for a belief are, in principle, always compatible with things' being otherwise than she believes. We can therefore see that it makes no difference to the skeptical problematic whether one pursues the strategy of moderation in its internalist or its externalist variant. On either view, it is, in principle, an open question *for the subject* whether her belief is true. And on either view, there is nothing the subject can do to extricate herself from this situation.

So let us ask at this point: What difference is there between the skeptic's account of knowledge and the position of moderation? They both have in common that the very best answer the subject can give to the question "Why do you believe that p?" is one that is compatible with the falsity of her belief. From the fact that I have the perceptual experience that p and that I have no reason to suppose that not-p, it does not follow that p. Nor does the fact that I have the perceptual experience that p and that my perceptual experiences are rarely misleading entail that p. There is, in principle, a gulf between the ground that I can put forward to justify my belief and the truth of my belief. The strategy of moderation is to argue that this gulf between the ground I can adduce for my belief and the truth of my belief does not entail that we cannot understand how someone can know something. If we understand the justification condition on knowledge in a different way from the skeptic—namely, in a way that doesn't imply that knowledge requires that I can adduce a ground that is incompatible with the falsity of my belief—then we can combine the possibility of error with the possibility of knowledge.

According to our reflections in Part One, however, the concept of a truth-guaranteeing ground that is available to the subject is indispensable for understanding knowledge. Now, advocates of positions of moderation think that it is possible to combine knowledge with a less demanding justification. However, this is impossible without turning a knowledge claim into a self-contradictory act. Because this position implies that someone who says, "I know that p," must be making both of the following claims simultaneously:

(1) P is true.
(2) For all I know, p may be false.

And this means that the subject must make two claims that are interrelated in such a way that the second retracts precisely what the first claims: namely, that p is true. The dogma of epistemology thus forces upon us the idea that someone who ascribes knowledge either to herself or to another must do something that it is impossible to do: namely, assert (1) and (2) simultaneously.[51]

The thought that one can resolve the paradox of knowledge by moderating the justification condition for knowledge—either by giving up its connection with the truth condition or by giving up its self-conscious character—proves to be an illusion. The difference between the skeptical position and the positions of moderation we have discussed is only apparent. The skeptic claims that the concept of finite knowledge

[51] On this point, compare my critique of positions of moderation in "Why Do Our Reasons Come to an End?" There I show that this incoherence in the strategy of moderation has its complement in an unstable diagnosis of the problem of skepticism, which arises from the fact that it must oscillate between two different interpretations of the problem.

is intrinsically paradoxical, because, on her account, we are obliged to give two mutually exclusive characterizations of the basis of knowledge. The strategy of moderation, by contrast, attempts to replace the concept of a truth-guaranteeing ground that is available to the subject with the concept of a less demanding ground. This ultimately leads to an account of knowledge according to which a subject entangles herself in an aporia whenever she applies the concept of knowledge to herself, because any such use of the concept requires that she make two mutually incompatible claims.[52] The upshot of their view is that the concept is not itself paradoxical, though its employments are. And that is not a way out of the paradox of knowledge but just another way into it.

Positions of moderation want to say that the skeptical characterization of the justification condition is "an artifact of theoretical preconceptions that we can reasonably dispense with."[53] Our reflections reveal that the opposite is true. Given the two epistemological alternatives we have sketched, we are faced with a dilemma. Either we agree with the skeptic and claim that only someone who bases her belief on a ground that guarantees its truth possesses knowledge. Then we need, adopting Blackburn's formulation, "guaranteeing states" as grounds for our beliefs—i.e., states that, as Blackburn puts it, "as a matter of necessity, could not have

[52] Advocates of the strategy of moderation accordingly express their position by saying that the skeptic is not in a position to see how we can acknowledge our fallibility and simultaneously understand how we can enjoy knowledge. Compare Cohen, "Contextualism and Skepticism" and "How to Be a Fallibilist." It is, indeed, correct that the skeptic is not in a position to combine our fallibility with the possibility of knowledge. But what we have shown here is that most contemporary epistemology is just as little in a position to do so.

[53] Williams, *Problems of Knowledge*," 197. See also, among others, Schiffer, "Contextualist Solutions to Scepticism," and Cohen, "Knowledge, Context, and Social Standards." On this view, we can be afflicted with skeptical doubt only if the latter is born of assumptions that, as Barry Stroud puts it, express nothing but "platitudes that we would all accept" (*The Significance of Philosophical Skepticism,* 82). What is right about this is that the standard against which our "epistemic practices" are to be measured must be immanent to them. Yet what must be brought to light through philosophical reflection is the necessity of this characterization of that standard, by highlighting the essential interconnection between the several ways in which that standard is characterized. And showing this has nothing to do with whether that standard appears to us as trivial or as immediately obvious, etc. That appearance can, at best, be a consequence of this necessity.

existed had not the beliefs formed in light of them been true."[54] But then it is unclear how we could ever have such grounds for beliefs if we simultaneously admit that finite subjects are liable to err. Either that, or we deny that we actually appeal to truth-guaranteeing grounds and accordingly loosen the justification condition for knowledge so that it is enough for the knowing subject to cite grounds that accomplish less.[55] But that makes it unclear how use of the concept of knowledge can be an intelligible activity. Thus, the dilemma in which we find ourselves is that we seem forced to choose between two different ways of saying that we do not understand the concept of knowledge.

---

[54] Blackburn, "Knowledge, Truth, and Reliability," 170.

[55] Blackburn calls the states correlated with these grounds "indicating states," which contrast with "guaranteeing states" (ibid.). We can understand these as states that give us some clue about how things are in the world but nothing more: they are indicators that point in a direction, which may be the false one.

# What Are Grounds?

## 1. The Rigorous Reading: Hume and Kant

At the outset of Part Two we distinguished two strategies for refuting the skeptic's position: diagnostic and transcendental. A diagnostic strategy has a particular advantage over a transcendental critique that we characterized as follows. While a transcendental critique can admittedly show that the skeptical position must be false, it does not give us any indication of how we are to actually understand this thing that strikes the skeptic as a riddle. A diagnostic strategy, by contrast, provides us with precisely such an understanding. However, as we have seen above, if the diagnosis is not correct, the resulting position, in seeking to refute the skeptical position, turns out to be a form of it. In the sections that follow, I will show that the correct diagnosis of the skeptical position traces it back to a presupposition that is open to transcendental critique. Diagnostic and transcendental critiques thus coincide here. For the presupposition that is responsible for the skeptic's position can be shown to be self-undermining. This presupposition, as we shall see, rests on a misunderstanding of the nature of grounds.

In order to understand how someone can know something, we have argued, we must understand how someone can form her beliefs on the basis of truth-guaranteeing grounds. Truth-guaranteeing grounds for beliefs are possible only if there can be a nexus between a subject and a propositional content that enables her to answer the doxastic why-question in a way that settles the question of the relevant belief's truth. A statement of the form "S perceives that p," as we typically think of it, seems to denote just this sort of a nexus between subject and propositional content. Accordingly, we argued that in order to understand perceptual knowledge, we must understand what it means to make a statement of that form. Now, the argument from the possibility of error aims to show that it is impossible to understand such statements as describing a nexus between subjects and propositional contents that would fall under the category of a truth-guaranteeing ground. For this argument drives the analysis of these statements into what appears to be an insoluble paradox.

The difficulty we have in making it intelligible how such a truth-guaranteeing nexus between subject and propositional content is possible, according to our reflections, derives from the fact that we are not yet in a position to reconcile the possibility of truth-guaranteeing grounds with the possibility of error. My thesis is that this is where our most fundamental difficulty lies.

This characterization of our difficulty in understanding knowledge may be unsettling. One might want to object that this difficulty is actually rooted in something even more fundamental. The fundamental difficulty that we face in trying to understand finite knowledge, on this objection, doesn't arise from the fact that we can't see how to accommodate the possibility of error without relinquishing the possibility of a truth-guaranteeing ground. The ultimate source of our difficulty is instead that the very idea of a truth-guaranteeing nexus that is both receptive and justificatory is unintelligible. For it demands that we think of a mental state that is intrinsically capable of justifying something, yet without itself standing in need of justification. The very idea of such grounds, the objection runs, makes no sense.[56] The argument is about how to conceive of mental states that involve an impact of the world on our senses, such as perceptual experiences. It is often argued that there

---

[56] This argument unites a wide variety of authors who are otherwise quite different, including Sellars, Davidson, BonJour, and Chisholm.

are only two ways of conceiving of such states and that both of them rule out the idea of a truth-guaranteeing nexus. According to the objection, one way to conceive of them is merely causally, as an effect of affection. But then they do not have propositional content. In that case, it is correct to think of them as states that do not stand in need of justification. But the reason they do not stand in need of justification is because they lie outside of the realm of things that are rationally linked to each other. For only sensory experiences that have propositional content can provide a subject with something that enables her to justify her endorsement of a particular propositional content as true. The only other option—so the objection goes—is that we conceive of them as sensory states that do indeed have propositional content. But then they are nothing other than beliefs. And in that case, they can admittedly serve to ground other beliefs, yet to do so they, too, must be grounded in turn.[57]

Let's consider this objection more closely. The objection seeks to claim that any sensory state that has propositional content stands in need of justification or grounding. But what is the basis for this claim? Proponents of the above objection never argue for this claim but presuppose it as self-evident. Yet the claim stands in need of argumentation. For it is does not simply go without saying that any sensory state

---

[57] This formulation of the objection to the category of truth-guaranteeing grounds can be found nearly verbatim in BonJour, *The Structure of Empirical Knowledge,* 69. BonJour speaks there of an insoluble "dilemma," as he also does in "Can Empirical Knowledge Have a Foundation?," 269–270. Chisholm's formulation of the objection is analogous to BonJour's, but draws a different conclusion from the argument—namely, that the foundation of our knowledge, because it cannot consist in sensible states that stand in no need of grounding, must instead consist in "self-justifying beliefs." (See Chisholm, "The Myth of the Given," 112f.) Davidson must likewise have in mind some such argument as the one above in support of his claim that only a belief can serve as a reason for a belief—i.e., the claim that "there is no use looking for a source of justification outside of other sentences held true" ("A Coherence Theory of Truth and Knowledge," 144). (Apparently, however, Davidson takes the argument to be so obvious that he doesn't even feel the need to mention it.) The thought that receptivity and normativity are incompatible with one another is also the central premise in Sellars's attempt, beginning in §45 of *Empiricism and the Philosophy of Mind,* to defend the idea that we must at some point have recourse to sense impressions devoid of all conceptual content if we are to make sense of how our purported knowledge of the world can be determined by the world itself, rather than merely constituting an empty play of concepts.

with propositional content is, *ipso facto,* in need of justification. To see this, consider the following. Imagine a subject with an infallible perceptual capacity. For a subject to have an infallible perceptual capacity means that it is impossible for her to enjoy a perceptual experience of things that does not represent things as they actually are. Let's further imagine that whenever this subject has a perceptual experience, she also believes that things are as her perceptual experience represents them to be. Thus, a subject with an infallible perceptual capacity would be able to have beliefs justified by her perceptual experiences, which, in turn, would stand in no need of justification in their own right. If it were, in principle, impossible for one to have a perceptual experience that failed to represent how things actually are, then one's perceptual experiences would have justificatory force yet without needing any justification of their own.

This line of thought shows that it is simply false to claim that we cannot coherently conceive of the category of a truth-guaranteeing ground that is both receptive and justificatory. Of course, one would immediately object that the idea of an infallible perceptual capacity cannot have any significance for us, for we are looking for an account of finite knowledge. But what does this actually mean? What we are looking for is an argument for the claim that we cannot understand the concept of a receptive nexus between subject and propositional content that guarantees the truth of a belief. The argument we formulated above has the form of a *reductio:* We can understand this concept only if it describes a nexus that arises from infallible perceptual capacities. Because the idea of infallible perceptual capacities would precisely foreclose the possibility of error—which we are not permitted to do if our aim is to understand finite knowledge—we cannot, therefore, understand this concept. But this should sound familiar to us. The argument that must implicitly underlie the objection to the category of a truth-guaranteeing ground that is both receptive and justificatory is the very same argument that leads to the paradox of knowledge. For the alternative that the paradox places before us is that we must either deny that perceptual experiences that serve as grounds for beliefs can be deceptive or admit that a perceptual experience that serves as a ground for belief cannot, in principle, guarantee the truth of that belief. One can formulate the above objection to the category of a truth-guaranteeing receptive nexus only if one is already implicitly presupposing the argument from the possibility of error.

What this means is that our actual problem lies in the paradox of knowledge that the argument from the possibility of error saddles us with and that makes skepticism unavoidable. For then we are compelled to claim that, in principle, perceptual experiences can at best have the status of premises on the basis of which we must then derive an answer to the question of how things are in the world. However, if that is so, then it is, in principle, impossible for us to ever settle the question in such a way that the question of how things are in the world is no longer open.

This is the rigorous reading of the skeptical problem, which is common to both Hume and Kant. Both Hume and Kant express the skeptical problem, as it applies to perceptual knowledge, in the form of a conditional: If we understand our purported knowledge of the world that sensibly affects us as, in principle, the result of an inference based on reflection upon a sensory experience as premise, then it is impossible for us to ever have knowledge of the world that sensibly affects us. For in that case it would be impossible for us to ever produce an argument that could guarantee the truth of a belief.[58]

As we have seen, however, it is the point of the argument from the possibility of error to show just this: namely, that our supposed knowledge of the world that sensibly affects us must be understood as the result of an inference for which our perceptual experiences serve as premises. We can describe Hume and Kant's shared description of the skeptical problem as "rigorous" because it entails that it is impossible to understand empirical knowledge if we accept this argument. If empirical knowledge of the world, in its fundamental instances, is inferential knowledge, then empirical knowledge of the world is simply impossible. And it is impossible for precisely the reason Hume and Kant highlight: namely, because a subject could have a truth-guaranteeing argument

---

[58] Hume's argument for this claim can be found in *An Enquiry concerning Human Understanding*, 152–153. For a similar argument as applied to knowledge by hearsay, see *Enquiry*, 109f. Kant formulates his own argument for this claim in the *Kritik der reinen Vernunft*, B276–277.

for a belief only if she could actually know that the sensory experience, on which her argument is premised, were caused by precisely the object that her sensory experience represents. That is to say, the subject could make a truth-guaranteeing argument for her belief only if she already enjoyed the very empirical knowledge that such an argument is meant to justify.

On the basis of these considerations, Hume concludes that we have no alternative but to embrace skeptical doubt. Because a subject cannot, in principle, have the requisite knowledge of the causes of her sensory experiences, empirical knowledge is impossible. For as Hume writes:

> By what argument can it be proved, that the perceptions of the mind must be caused by external objects, entirely different from them, though resembling them (if that be possible) and could not arise either from the energy of the mind itself, or from the suggestion of some invisible and unknown spirit, or from some other cause still more unknown to us?[59]

Because it is a "question of fact" whether and which (if any) of a subject's "perceptions" result from external objects, the truth (or falsity) of the beliefs about the world that the subject infers from this basis can be determined only "by experience" according to Hume.[60] But when it comes to explaining how "experience" can provide us with knowledge of the world, experience itself "must be entirely silent."[61] If empirical knowledge is, in the fundamental case, inferential knowledge, then "the mind [...] cannot possibly reach any experience of [its perceptions'] connexion with objects"—i.e., it cannot possibly acquire through experience an answer to the question of how such experience is hooked up with objects in the world.[62] Thus, Hume concludes that "the supposition of such a connexion" between experience and objects in the world "is, therefore, without any foundation in reasoning."[63]

[59] Hume, *An Enquiry concerning Human Understanding*, 152f.
[60] Ibid. 153.
[61] Ibid.
[62] Ibid.
[63] Ibid.

Kant famously takes up this Humean diagnosis and reformulates it in the following way: If we start with the thought that "inner [experience] is the only [kind of] immediate experience," then this means that we can "only *infer* [the existence of] external things."[64] Yet if we must thereby "infer *particular* causes from given effects," this sort of inference can only ever be "unreliable," "because the cause of our representations that we (perhaps wrongly) ascribe to outer things could lie in us."[65] If we presuppose that, in the fundamental case, our knowledge of the world that sensibly affects us takes the form of an inferred conclusion, then skepticism is unavoidable, according to Hume and Kant's rigorous reading of the skeptical problematic.

For Hume and Kant it is clear that the argument that results in such an inference must rest upon of causal considerations. That is, it must contain a reflection on the cause of our perceptual experience. Only if it takes this form, Hume and Kant claim, can we understand what we believe about the world as something whose truth is dependent on how things are in the world. If this inferentialist account of the form of empirical knowledge is compulsory, then it follows that whenever I come to believe something on the basis of a perceptual experience—e.g., the perceptual experience that there is a white teacup before me—my belief is to be construed as the result of an inference of the following sort:

(1) I have the perceptual experience that there is a white teacup in front of me.
(2) The cause of (1) is a white teacup located in front of me.
(3) Therefore, it is true to believe that there is a white teacup in front of me.

But because premise (2) is something we cannot ever know to be true— "for of course," as Davidson puts it, "we can't get outside our skins"—the inference to (3) stalls out.[66] And that is precisely why Hume and Kant

---

[64] Kant, *Kritik der reinen Vernunft*, B276, emphasis in original.
[65] Ibid., emphasis in original.
[66] Davidson, "A Coherence Theory of Truth and Knowledge," 144.

hold that skepticism is unavoidable within this inferential construal of empirical knowledge.[67] Skepticism is the ineluctable flipside of any inferentialist account of empirical knowledge. For on an inferentialist view we have only the following two options. Either we conclude that one cannot, in principle, enjoy empirical knowledge of how things are in the world because one cannot, in principle, construct an argument that can guarantee the truth of one's belief about how things stand in the world. That is the skeptical position. Or we deny that someone has knowledge only if she has a truth-guaranteeing ground for her belief. We would then accept that a less demanding justification is sufficient for knowledge. That is the epistemologist's position of moderation, which we have shown to be just another form of skepticism that is distinguished from the former one only in that it does not recognize itself as a skeptical position.

This constellation of options makes it clear why it is completely misguided to interpret skepticism as the result of, say, an immoderate demand for certainty or as an expression of a desire for infallible judgments.[68] For the skeptic attempts to do nothing more and nothing less than to hold on to the idea that when someone knows something, she cannot be wrong. Therefore, we can succeed in understanding knowledge only if

---

[67] Various authors accordingly think that Hume and Kant's rigorous reading overshoots its goal. These authors think that the skeptical problem that confronts us rests solely on our (mistaken) belief that the inference from (1) to (2) must be grounded in specifically causal considerations—i.e., considerations regarding the cause of (1). That is how a phenomenalist such as Ayer would view the matter (see *The Foundations of Empirical Knowledge,* esp. 38–39, 82–83, 123). But this involves a misunderstanding. If, in the fundamental case, the belief that I come to hold on the basis of sense impressions rests on an inference, then the thought that this inference secures something less than a guarantee of truth—a thought that even Ayer affirms—must deeply unsettle us. For the skeptic's argument is indifferent to whether the considerations underlying our inference from our sense impressions to the truth of our empirical beliefs about the world are to be understood causally or in some other manner.

[68] See, for example, Ayer, *The Foundations of Empirical Knowledge,* 39. See also Brandom, "Knowledge and the Social Articulation of the Space of Reasons," 899. A crucial mistake of Brandom's is that he fails to see that the only correct claim common to both the skeptic and the dogmatist (to use Brandom's term) is the idea that a justification that suffices for knowledge must foreclose the possibility that the judgment in question is false.

we can manage to give up the assumption that seems to make a choice between these two options unavoidable.

## 2. Grounds and Facts

In what follows I will begin to describe the presupposition that underlies the denial of the possibility of truth-guaranteeing grounds for perceptual knowledge (and analogously for knowledge by hearsay). This presupposition can be described at various levels, and I will progressively peel away some of these layers of the onion until we are at the relevant level of depth. I will initially describe the presupposition at a level where it takes the form of a particular understanding of the nature of grounds. In Part Three we will then see that this (mis)understanding of the nature of grounds has its roots in a more fundamental misunderstanding of the nature of knowledge. Here and throughout, I will address this presupposition—i.e., the first layer of its description— as it applies to perceptual knowledge, though the discussion will be a model for other instances of empirical knowledge as well (e.g., knowledge by hearsay).

Theories of perceptual knowledge that deny the possibility of truth-guaranteeing grounds for perceptual knowledge are defined by the following thought: they hold that the best possible receptive ground available to a subject for believing something about the world is compatible with the subject's coming to a false judgment about the world on its basis. On this account, the best possible receptive ground is one that can ground both true and false judgments about the world. I will accordingly call this the "common-ground thesis."

They accept this thought because they take the argument from error to be compelling. But this thought is not free from presuppositions. And one should only accept it if the presuppositions, on which it depends, are correct. One of its crucial presuppositions is this: Receptive grounds for beliefs about the world must be available to the subject independently of whether things in the world are as the subject believes them to be on their basis. For one can claim that the best possible receptive ground on which a subject can ever base her belief is compatible with the falsity of that belief only if one thinks that receptive grounds for beliefs must be available even when things are not as one believes them to be on that basis. Theories of perceptual knowledge that deny the possibility of truth-guaranteeing grounds for perceptual knowledge stand or fall with this presupposition—i.e., with the idea that it is in the nature of receptive grounds to be, in this sense, independent of the world. If we peel away the outermost layer of the dogma of epistemology—according to which a subject can justify her belief in a manner that suffices for knowledge even when her belief is false—what we discover is another dogma underlying it: the dogma of world-independent grounds.

I want to work out the significance of this description of the presupposition of skepticism (and, as a variation of it, of positions of moderation) by distinguishing it from an apparently similar critique, which has been developed by Davidson, Burge, and others.[69] Burge characterizes the presupposition underlying most of the dominant traditional theories of empirical knowledge that he seeks to oppose in a similar way by holding that, according to those theories, perceptual experiences are mental states that are intrinsically independent of the world. He understands this thought about the world-independence of perceptual experiences in a particular way. According to Burge, it is the thought that sensory experiences are intrinsically world-independent in the sense that the concepts that determine the content of these experiences are completely independent of the environment in which a subject employs them. But this presupposition is false, on Burge's view. The meaning of our concepts is partly determined by the nature of the objects in our environment that normally fall under them. To take an example: When I have the sensory experience of a white teacup, the content of which I express in saying, "I have the sensory experience of a white teacup," this content distinguishes my sensory experience from the sensory experience

---

[69] See, for example, Burge, "Other Bodies" and, especially, "Cartesian Error and the Objectivity of Perception." That this critique of inferentialism—which, when it is not couched in expressly epistemological terms, as it is here, is typically called "Cartesianism"—as made prominent by Burge and Davidson is still fundamentally flawed, because it fails to identify and jettison the crucial premise of inferentialism, is also argued by McDowell, "*De Re* Senses."

that my counterpart on Twin Earth would characterize using the same words. In particular, these sensory experiences are distinct because the meaning of the concept "teacup" for my counterpart on Twin Earth is not determined by those objects that in our environment on Earth normally cause a sensory experience whose content is described by the concept "teacup." The meaning of the concept "teacup" for my counterpart on Twin Earth is instead determined by those objects that in the environment of Twin Earth normally cause a sensory experience whose content is described by that concept.

Davidson similarly describes the presupposition of skepticism as it pertains to empirical knowledge as follows: Skeptical theories presuppose that empirical beliefs are world-independent cognitive states in the sense that one can identify them as this or that particular belief without thereby assuming that the purported object in the world to which it refers is—in most cases—the cause of the belief in question.[70] Davidson argues that this thought—that empirical beliefs are, in this sense, world-independent—is false. We must rather come to see that it is part of what it is to have beliefs that the majority of the beliefs someone forms are caused by precisely those objects in the world to which they refer and, thus, that the majority of someone's beliefs are true.

Yet Burge and Davidson's descriptions of the presupposition on which skepticism depends are insufficient. Their descriptions do not by any means solve the problem of skepticism. For according to Burge and Davidson, it is not the object that I actually see in the world that determines the intrinsic character of my sensory experience or my belief; instead, this is determined by an object that, *in most cases,* is the cause of my sensory experience or belief. The view Burge and Davidson develop thus does not provide an intrinsic difference between the sensory experience that I have when I see a white teacup and the one that I have when I merely hallucinate a white teacup. On the present view, the difference between these two experiences, namely that in one case the cause of my experience is a white teacup, while in the other case it is not, is external to the experiences. Yet if this difference between the two cases of

[70] See Davidson—e.g., "A Coherence Theory of Truth and Knowledge" and "The Myth of the Subjective."

a sensory experience is external to the experiences—i.e., if there is no intrinsic difference between the experience I have when I see something as opposed to the one I have when I hallucinate—then the insight that sensory experiences and beliefs are world-dependent in the specified sense does not bring us closer to solving the problem that is our concern: namely, how to make sense of the idea that a subject can form a belief on the basis of a ground that rules out the falsity of that belief. This problem is unaffected by the insight that most of our beliefs must be true. The general insight that most of our beliefs must be true cannot satisfy us until we solve the problem of how we can know whether a particular belief of mine actually is true. And once we understand how to solve the latter problem, the general insight that Davidson's reassuring strategy provides—namely, that to have beliefs at all already ensures that most of one's beliefs must be caused by the very objects in the world to which they refer—is rendered superfluous.

The crucial presupposition of skepticism accordingly should not be described in terms of the general thought that sensory experiences are world-independent. As we have seen above, one can give up that thought while retaining the crucial presupposition of skepticism: namely, that the best possible mental basis we can have for a belief is nevertheless compatible with that belief about the world being false. Our task must instead be to take this thesis—what we called the common-ground thesis—off the table altogether. And in order to do so, we must provide a more fundamental characterization of the world-independence of sensory experiences than any position that denies the possibility of truth-guaranteeing receptive grounds.[71]

## 3. A Transcendental Argument

A transcendental argument against a skeptical position, properly understood, consists in showing that in formulating her argument, the skeptic must appeal to a premise to which one is not entitled if one denies precisely what her skeptical argument seeks to show is impossible. In the

---

[71] On this point, see also Child, "Vision and Experience," 303.

present case, the premise in question—the premise that the skeptic must invoke in order to formulate her argument against the possibility of empirical knowledge—is the presupposition that we do have grounds for empirical beliefs but not truth-guaranteeing grounds. In what follows, I will formulate a transcendental argument against the skeptical position by focusing on this premise. The argument aspires to show that the skeptic's "unworlding of grounds", as we might put it, ends up rendering impossible precisely the thing that the skeptic must appeal to in articulating her doubt—namely, that there are receptive grounds for beliefs at all. Our transcendental argument consists of three steps.

*The first step.* Judging, and correlatively, believing something, is a free, rational activity. To judge is to endorse a conceptual content as true and to be guided, in doing so, by the standard of truth, which one's judgment claims to fulfill. If we understand the concept of judgment in this way, we think of a judgment as the target of a particular form of explanation: a normative, self-conscious explanation. We expressed this connection between the idea of judgment and the idea of such a form of explanation by saying that it is constitutive of judgment that the judging subject can make her judgment intelligible by adducing grounds that represent the judgment as true or as likely to be true. This concept of judgment is the starting point for all skeptical positions. For the skeptic wants to claim that a particular sort of ground, one that would be required for us to have knowledge, is unavailable to us—namely, a ground that would guarantee the truth of the judgment it justifies. The best possible ground that is available to us, according to the skeptic, accomplishes less.

*The second step.* The judgments and, correlatively, the beliefs to be explained are supposed to have a conceptual content whose truth is dependent on how things are in the world. Consequently, a subject can have such beliefs only if she is able to ground her belief in some mental act through which she is receptive to how things are in the world. Thus, a subject can have an empirical belief, in this sense, only if she has grounds that reflect precisely this dependence on the world. In order to understand how a subject can enjoy empirical beliefs, therefore, we must conceive of the believing subject as a sensible being who enjoys mental states that result from an impact of the world on her sensibility and that can serve as grounds for belief. Our subject needs receptive grounds. Sensory experiences with conceptual content seem to be able to provide such grounds, for sensory experiences with conceptual content, on any account of them, are mental states of a subject that result from an impact of the world on her sensibility.

Now, the account that is common to both horns of the dilemma between skepticism and positions of moderation holds that the best possible sensory experience that can serve as a subject's ground for believing something is connected with the fact to which it refers in precisely the same way that a belief is connected with the fact to which it refers: namely, in such a way that one can enjoy the relevant state independently of whether things are as one's experience represents them to be. That is the gist of the common-ground thesis.[72] However, if a sensory experience is, in principle, connected with the fact to which it makes reference in precisely the same way as a belief is, then we are faced with the question of how to account for these experiences. For if these experiences are connected with the fact to which they make reference in precisely the same way as a belief, then it is ruled out from the start that we might account for them in terms of the fact to which they refer. However, if it is ruled out from the start that we can account for sensory experiences in terms of the facts to which they refer, then the only other account that is left is one that decomposes a sensory experience into two mental states: (1) a state conceived merely causally, as an effect of affection, lacking all conceptual content, to account for the sensible character of these experiences, and (2) an empirical belief, in order to account for the conceptual content of these experiences.

*The third step.* This analysis of receptive grounds undermines itself. For in order to account for the idea of a receptive ground, this analysis

---

[72] A "strict account," to use Strawson's phrase, of the mental act that constitutes this common basis would be one "which confines itself strictly within the limits of the subjective episode, an account which would remain true even if he had seen nothing of what he claimed to see, even if he had been subject to total illusion." See Strawson, "Perception and Its Objects," 43.

has to presuppose the intelligibility of the very belief that the idea of a receptive ground was supposed to make intelligible in the first place. If we connect this result back up with our first step, it follows that the skeptic is not entitled to invoke the idea of a subject who can form empirical beliefs on the basis of receptive grounds—an idea that forms a central part of her claim that the truth of those beliefs can only ever be problematic.

WE HAVE THUS SHOWN that the "unworlding of grounds" as it characterizes all positions caught in the epistemological dilemma is self-undermining. The "unworlding of grounds" is not to be rejected simply because such grounds cannot explain empirical knowledge. It is to be rejected because it makes unintelligible the very idea of receptive grounds and hence the idea of empirical belief. If the best possible sensory experience on the basis of which someone can acquire a belief is one that is available independently of whether things are as she believes them to be on its basis, then the very idea of a subject who can so much as have a ground for belief whose truth she understands to be dependent on how things are in the world becomes unintelligible. The skeptic is not entitled to assume the intelligibility of the idea of grounds for empirical beliefs—though she must indeed suppose it to be intelligible in order to claim that such grounds can never guarantee the truth of one's belief.

The above argument is at once a diagnosis of the skeptical position as well as its transcendental refutation. Conjoining diagnosis with refutation, the argument shows not only that the skeptic's position is self-undermining, but also why it is. It is self-undermining because of the way in which it understands the nature of grounds for empirical beliefs. In order properly to grasp the nature of grounds for empirical belief, we must give up the idea that a receptive ground for belief must be available independently of whether things are as the subject believes them to be on its basis. Instead, we have to conceive of a receptive ground for belief in terms of a mental state that is, in the fundamental case—i.e., the case without which we could not understand the idea of receptive grounds and hence of empirical beliefs—dependent on things being as the subject believes them to be on the basis of this ground. A sensory experience that is dependent on things being as the subject believes them to be on the basis of this experience (or would believe them to be, were she to endorse the content of the experience in question) is precisely such a ground. Moreover, it is a receptive ground that guarantees the truth of one's belief. For insofar as it is sensory, the world-dependence that is characteristic of such an experience is a form of causal dependence. It is a sensory experience that is caused by the object of which it is an experience. And this provides us with just what we need: namely, a state that is, as such, justifying and yet does not re-attract the question that it serves to answer because its concept already contains an explanation of this very state—namely, an explanation in terms of the very object that is its content.

With this, we arrive at the following understanding of the nature of receptive grounds. A receptive ground for belief, in the fundamental case, consists in a sensory experience, which, as such, is caused by the object of which it is an experience.

Our question was: How are beliefs, whose truth depends on how things are in the world, so much as possible? Our answer is: Such beliefs are possible in virtue of sensory experiences that have the same conceptual content as the beliefs they explain but that differ from beliefs insofar as they can be enjoyed (in their respective characteristic ways) only if things are as the subject who enjoys them represents them as being. If we then apply this insight to the question we posed at the end of Part One—namely, What does it mean to describe someone as perceiving that p?—then we can say: Someone who perceives that p enjoys the fundamental case of a ground for an empirical belief. She has a conceptual representation of how things are that is impressed on her—in the way characteristic of a perception—by what she perceives. Seeing that things are thus and so is a case of being causally necessitated conceptually to represent things as being thus and so by the object that one sees.

The central difference between the relation a subject bears to the content of her perception and the relation she bears to the content of her belief lies in the fact that the former involves a conceptual content being impressed upon her. When a subject believes something, her relation to the conceptual content of her belief is, as we said, a spontaneous relation, to use Kantian terminology. That a subject believes something means that she endorses a particular conceptual content as true. By contrast, to enjoy a perception that constitutes a receptive ground for a belief is to have a conceptual representation that is the result of causal necessitation—a necessitation that, in the case of perception, flows from the very object that it represents. The essential difference between a sensory experience and a judgment, which enables the former to explain how empirical belief is possible, thus lies in the fact that a sensory experience is not a deed on the part of the subject, as a judgment is, but is instead something she suffers—something that, in the non-delusive case, is impressed upon her by the object that is both the conceptual content and the cause of that experience. This explains why a particular sort of why-question does not apply to sensory experience. One cannot ask a subject what her grounds are for having a certain sensory experience (e.g., the sensory experience that there is still apple juice in the fridge), because she is not responsible for the fact that she has this experience—i.e., this actualization of her conceptual capacities is not the result of a decision on her part.

With this concept of perception, we have equipped ourselves with the concept of an act that makes it intelligible how someone can have an empirical belief. But we have gained even more than this. For the very concept of perception that we developed above, which makes it intelligible how someone can have an empirical belief, is likewise capable of rendering intelligible how someone can acquire knowledge on the basis of a perception. For perception, so understood, falls under the category of a truth-guaranteeing ground. Someone who enjoys a sensory experience that one cannot even have unless things are as one would believe them to be on its basis, has a ground for her belief that rules out the possibility that her belief might be false. Someone who enjoys a sensory experience that is, in this sense, world-dependent accordingly has just what we have been searching for: a ground for knowledge. The fundamental case of a ground for empirical belief is one that serves as a ground for knowledge. *The fundamental case of a ground for belief is a truth-guaranteeing ground.*

At the outset of our inquiry, it seemed impossible to understand how someone who grounds her belief on a perception can thereby answer the doxastic why-question in such a way that it does not remain open. Yet our transcendental reflections have shown us that this is precisely what we must understand in order to see how a subject can have grounds for empirical belief in the first place.

Our answer to the question of how we must understand a factive statement of the form "S perceives that p," as we have developed it up to this point, therefore holds that its factive sense is irreducible. That is to say, such statements do not derive their factive sense from a statement about an act that lacks a factive sense, such as the statement "I have the sensory experience that p," conjoined with the claim that p. It is instead a statement that describes an act in which a subject stands in an irreducible causal relation to the very fact that makes up the conceptual content of that act.

This does not mean that it is wrong to explain the concept of perception in terms of the concept of a sensory experience. Quite the contrary. That is precisely what we did above. Someone who perceives something has a sensory experience. But it is not always the case that one perceives something when one enjoys a sensory experience. One can enjoy a sensory experience without perceiving anything—e.g., when one is hallucinating or dreaming. The concept of a sensory experience is broader than the concept of perception, precisely because it not only describes the mental basis one has when one acquires empirical knowledge through it but also the sort of mental basis one has in the infelicitous case, when it merely appears to one as if things were thus and so. Yet how are these things compatible? How can we claim that the factive sense of statements of the form "S perceives that p" is irreducible while simultaneously employing the concept of a sensory experience to explain what it means for someone to perceive something?

To be able to make both claims simultaneously, we have to recognize that a statement of the form "I have the sensory experience that p" has a disjunctive sense.[73] When we say, "I have the sensory experience that p," we are not describing a mental act that can occur both in cases when

[73] This is the same conclusion to which McDowell, Child, Snowdon, Willaschek, Rödl, Hinton, and Williamson, among others, have come. Each of these authors explicitly endorses a "disjunctive conception of sensory experience." (On this point see the following footnotes.) However, not everyone who argues for a disjunctive conception of sensory experience has the same view of the rationale—and hence the point—of this conception. For example, Snowdon erroneously believes that this understanding

we are perceiving something as well as in cases where things merely appear to us as if they were thus and so. Rather, in such a statement we are describing *either* a perception *or*, on the other hand, a mental act in which things merely appear to us as if they were thus and so. The concept of a sensory experience—which is neutral with respect to these two cases, i.e., the case in which one recognizes how things are through one's senses and the case in which one does not—is not more fundamental than the factive concept of perception. The reverse is true. The concept of a sensory experience, which is neutral with respect to the two cases, is an abstraction from a more fundamental description of an act either as a perception or as the illusion of a perception. That does not, of course, mean that there is no description that can be applied to the cases in which we perceive what is the case as well as to the cases in which it merely appears to us as though we perceive what is the case. In both cases, we can say, for example, "I have the sensory experience that p." But there is not some act (some type of act) that is common to both sorts of case covered by this description.[74] This statement instead describes either the obtaining of the particular sort of causal relation between me and an object,[75] which is characteristic of perception, or, instead, the mere appearance of such a relation.[76]

requires us to challenge the idea that perception is an essentially causal notion. I will return to this point in what follows.

[74] See the accounts given in Child, "Vision and Experience"; Snowdon, "The Objects of Perceptual Experience." All the cases that Grice and Pears, for example, adduce in order to show that perceptual knowledge must rest on some sort of causal reasoning (even if such reasoning, as is always admitted, need not be consciously performed or registered) already presuppose precisely this reducibility of the factive sense of the concept of perception. See Grice, "The Causal Theory of Perception," as well as Pears, "The Causal Theory of Perception."

[75] This is how Snowdon characterizes the disjunctive conception in "Perception, Vision, and Causation," esp. 200f. On this point, see also the descriptions in Hinton, "Visual Experiences," Hinton, *Experiences,* and Willaschek, *Der mentale Zugang zur Welt,* 217f; and Williamson, "Is Knowing a State of Mind?"

[76] See Snowdon, "Perception, Vision, and Causation," 203. Thus, the function of such a statement is not to say that there is a mental act to which we relate just as we relate to the world in that act. See also Snowdon, "The Objects of Perceptual Experience," 137, as well as Evans, "Self-Identification," in *The Varieties of Reference,* 227–228.

But aren't we often uncertain whether we see or hear something? Sometimes I am uncertain whether I just heard the telephone ring. Did it just ring, or am I imagining things? Or sometimes I am uncertain whether I see a dark figure walking in the park at night. Was it perhaps just my imagination, because I am afraid of walking through the park at night? Naturally, we sometimes go back and forth about these questions. But what significance does this uncertainty have? When I ask myself whether I really heard the phone ring, I am not asking myself whether my sensory experience was really caused by the ringing of the telephone. What I am asking myself is just this: whether I really heard the telephone ring. If I then proceed to pick up the phone and hear nothing but the awful dial tone, I am not establishing that I was mistaken about the cause of my sensory experience. What I am establishing is that it only appeared to me as though I heard the telephone ring. Sometimes we are uncertain. Yet our uncertainty does not pertain to the causes of our sensory experiences as something that is separable from the experience. What we are uncertain about in these moments is whether we really perceived something or whether it only appeared to us as though we did.[77]

## 4. Causality or Normativity: A False Dichotomy

As we saw at the beginning of Chapter V, section 1, one of the arguments that might lead one to deny the possibility of truth-guaranteeing grounds maintains that receptivity and normativity are two mutually exclusive characterizations of a mental act. On this view, to represent an act as receptive means conceiving of it merely causally, as an effect of affection. But then the act cannot be normative—i.e., it cannot serve, just as such and in the absence of further reflection, to reveal a belief to be true. Or alternatively, an act can be normative, i.e., have a justificatory character.

---

[77] One aspect of the disjunctive conception of sense impressions is, therefore, that self-ascriptions of these acts are essentially corrigible. Hence, the self-ascription of mental acts, in the fundamental case, should itself be understood as an act of knowledge. (We will discuss this point at some length in Part Three.)

But then it cannot be receptive. Or so the argument goes. What we found, however, is that a subject can form empirical beliefs only if she can justify (some of) her beliefs through sensible acts that are caused by the very objects they represent. It follows from this that we have to reject the apparent dichotomy between receptivity and normativity as based on a misunderstanding. For in order to explain the possibility of empirical beliefs, we must appeal to acts that are both receptive and normative at once. More precisely, we must make reference to acts whose receptivity cannot be described without describing their normative character and *vice versa*. For, as we have seen, one cannot describe the cause of such acts without describing their conceptual content. It is the conceptual content of such an act that enables one to describe its cause. At the same time, one cannot describe the conceptual content of these acts without describing their cause. The description of the conceptual content of these acts depends on a description of the objects that cause them. It is the description of the objects that cause these acts that allows us to describe them as having a particular conceptual content, whose description, in turn, allows us to describe the objects of these acts. It characterizes the acts that explain empirical beliefs that they exhibit a normative receptivity.

The idea of such normative receptivity may well invite the following objection. If one claims that there are sensible acts that are dependent on the objects that constitute their conceptual content, then one is compelled to deny that the concept of such an act is genuinely causal. We exploited this causal sense of the concept in our characterization of perceptions as something self-evident. But we were not entitled to do so. For an act is either causally linked to its object, in which case the occurrence of the act is something that is logically independent of that object, or the occurrence of a particular act may logically depend on its object, in which case the object cannot be the cause of the act. So the objection goes. Thus Snowdon argues that any theory that denies that the concept of perception can be analyzed into independent elements must also deny that causality is a necessary element in perception—a consequence Snowdon himself accepts.[78]

---

[78] See Snowdon, "Perception, Vision, and Causation" and "The Objects of Perceptual Experience."

But what is this objection based on? The objection has to assume that the idea of a causal relation between two elements—in this case, between the object and the perception of the object—presupposes their mutual independence of one another. That is Hume's famous account of causality, which holds that a causal relation can obtain between two elements, let's say A and B, only if our fundamental descriptions of these elements are such that, under those descriptions, A cannot be derived from B, nor B from A.[79]

When we say that the statement "S sees that p" describes an act in which a subject stands in a causal relation to the object that constitutes its conceptual content, therefore, we are rejecting the Humean doctrine of causation. For we are denying that we can, in this case, describe the effect independently of its cause. Our analysis of perception accordingly compels us to dispute the validity of the Humean doctrine of causation—at least as it pertains to perception. What exactly this means is something we will work out step-by-step in what follows, until we arrive, in Part Four, at an adequate understanding of the relevant concept of causality characteristic of perceptual knowledge. For the moment, it suffices to point out that Hume's doctrine is incompatible with our analysis of perception and that we accordingly have reason to reject it.[80] Anscombe argues against the unrestricted validity of this doctrine along different lines. Anscombe claims that the Humean doctrine of causation cannot pertain to all phenomena, because our understanding of a general concept of causality as a relation between two elements is actually derivative when compared to an understanding of quite particular causal concepts. Anscombe's examples include concepts such as "scrape, push, wet, carry, eat, burn, knock over, keep off,

---

[79] For a discussion of this objection, see also Child, "Vision and Experience: The Causal Theory and the Disjunctive Conception," esp. 306f.

[80] Snowdon accepts the Humean doctrine of causation at face value and thus believes he must deny that causality is part of our concept of perception. See Snowdon, "Perception, Vision, and Causation," 201. This misses the real point of critiques of the causal theory of perception. The issue is not whether we must deny that perception is causal, but whether we can maintain that this sort of causality is irreducibly normative. This misunderstanding can also be found in Hyman, "Vision and Power" and "Vision, Causation, and Occlusion."

squash, make (e.g., noises, paper boats), hurt."[81] According to Anscombe, it is a mistake to believe that these causal concepts should be understood as posterior to a general concept of causality, in terms of which they are to be understood. The idea of a general concept of causality, in Anscombe's view, is instead an abstraction from such particular causal concepts, our understanding of which is more fundamental.[82] The concept of perception, we might now interject, is likewise a particular causal concept of the sort Anscombe identifies.[83]

---

[81] Anscombe, "Causality and Determination," 137. See also Anscombe's papers "Memory, 'Experience,' and Causation" and "The Causation of Action." On this point, see also Child's defense of his own critique of the causal theory of perception in "Vision and Experience," and Child, *Causality, Interpretation, and the Mind,* esp. 103–105.

[82] Another way to reject the Humean doctrine would be to show that its scope is limited. It is valid, on this view, only as restricted to the realm of inanimate nature. One might grant that the inanimate realm can indeed be thought of as a domain of autonomous entities—i.e., as a domain of things whose intrinsic nature is independent of other things. For precisely this reason, the Humean doctrine of independent existence as an essential feature of causal relations would neatly pertain to this realm. But neither the realm of animate nature, nor the realm of the mental, as a special form of animate nature, can be understood in the manner of inanimate nature—viz., as a realm of autonomous and mutually independent entities. To demand that it is an essential feature of causal relations that cause and effect must be logically independent of one another would therefore amount to a demand that one be able to understand the realm of animate nature—and specifically, for our purposes, the realm of the mental—on the model of inanimate nature. Hinton presents an argument along these lines in the course of defending his critique of the so-called causal theory of perception, in the sense articulated by Grice. See Hinton, *Experiences,* 80–81.

[83] And, we might add, the concept of hearsay must be understood in an analogous way. Inferentialist conceptions of knowledge by hearsay—analogous to inferentialist conceptions of perceptual knowledge—rest on the thought that the best possible nexus between a subject and the world that hearsay is able to establish is one that is, in principle, weaker than it would need to be in order to guarantee the truth of the belief based on hearsay. Here, too, the presupposition underlying this thought is that the best possible case of hearsay, on the basis of which one comes to believe something, is one that can obtain independently of whether things are the way as one comes to believe they are. And here, too, we must reject inferentialism, in order to understand knowledge from hearsay. The fundamental sense of the statement "S learned from so-and-so that p" must consist in describing a receptive act in which someone enjoys a conceptual representation of how things stand, which is caused—in the way characteristic of learning something through hearsay—by the fact that things are as one represents them to be. Just as in the case of perception, someone who learns from the newspaper, say, how things stand in the world, has a conceptual representation of how things

## 5. The Primacy of Knowledge

Our recognition of the disjunctive sense of statements of the form "S has the sensory experience that p" has the happy result that it enables us to resolve the paradox of knowledge. The skeptic holds that we must affirm and accept the paradox of knowledge. It is impossible, according to the skeptic, to combine the idea that knowledge requires truth-guaranteeing grounds with the idea that knowledge is fallible. By contrast, our recognition of the disjunctive sense of statements of the form "S has the sensory experience that p" enables us to combine the idea that knowledge requires truth-guaranteeing grounds with the fallibility of knowledge. For it says that those sensory experiences that explain the possibility of error are not the same mental states as those that are truth-guaranteeing grounds for knowledge. A subject who believes something on the basis of a sensory experience believes it *either* on the basis of a truth-guaranteeing ground *or* on the basis of something less than a truth-guaranteeing ground, e.g., on the basis of the mere appearance of a truth-guaranteeing ground.

What entitles us to have a disjunctive conception of sensory experiences as grounds for belief is our refutation of the idea that grounds for belief must be available to the believing subject independently of the truth of the belief based on them. We must instead understand the receptive ground of someone's belief, on the basis of which she acquires empirical knowledge, as something that is available to her *in virtue of the fact* that constitutes the conceptual content of her belief.

Now one may initially have the impulse to object that this account of the nature of grounds doesn't really solve the problem of knowledge but only relocates it to a different level. For even if it is true that someone who sees that there is still apple juice in the fridge has a reason to believe that there is still apple juice in the fridge—and, indeed, a reason that rules out the possibility that her belief be false—the skeptical

stand that is imposed upon her by the newspaper's report of the facts that her conceptual representation represents. Because they cannot see this possibility, here, too, the critiques of inferentialism articulated, e.g., by Burge or Coady, miss the crucial point. See Coady, *Testimony: A Philosophical Study,* as well as Burge, "Content Preservation" and "Interlocution, Perception, and Memory."

question then shifts to how I can ever know whether I actually see that there is still apple juice in the fridge or whether it merely appears to me as though I see this.[84] And this knowledge, so the objection goes, is still completely incomprehensible, for all that we have said so far. We have done nothing to show how it is possible to know that one perceives something. And so long as we have not made it intelligible how someone can know this, we haven't made any progress toward explaining how someone can know on the basis of her perception that there is still apple juice in the fridge. For one can only have the latter knowledge if one has the former.

Our original question was how we can justify our beliefs about how things are in the world through a receptive experience. The skeptic's insight was that if we have to base our beliefs about how things are in the world on experiences that are, in principle, compatible with the falsity of the belief we form on their basis, then it is impossible to understand how our beliefs can amount to knowledge. The above objection claims that our foregoing arguments and considerations haven't really altered this situation. Even if one accepts the considerations we have offered above, we still cannot understand how someone who believes something can be in a better situation than the one the skeptic envisions. For the unsettling question that still seems to confront someone who attempts to justify her belief that there is apple juice in the fridge through a corresponding perception is how she can justify her belief that she perceives that there is still apple juice in the fridge and is not merely suffering the appearance that she perceives that this is the case, when, in fact, she does not. And the objection is that precisely the same problem arises for the justification of this belief as arose for the justification of the original one: namely, that there is no answer to this question that

---

[84] This is how Cavell, for example, objects to this strategy of resolving the skeptic's doubt. See *The Claim of Reason*, 41f. See also Glendinning, *On Being with Others: Heidegger, Derrida, Wittgenstein*, 138–140. A similar argument can be found in Wright, "(Anti-)Sceptics Simple and Subtle: G. E. Moore and John McDowell." I discuss this objection in Kern, "Einsicht ohne Täuschung: McDowells hermeneutische Konzeption von Erkenntnis," esp. 928–930. For a critique of this objection that discusses Wright's formulation of the objection, see also McDowell, "The Disjunctive Conception of Experience as Material for a Transcendental Argument."

does not either lead into an infinite regress, arbitrarily break off, or loop around in a circle. It would appear that we are once again faced with Agrippa's trilemma.

If this objection were correct, it would confront us with Agrippa's trilemma at precisely the point where we thought we had undermined the foundations on which it rests. What is right in the above reasoning is that we cannot yet claim already to have a positive understanding of how it is possible for someone to have the sort of grounds that are required for knowledge—i.e., truth-guaranteeing grounds. But we can already see that the above objection fails to appreciate our account of knowledge. For to claim that the subject's belief that she actually perceives something only reactivates the original problem—namely, the problem that one cannot, in principle, have a ground for this belief that guarantees its truth—already presupposes a rejection of precisely the account of grounds we gave above. For it is only if one understands a subject's ground for belief as something that must be independent of the fact that she believes, on its basis, to obtain, that one can object that truth-guaranteeing grounds for the belief that one is perceiving something are, in principle, impossible. We called this understanding of grounds the dogma of epistemology. And the above objection can arise only if one is still holding on to this dogma. For the understanding of the nature of grounds we have suggested—namely, as something that, in the case of a receptive ground, cannot be had independently of the truth of the belief for which it is a ground—already entails an account of how someone who perceives something can know that she perceives something. If a perception is an irreducibly factive mental state that provides a receptive ground for belief, then a subject who perceives that p has a ground to believe that p just in virtue of being in that mental state. If she decides, on such an occasion, to believe that p on the basis of such a ground, this means that she recognizes the ground she has as a ground for knowledge and hence acquires the knowledge that p. In such a case, the knowledge she comes to have about her environment—namely, that p— and the knowledge she comes to have about herself—namely, that she perceives that p—are not two separate acts with their own distinct grounds. Rather, her belief that p on the basis of her perception that p and her recognition of her perception that p as a perception are two aspects of one and the same act. Her belief that p on the basis of her perception that p realizes two kinds of knowledge in one and the same act: knowledge about how things are around her as well as self-knowledge about how she knows these things around her.

We have argued that someone who perceives that there is apple juice in the fridge, just by being in that mental state, thereby has a receptive ground for believing that there is apple juice in the fridge. And it follows from this that coming to believe that there is apple juice in the fridge on the basis of this receptive ground and coming to believe that one perceives that there is apple juice in the fridge cannot be understood as two logically separable acts requiring different respective grounds. Knowing that there is apple juice in the fridge on the basis of one's perception that there is apple juice in the fridge and knowing that one perceives that there is apple juice in the fridge, on this account, have to be understood as two aspects of one and the same act of recognizing the ground one has for knowledge as a ground for knowledge.

Thus, the answer that we should give to the question of how someone can know that she actually perceives that there is still apple juice in the fridge is this: She can know this on the basis of a ground that she has in virtue of the very fact that she believes to obtain on the basis of that ground. If someone perceives that there is apple juice in the fridge, she is in a position to know that she perceives this on the basis of a ground that she would not have if the fact that she believes to obtain on the basis of this ground did not obtain. The insight that perceptions are irreducibly factive mental states that equip a subject with a receptive ground for believing what she perceives, entails that someone who perceives that there is apple juice in the fridge is in a position to know that there is apple juice in the fridge and to know that she is perceiving that there is apple juice in the fridge in virtue of one and the same receptive ground: namely, by perceiving that there is still apple juice in the fridge.

One can raise the above objection—i.e., the objection that our account of knowledge still leaves open the question of how someone can know that she is actually perceiving that there is still apple juice in the fridge—only if one refuses to understand a receptive ground as something that, in the fundamental case, is dependent on precisely the fact that one believes to obtain on the basis of that ground. If one instead understands a perception as an irreducibly factive mental state that equips a subject with a receptive ground for belief, then the knowledge of one's environment one acquires through perception, on the one hand, and the kind of self-knowledge one has when one knows that one perceives something, on the other, cannot be analyzed into two independent acts of knowing, whose possibility can be investigated separately.

It is, admittedly, true that we have not yet given a positive account of how it is possible to actually enjoy such world-dependent receptive grounds for belief—grounds by means of which one can know something about one's environment as well as about oneself. But we have shown at least this much: we have shown that one cannot logically separate the knowledge that one is actually seeing that there is apple juice in the fridge from the knowledge that one has when one recognizes on the basis of that experience that there is apple juice in the fridge. The account of knowledge that we seek must therefore be one that makes sense of how a unitary act of knowledge can have these two sides.

So let us take stock. We have shown that we can understand how empirical beliefs are possible only if we understand a receptive ground for belief as something that, in the fundamental case, is dependent on things being as one believes them to be on that basis—grounds that therefore guarantee the truth of the latter belief. That is to say, we have realized that the sort of ground that someone must be able to have for her belief in order to have any empirical beliefs at all is precisely the sort of ground that guarantees the truth of her belief and hence qualifies it as knowledge. The fundamental case in which someone believes something—i.e., the case in the absence of which one could not understand any others—is consequently one in which she knows something.

The insight that we have gained in the course of the foregoing reflections is thus that the concepts we invoked in our initial account of the concept of knowledge—viz., the concepts of belief, truth, and grounds—cannot be more fundamental than the concept of knowledge itself. The concept of knowledge, we have to conclude, is itself a fundamental concept: it describes a unity of elements, our understanding of which is not more fundamental than our understanding of knowledge itself. Quite the contrary. When we understand these elements, what we are understanding is precisely the unity to which they belong—namely, knowledge.

With this insight into the fundamental character of the concept of knowledge, we are taking the conceptual order that has been unquestioningly presupposed throughout epistemology up to this point and turning it on its head. For the dogma of epistemology, according to which a ground must, in principle, be the sort of thing that a subject can enjoy independently of whether or not the belief it serves to ground is true, rests on the assumption that the concepts we employ to elucidate the concept of knowledge are themselves independent of an understanding of what knowledge is. The assumption here is that we can understand how someone can hold a belief, or have a ground for a belief, or even hold a true belief, without yet needing (or being able) to understand how someone can know something. To understand how someone can know something, on this line of thought, is not a prerequisite for being able to understand how someone can believe something for reasons. An exemplary expression of how this unquestioned assumption makes its way into contemporary epistemology can be found in Crispin Wright, who writes: "Knowledge is not really the proper central concern of epistemologico-sceptical enquiry [ . . . ]. We can live with the concession that we do not, strictly, *know* some of the things we believe ourselves to know, provided we can retain the thought that we are fully justified in accepting them."[85]

Wright's first thought here is that it is more difficult to understand how it is possible "to know that p" than it is to understand how it is possible "to be fully justified in accepting p." His second thought is that we can learn to live with the admission of skepticism, according to which knowledge is impossible, so long as we can manage to understand how it is possible for someone to nevertheless be fully justified in accepting a particular claim. Yet as we have seen, the only reason one could have for believing that we can live with skepticism is that one cannot see any way out of the dilemma between skepticism and a position of moderation. However, positions of moderation are not alternatives to skepticism but only alternative expressions of it. This dilemma, we have

---

[85] Wright, "Scepticism and Dreaming: Imploding the Demon," 88.

now realized, rests on a misunderstanding: namely, the misunder-standing that holds that "being fully justified" is more fundamental than knowing. The dilemma rests on the misconception that we can understand how someone can be "fully justified" in believing something without already understanding how someone can know something. And we have now seen that this is impossible. For we have realized that the ground that someone needs in order to have knowledge is precisely the same as the ground she would need in order to have something that, according to Wright, is simpler to understand: namely, justified beliefs. That is to say, we have realized that the fundamental case of a ground for belief is one in which that ground puts the subject in a position to know something. The fundamental case of a ground for belief is a ground for knowledge.

# PART THREE

## *The Nature of Knowledge*

KNOWLEDGE IS A FUNDAMENTAL ACT OF MIND. THIS INSIGHT INTO the fundamental character of knowledge can be unsettling. For in claiming that knowledge is fundamental, we do not wish to deny that knowledge is a complex act containing elements that can also obtain independently of whether someone knows something. Indeed, we maintained that this possibility constitutes the central hallmark of finite objective knowledge. We thus want to claim two things at once: We want to say that one cannot know something about the world without having a sufficiently justified true belief about the world. While, simultaneously, we want to say that knowledge is fundamental for having grounds for beliefs, for having true beliefs, and even for having beliefs at all. How do these two claims fit together?

One might think that they cannot fit together. We have only two options here. We can either claim that the concept of knowledge is more fundamental than the concept of a true and sufficiently grounded belief. But then we cannot explain the concept of knowledge in terms of the concept of a true and sufficiently grounded belief. Or, on the other hand, we can persist in explaining knowledge in terms of true and sufficiently grounded belief, but then we must admit that the concept of knowledge is not fundamental. So the objection goes.

But what is the presupposition underlying this objection? The objection must assume that there are only two alternatives for understanding the concept of knowledge. Either the concept of knowledge consists of various elements, in which case these elements, into which it can be analyzed, are more fundamental than the concept of knowledge that contains them. Or, alternatively, the concept of knowledge does not consist of various elements but is itself an unanalyzable element. Given these two alternatives, the insight we gained in Part Two seems to be incoherent.

In what follows, I will attempt to undermine the assumption that these two alternatives exhaust the space of possible interpretations of the concept of knowledge. For this presupposition—which makes it look as though we were forced to choose between the aforementioned alternatives—takes for granted that the concept of knowledge must constitute an analytic unity. By an "analytic unity" I mean one that consists of elements that are more fundamental than the whole they collectively make up. The concept of knowledge, as our previous reflections have shown, cannot be such a unity. But it does not follow from this that the concept of knowledge, as we have characterized it, doesn't constitute a unity of various elements at all. Knowledge is neither the collective product of elements that can be conceived of independently of one another, nor is it an ultimate and non-compound element in its own right. The concept of knowledge, as I will suggest in what follows, instead constitutes a different sort of unity. It exhibits the unity of a rational capacity. Rational capacities are, as I will suggest, unities of just the sort we need in order to understand knowledge. For they are non-analytic unities. In contrast to analytic unities, a non-analytic unity is one that, to put it abstractly, consists of elements that are not more fundamental than the complex they collectively make up. Quite the contrary. In a non-analytic unity, the elements that make it up are precisely dependent on the unity in which they appear.

Our guiding idea in what follows will be that rational capacities are exemplary instances of non-analytic unity. This thought will enable us to combine the apparently incompatible characterizations of knowledge given above. If the concept of knowledge, in its fundamental employment, describes a rational capacity, then it consists in a unity of elements that are themselves dependent on the unity they serve to constitute.

The conclusion to draw from our reflections is accordingly that the fundamental employment of the concept of knowledge—i.e., the employment that is fundamental for our understanding of it—does not consist in characterizing a singular act, as previously supposed, but instead consists in characterizing something that lies on a different logical level: a rational capacity. The so-called analysis of knowledge in terms of true and sufficiently justified belief is, properly understood, the articulation of a more fundamental characterization of knowledge: knowledge as an act of a rational capacity for knowledge.

In order to understand what knowledge is, we have to understand what a rational capacity for knowledge is. We will do so by first investigating the notion of a rational capacity. Our next step will be to apply this general account to the case of knowledge and develop the specific idea of a rational capacity for knowledge in light of this general account. We will thereby show that the dilemma of epistemology, which we reconstructed in Part Two, is not just an expression of a misunderstanding of the nature of grounds. On a deeper level, it is the expression of a misunderstanding of the nature of knowledge. It expresses a misunderstanding about what knowledge is.

# Rational Capacities

## 1. The Category of a Rational Capacity

We can come to see how it is possible for someone to know something if we understand an act of knowledge as the exercise of a rational capacity for knowledge. That is the thesis I will develop in what follows. But because the sort of knowledge that we are seeking to understand is the knowledge of empirical facts, we can put this thesis more precisely: We can understand knowledge of empirical facts if we understand it as the actualization of a rational capacity for knowledge that is essentially receptive. For the concept of a rational capacity, as we shall see, is exactly what we need to bring into view in order to understand the peculiar sort of unity exhibited by the concept of knowledge.

The thought that the concept of knowledge is not analyzable in terms of more fundamental concepts has recently been explored from a number of different directions—for example, in work by Colin McGinn, David Owens, and Timothy Williamson, among others. But no one has yet connected this idea with the thought that knowledge must be understood as an act of a rational capacity for knowledge.[1] The thesis of

---

[1] See McGinn, "The Concept of Knowledge," 24–25; Owens, *Reason without Freedom: The Problem of Epistemic Normativity,* 46; Williamson, "Is Knowing a State of Mind?," 543.

the "unanalyzability of knowledge"[2] is accordingly understood as a negative claim. It merely claims that it is impossible to provide a complete analysis of the concept of knowledge. Yet this fact—that knowledge is, in this sense, unanalyzable—is presented as something inexplicable: a point where our philosophical insight into the nature of knowledge simply reaches its limits. Owens, for example, argues as follows. He begins by analyzing knowledge as a cognitive state in which one has compelling reasons for the truth of one's belief: "to know that p is to have a conclusive ground for p."[3] Owens then asks whether this account constitutes an analysis of knowledge. And he quite rightly maintains that it cannot constitute such an analysis so long as we do not have an account of what a "conclusive ground" is. Owens's thesis is then that it is impossible to more nearly explain what a conclusive ground is. The best one can do is provide examples of conclusive grounds—Owens goes on to do this and then concludes with the comment: "I gave some examples of conclusive grounds [ … ] but [ … ] since I didn't tell you what a conclusive ground was, neither did I tell you what knowledge was [ … ]. Fortunately, my purposes in this book do not require a reductive analysis of knowledge, or even the assurance that such an analysis is possible."[4]

It is a genuine insight to see that knowledge is not reductively analyzable. But this insight remains philosophically unsatisfying so long as one does not understand why knowledge eludes analysis in this way.[5] The significance of the claim that knowledge is not reductively analyzable lies in its justification. For the justification of this claim will

---

[2] Owens, *Reason without Freedom,* 47.

[3] Ibid., 46.

[4] Ibid., 47.

[5] Owens thinks he can defend his position by claiming that the purposes of his book do not require a reductive analysis. The aim of his book is to work out the essence of theoretical reason. However, if we are right to claim that we cannot understand theoretical reason without also understanding knowledge, then one cannot have an understanding of theoretical reason in the absence of a positive account of why a reductive analysis of knowledge is impossible. Williamson, by contrast, has an argument for the unanalyzability of knowledge, but only a negative one. Knowledge is indispensable for particular explanatory purposes. That is to say, we cannot replace knowledge with any other cognitive state and still employ the sort of explanation that knowledge enables. See Williamson, "Is Knowing a State of Mind?," esp. 549f.

have to contain a positive account of the nature of knowledge. The reason knowledge is not reductively analyzable is that the fundamental employment of the concept of knowledge consists in describing a rational capacity for knowledge. The claim that knowledge is unanalyzable, in a particular sense, and the claim that an act of knowing is to be understood as an act of a rational capacity for knowledge are, for us, two sides of the same coin. Hence, it would involve a fundamental misunderstanding of the unanalyzability thesis to interpret it as a claim about the limits of our philosophical insight. If any single act of knowing is to be understood as an act of a rational capacity for knowledge, then our inability to analyze the concept of knowledge into more fundamental concepts does not represent a limitation of our understanding of knowledge but instead articulates a feature of our positive understanding of it.

In order to understand knowledge, we must therefore understand what it means to have a rational capacity for knowledge. I will develop such an account by first laying out some of the logical features that characterize rational capacities in general. My next step will be to indicate how these general features apply to the sort of capacity at issue here: namely, a capacity for perceptual knowledge. The aim of the reflections that follow is not to lay out all the features characteristic of rational capacities. The sole goal is to spell out those features that show that and how our understanding of the nature of knowledge in terms of a rational capacity deepens the understanding of the nature of grounds for knowledge that we developed in Part Two.

This will enable us to argue that the dilemma of epistemology that we arrived at in Part Two stems from the failure to see that the fundamental account of knowledge consists in the description of a rational capacity—a description according to which the following holds:

S knows that p = S's belief that p is a perfect exercise
of her capacity for knowledge.

All further explanations or accounts of knowledge thus have no other purpose apart from helping us to understand what is contained in this formulation.

To work out the features of rational capacities that are essential for our inquiry, I will draw on a philosophical tradition whose relevance for contemporary epistemology has been seriously underestimated, to say the least. Our most significant reflections on the nature of capacities are, of course, due to Aristotle—which is why it is no surprise that the authors who are most central to our present enterprise, namely Gilbert Ryle, Anthony Kenny and Michael Thompson, crucially draw upon the Aristotelian tradition. One thing that unites these authors is that they approach the question of what rational capacities are by asking what role rational capacities play in our thinking. We will adopt the same approach by asking how we represent rational capacities, i.e., by inquiring into the form exhibited by the expressions we use to describe them.

Let's think of someone who possesses a rational capacity, such as the capacity to swim. Let's think of Lisa, who is a good swimmer. How do we represent her when we represent her as the bearer of such a capacity? When we represent someone as possessing a rational capacity, we represent her as having a capacity for doing something—e.g., for swimming, or reading, or dancing. Capacities are accordingly named after the things they are capacities to do. We say, for example, "Lisa can/is able to $\varphi$," where '$\varphi$' stands for a particular activity, such as swimming, reading, or dancing. It is characteristic of such statements that they can be true even if Lisa is presently lying in bed asleep. When we make such a statement about Lisa, we are accordingly making a claim about her that doesn't describe a particular, individual state or action of hers— neither one she has performed in the past nor one she is performing right now. Rather, we are saying something general about her, which doesn't pertain to any particular occasion or point in time.

Rational capacities belong to that class of things that we describe through general and timeless statements. If, by contrast, we describe an action or a state, we describe something singular, which takes place at a determinate point in time. We might say, for example, "Lisa is presently $\varphi$-ing" or "Lisa $\varphi$-ed—previously, yesterday, etc." When we say that someone has a certain capacity—such as the capacity to swim—we are not thereby saying that she occupies (or occupied) a particular state at a particular time or that she performed a particular action at a particular time. We are instead making a claim that goes beyond whatever she is doing here and now. Unlike states or actions, which are particular temporal events, capacities are, as Kenny says, "inherently general."[6] There is no such thing as a capacity for doing things "only on one particular occasion."[7] "This is true," as Kenny remarks, even of capacities that "of their nature can be exercised only once," such as the capacity to kill oneself.[8] Even if it is in the nature of a capacity that it can be exercised only once, it is nevertheless "inherently general" in the sense that someone who has the capacity in question is in possession of something that she might have exercised on a different occasion from the one on which she actually did exercise it. To possess a capacity is to possess something general that cannot be exhaustively described by saying what one is doing at a particular time.[9]

Yet even though claims about capacities are not claims about particular temporally determinate states or actions, they nevertheless intrinsically refer to temporally determinate states and actions: namely, those states or actions that actualize the capacity in question. Claims about capacities are, in this respect, like claims about dispositions, which Ryle aptly characterizes as follows:

> Dispositional statements are neither reports of observed or observable states of affairs, nor yet reports of unobserved or unobservable states of affairs. They narrate no incidents. But their jobs are intimately connected with narratives of incidents, for, if they are true, they are satisfied by narrated incidents. "John Doe has just been telephoning in French" satisfies what is asserted by "John Doe knows French."[10]

A capacity is something general that intrinsically refers to a potentially infinite series of states or actions, namely all those states that actualize the capacity in question. Actions that actualize a capacity may differ from one another in every respect apart from the fact that they all, insofar as they are actualizations of a capacity, contain one selfsame

[6] Kenny, *Will, Freedom, and Power*, 135.
[7] Ibid.
[8] Ibid.
[9] See Kenny, *The Metaphysics of Mind*, 69.
[10] Ryle, *The Concept of Mind*, 125.

common element: the very capacity they actualize. Someone who can ski never skis down the mountain in precisely the same way. Sometimes she swings out leisurely curves, sometimes she cuts her turns short and brisk. Even the individual motions she makes may differ in many respects. The motions she makes in skiing over ice slicks are surely (or very likely) different from those she makes when floating through deep powder, as will be the motions she makes when skiing a steep black diamond as opposed to those she makes when skiing an intermediate or bunny slope. But what manifests itself in all these various skiing activities is not something that is merely similar between the various cases, in the sense that various particular runs down the mountain may be more or less similar. No. It is one and the same element that sustains itself through all the members of this potentially infinite series of actions. In this respect, capacities are like dispositions. When confronted with acts that actualize capacities or dispositions, we are, as Michael Thompson puts it, presented with an element "[that] is essentially one and the same, unchanged, unexhausted, and not merely similar, through a potentially unlimited series of individual acts."[11]

When we say that it belongs to the nature of capacities that they are, in principle, able to manifest themselves in an unlimited number of performances, this means that capacities are something that cannot exhaust themselves or come to an end in any single performance. One cannot say that a particular action "fulfills" a capacity in the sense that one might say it fulfills a wish. Capacities are not fulfilled through individual acts but instead are actualized, manifested, or instantiated in them.[12] This does not, of course, mean that it is impossible to lose a capacity. It is possible for a capacity to, in that sense, come to a temporal end. So claims about capacities, as Ryle points out, can also have a temporal form and, accordingly, take tenses.[13] We can very well say: "Peter

---

[11] Thompson, *Life and Action*, 158. This does not, of course, mean that one cannot improve one's exercises of a capacity and, in that sense, improve one's capacity. Quite the contrary. Many or even most capacities are just like this. But what one is improving in such cases is the very same "element" that sustains itself as the same element in all the acts that manifest the capacity in question.

[12] See ibid.

[13] See Ryle, *The Concept of Mind*, 125. See also Kenny, *Will, Freedom, and Power*, 134.

could (was able to) see until the age of seven." But when something like this happens, that is not an "achievement" that can be explained by the capacity in question. The fact that a particular action was one in which this capacity met its end cannot be explained by reference to the relevant capacity but must be explained by something else—e.g., by the fact that Peter was in an accident, or suffered some sort of disease, etc. The fact that capacities can have a duration does not affect their characterization as something that cannot be concluded or finalized in a particular performance but only instantiated and manifested there.

Capacities are thus characterized by a feature that is also exhibited by principles or rules. A rule is likewise something general that can manifest itself in a potentially infinite series of events or performances. Wittgenstein expresses this by saying that it belongs to the concept of a rule that one cannot follow it only one time.[14] Yet rules and principles are not the same as capacities. Wherein lies the difference? Let's imagine an imperatival rule such as the following: "You must wash your hands before eating." Now let us further imagine that not a single person actually knows this rule. It follows that no one could ever have governed her behavior by that rule in the sense that the rule cannot have been the ground for which anyone ever did anything—even when people occasionally (or even regularly) washed their hands before eating. It is nevertheless possible to judge whether (and with what frequency) everyone's behavior is in actual agreement with this rule. And it is equally possible that, after adjudicating this question, we might conclude that there is not and never has been a single act that actually agrees with the rule.

A rule is therefore the sort of thing that particular acts can either agree with or not, even though not a single one of the acts in question were actually determined by the rule. That is to say, rules are standards of acts; but they are standards that might not be actualized by a single act. The fact that a particular act agrees with this or that rule does not

[14] Wittgenstein, *Philosophical Investigations,* §199: "It is not possible that there should have been only one occasion on which only one person obeyed a rule." See also §218: "Instead of the rule, we might imagine rails. And infinitely long rails correspond to the unlimited application of a rule." See also Wittgenstein's discussion in *Remarks on the Foundations of Mathematics,* 323–324.

imply that the rule in question has an explanatory role in the account of this act.[15] When someone performs an act that agrees with a particular rule, not just *by accident* but in virtue of the fact that she determines her act through the rule in question, this entails that she stands in a reflective relation to that rule, which she has recognized as a ground for what she does.

Things are quite different when it comes to capacities. When we judge whether someone acts in agreement with a rational capacity, we are assessing her acts with reference to something that does not so much as exist if it does not in some sense explain what happens when a subject acts in agreement with it. As Kenny puts it: "A skill or ability is always a positive explanatory factor in accounting for the performance of an agent."[16] In contrast to rules, rational capacities, just like skills and abilities, are the sort of general thing that exists only if it in some sense explains someone's acting in accordance with it. In this respect, capacities are like dispositions, which, as Thompson puts it, "on any account [ . . . ] must have some sort of explanatory standing in respect of what happens when it is manifested in an individual action."[17] When someone has a capacity—say, the capacity to swim—this means that her acts of swimming agree with the capacity in question not just accidentally but precisely in virtue of the capacity in question. Thus, the situation we encountered with rules is ruled out from the very outset when it comes to capacities. It cannot be the case that we find an action in agreement with a capacity without the capacity having "some sort of explanatory standing in respect of what happens" when she acts that way.

---

[15] That is why we can only understand how a rule can be efficacious in determining a subject's acts by understanding the subject as someone who grants it the status of a ground for doing something. It is precisely this aspect of rules that serves as the foundation for Brandom's attempt to explain the idea of something that enjoys normative status—such as knowledge—in terms of the idea of recognition of epistemic rules. See Brandom, *Making It Explicit*, esp. chaps. 1–4. The philosophical significance of the category of capacities, as it will turn out, consists in the fact that it undermines from the very outset the problem into which one falls when one treats the idea of a rule as fundamental for the explanation of knowledge. We will come back to that in the course of our inquiry.

[16] Kenny, *Freedom, Will, and Power*, 133.

[17] Thompson, *Life and Action*, 160.

Because our concern in what follows is to understand knowledge, the philosophical significance of introducing the category of a rational capacity lies, *inter alia,* in the fact that we thereby introduce the category of something general that is, in a particular sense, the "cause" of the performances that manifest it.[18] It is still going to take some work before we are able to determine this explanatory aspect of rational capacities more precisely. For the discussions that immediately follow, however, we will simply work with the mere fact that capacities have this feature. Because this explanatory aspect is not a logical feature unique to capacities but one that is shared by other things—such as habits—I first want to work out the distinction between capacities and habits. For one way to describe the misunderstanding under which the analytical approach to knowledge labors is to say that it treats knowledge as a mental act that manifests a sort of habit. But knowledge is not a habit: it is a rational capacity.

## 2. Rational Capacities as Constitutive Unities

The minimal characterization of capacities that we have developed thus far describes them as "causes," in a particular sense, of a potentially infinite series of acts or states. This feature is something they share with habits. A habit, too, is something that can exist only insofar are there are subjects that keep on performing acts that agree with the habit precisely because they actually have the habit in question. When we say that someone is a habitual smoker, we are not describing any particular action at a particular time. Rather, as in the case of capacities or abilities, we are making a general claim that does not have reference to any

---

[18] Compare Heidegger, when he writes in his commentary on Aristotle: "Power is hence a derivative concept of causality [...]. A power has the character of being a cause." See Heidegger, *Aristoteles: Metaphysik IX, 1–3: Vom Wesen und Wirklichkeit der Kraft,* 79–80. Heidegger takes this characterization of capacities to be self-evident. However, as I will argue in Part Four of this book, the philosophical significance of the concept of a capacity in our account of knowledge will depend on how we understand the kind of causality that goes with the concept of a capacity, which will be our concern in Part Four.

particular point in time. We are characterizing the subject through something general that serves to explain, in a particular sense, the acts she performs that are in agreement with that general thing—e.g., her acts of smoking. What we want now is an account of the logical features relevant to our understanding of knowledge that distinguish a rational capacity from a habit. According to Hegel, habits tend to be "skipped over as something contemptible in scientific treatments of the soul and the mind" or else avoided "because they belong to the most difficult [of its] features."[19] If Hegel is correct in this assessment that a habit is one of the "most difficult features" of the mind to understand, then our goal in what follows cannot be to give a complete account of the concept of habit. Our only aim is to characterize it sufficiently to distinctly bring out the difference between a habit and a rational capacity in such a way that we can understand why an act of knowledge cannot be conceived of as an act of habit but must be thought of as the act of a rational capacity.

Hegel characterizes habit by saying that it is a "determinacy of feeling, or even intelligence, will, etc., that has been made natural, mechanical" and is accordingly "quite properly called a second nature."[20] Hegel writes: "Habit is [ . . . ] *nature,* for it is an immediate being [Sein] of the soul—[it is] a *second* [nature], for it is an immediacy posited by the soul, an in- and transforming of corporeality that pertains to determinations of feeling as such and to determinations of representation and will as corporealized [verleiblichten]."[21]

Hegel here isolates two features as characteristic of habits. First, a habit is a "determinacy" of the soul of a subject that has immediate efficacy within the subject who is determined by that habit. That is its natural aspect. Second, a habit is a determinacy of the soul of a subject that is due to a specific process that Hegel describes as an "in- and transforming of corporeality." In this respect, a habit is not a first but a second nature. Hence, a habit is a sort of determinacy of a subject that is intrinsically bound up with a specific process of acquisition. If someone

[19] Hegel, *Enzyklopädie der philosophischen Wissenschaften im Grundrisse (1830),* §410, Remark.
[20] Ibid.
[21] Ibid.

has a habit, that means she has acquired a "determinacy" through an "in- and transforming" of her corporeality that is now immediately efficacious within her.

The features Hegel invokes in his account of habit in order to explain why a habit is often called a "second nature" are not, however, unique to habits. For such features are also characteristic of particular sorts of capacities: namely, to all capacities that are not innate.[22] It is for this reason that Aristotle is able, in book IX of his *Metaphysics,* to characterize all non-innate capacities in precisely the same way Hegel characterizes habits. Aristotle divides capacities into two fundamentally different sorts: those that are "innate," and those that one "must acquire by previous exercise."[23] To have a capacity that is not "innate" means to have a capacity that one comes to possess by engaging in activities that themselves already bear some intrinsic reference to the capacity that is to be acquired through them.[24] Someone learning how to play tennis may begin by hitting around a large, heavy foam ball rather than a regulation tennis ball. And in hitting around that foam ball, she is certainly not yet playing tennis in the way a skilled tennis player would play tennis. Yet by beginning with the strokes necessary to hit the large foam ball, one starts to realize, in a simplified form, the movements of a standard topspin stroke. One thereby begins to undertake the "in- and transforming of corporeality" that makes a proper tennis player.

However we may end up further characterizing rational capacities in what follows, we can already say this much here: a rational capacity is something whose possession requires that there are specific acts of exercising it through which the capacity in question can be acquired. We will be able to more precisely specify how to account for these acts in the case of a capacity for knowledge in Part Four, once we have worked out the requisite features of rational capacities. For the moment,

---

[22] On this point, see Michael Wolff's extensive analysis, in which he provides a detailed reconstruction of Hegel's understanding of the specifically bodily reference of rational abilities, in *Das Körper-Seele-Problem: Kommentar zu Hegel, Enzyklopädie §389.*

[23] Aristotle, *Metaphysics,* IX.5, 1047b33–34.

[24] On the relation between performance and acquisition, see Miles Burnyeat, *Notes on Eta and Theta of Aristotle's Metaphysics,* 117. We will dwell on the distinctive character of acquiring rational abilities at some length in Part Four, Chapter X, sections 1 and 2.

it is sufficient to seize on the idea that the possession of rational capacities is to be understood through the idea of acts of repetition that, in some sense, already make reference to the capacity in question. Things are similar in the case of habits, which Hegel, following Aristotle, describes by saying, "this self-in-forming of the particular or corporeal [aspect] of determinations of feeling in the being of the soul appears as a *repetition* of the same and the acquisition of the habit [appears] as *practice (Übung)*."[25]

Thus, what unites habits and capacities that are acquired through "exercise" is that they are, in this sense, a kind of "second nature." Their status as "second nature" means that a subject, by repeating particular activities, comes to possess a "general mode" of action, feeling, thought, judgment, etc. that has immediate efficacy in her behavior.[26] It is this idea of immediate efficacy that is supposed to be expressed in the characterization of habits and capacities as a sort of "nature." And it is the idea of acquisition through exercise that is supposed to come out in the characterization of particular capacities and habits as a "second" nature. So where does the distinction between habits and rational capacities lie?

Ryle characterizes their difference as follows: "Habits are one sort, but not the only sort, of second nature, and [ ... ] the common assumption that all second natures are mere habits obliterates distinctions which are of cardinal importance for the inquiries in which we are engaged."[27] Ryle goes on to adduce essentially two differentiating features between rational capacities (what he calls "intelligent capacities") and habits. But both these features are, *prima facie*, of little help in understanding the distinction. For as we shall see, they themselves presuppose that we already understand the distinction in question. Ryle's

---

[25] Hegel, *Enzyklopädie der philosophischen Wissenschaften,* §410.

[26] Ibid., §410, Remark.

[27] Ryle, *The Concept of Mind,* 42. Similarly, Michael Tomasello has come to the conclusion, in the course of his anthropological investigations, that the categorical and decisive difference between various capacities lies not in the fact that some are possessed from birth whereas others are acquired thereafter but rather in the different ways in which capacities are acquired. See Tomasello, *The Cultural Origins of Human Cognition,* 33–55. This thesis also finds expression in, *inter alia,* bk. IX of Aristotle's *Metaphysics.*

first observation is that habits have "sources" whereas rational capacities have "methods."[28] His second claim is that habits are acquired through "[d]rill (or conditioning)" whereas rational capacities are acquired through "training."[29] I will not contend in what follows that Ryle's description of these features is completely false. Quite the contrary, he is attempting to capture something that just cannot be made clear in this manner. Regardless of whether we already have an understanding of what a rational capacity is, it is simply not clear what either of these contrasts is meant to signify. For "training" clearly cannot mean something like "inculcated through textbooks," if rational capacities are meant to include things like reading and skiing. Nor can "drill" mean something like "subjected to sanctions," if habits are to include things like habitual smoking. Similarly, the fact that actualizing a rational capacity rather than a habit involves following a "method" cannot simply mean going about the activity in question in a general way. For someone indulging a habit, too, instantiates a general way of doing something. Likewise, the fact that habits have an "origin" cannot mean that they have a temporal beginning in individual subjects, because rational capacities are like that, too.

I therefore think that we should understand the concepts Ryle deploys in order to distinguish habits from rational capacities as summarizing descriptions of a number of specifically logical distinctions between habits and rational capacities. And we can attain greater clarity about these logical distinctions if we reflect on the respective relations in which a habit and a rational capacity stand to the acts that fall under them. My aim in what follows is to spell out these logical distinctions in more detail.

We followed Hegel in saying that a rational capacity is like a habit in that both are "general ways of acting."[30] Let's consider an example of a habit. One of my habits is to go jogging in the morning, then shower, and then have toast with Nutella. My friend Rachel has a smoking habit. My cat is in the habit of curling up on the windowsill on sunny

---

[28] See Ryle, *The Concept of Mind,* 134.
[29] Ibid., 42.
[30] Hegel, *Enzyklopädie der philosophischen Wissenschaften,* §410, Remark.

afternoons, wrapping her tail around her ears, and napping for a while. Let's contrast these descriptions of habits with a description of the rational capacity that we will take as our guiding example in what follows—the capacity to ski.[31] A standard skiing textbook describes the execution of parallel short turns as follows:

> The turn begins with an explosive extension of the legs in which one firmly supports oneself on the downhill pole. Assume the traversing stance. Then rapidly pull the skis upward. (One may experience some heel-tap). At almost the same time, one then swings one's legs—but not one's hips—quickly in the direction of the turn. As one begins the turn, immediately increase the pressure on the outer ski and turn one's outer leg in preparation. One's rump will be leaned distinctly over the outer ski [ . . . ].[32]

The glaring difference between our description of the acts that make up various habits and the above description of the acts involved in parallel short turns lies in the fact that the concepts we used to describe the acts of a habit are intelligible independently of our using them to describe them as acts of a habit. Eating toast with Nutella, jogging, showering, etc.—these are all acts that we describe using concepts that can be independently understood and deployed regardless of whether or not what we have in view is their unity in a habit. We might put this point by saying that the description of a habit is the description of a mere sum of acts, each of which can be characterized independently of the habit in question. "Jogging" does not intrinsically involve "eating toast with Nutella." Nor does "curling up on the windowsill" essentially entail "wrapping one's tail around one's ears." Acts of a habit fall under concepts that we can make sense of independently of their reference to

---

[31] For the use of this example, see also Christiane Schildknecht, *Aspekte des Nichtpropositionalen,* 9. Schildknecht deploys it as evidence for the claim that "knowledge how" cannot be reduced to propositional knowledge. One reason for my adoption of this example is that my argument aims to undermine a certain account of the distinction between "knowledge how" and "knowledge that" by claiming that "knowledge that" itself consists in the actualization of a capacity.

[32] Deutscher Verband für das Skilehrwesen e.V., ed., *Ski-Lehrplan* 1:78.

the sort of unity to which they belong when they are habitual. The combination of acts into the sort of unity of activities that constitutes a habit is not essential to the acts thus combined.

The same is not true of the concepts we use to describe how to ski parallel short turns. We cannot understand what an "explosive extension of the legs" is, what it means to "firmly support oneself on the downhill pole," and what it means for one to "assume the traversing stance" except insofar as we grasp these concepts in relation to the totality of concepts that collectively provide a description of how to ski parallel short turns. For what does it mean to "assume a traversing stance"? What is meant here is the posture of my upper body, leaning slightly forward—not bent so far that I am looking at the ground but rather bent at just the angle one assumes when one is skiing. Hence, one understands what the traversing position is only insofar as one specifically understands that what is being described here is skiing (and not some other activity). Similarly, to properly understand what it means to "firmly support oneself on the downhill pole" or to "rapidly pull the skis upward" depends on one's understanding it as part of a description of how to ski parallel short turns.

What the example suggests is that, in contrast to the concepts we employ in describing a habit, the concepts we employ in describing a rational capacity owe their content to the fact that they form part of a description of a specific unity of acts. The concepts we employ to describe the capacity to ski parallel turns are unintelligible when considered independently of our understanding of the specific unity of acts whose elements they describe—i.e., the unity that we understand when we understand these concepts as describing the capacity to ski parallel short turns. The acts that are involved in a rational capacity accordingly belong to a sort of unity that is logically different from the sort of unity to which acts of a habit belong. Whereas a habit is a unity of acts that can be severally understood independently of any understanding of the unity in which they habitually come together, a rational capacity is a unity of acts that can be understood only if and insofar as one understands the unity in which they are combined. Let us call the sort of unity exhibited in a habit an analytic unity. By an "analytic unity" I mean the sort of unity whose elements are characterized by their logical independence of the unity in which they figure. Correlatively, we can call the sort of unity exhibited by a rational capacity a non-analytic or, positively, a constitutive unity. By a "constitutive unity" I mean the sort of unity whose elements are characterized by their logical dependence on the unity they jointly make up.

Thus, when we characterize the actions that Jim is currently performing on the slopes as exercises of his capacity to ski parallel short turns, this means that, in our descriptions of his individual performances—e.g., that he is explosively extending his legs, etc.—we view those acts in light of something that is not itself an act, but a unity of acts.[33] By contrast, when we characterize an action as the exercise of a habit—as in the case of my morning shower—our identification of the action in question (e.g., as an act of showering) is by no means dependent on our seeing it as an integral part of my morning routine, which includes other actions, such as jogging and making toast. What it means to shower can be understood independently of the fact that my morning routine also involves jogging and eating toast with Nutella. That morning shower could just as easily be combined with other acts to form a different habit—as, indeed, it likely is in the morning routines of other people. One person does one thing after her shower, another person something else.

We can further elucidate this initial distinction between habits and rational capacities by drawing on Rawls's well-known distinction between the "practice conception of rules" and "the summary conception of rules." This distinction was taken up and elaborated by Searle and others in terms of the canonical contrast between "constitutive" and "regulative" rules.[34] In line with this distinction, habits are just like

---

[33] Ryle expresses this point as follows: "Now a skill is not an act. It is therefore neither a witnessable nor an unwitnessable act. To recognize that a performance is an exercise of a skill is indeed to appreciate it in the light of a factor which could not be separately recorded by a camera. But the reason why the skill exercised in a performance cannot be separately recorded by a camera is not that it is an occult or ghostly happening, but that it is not a happening at all" (*The Concept of Mind*, 33).

[34] Rawls, "Two Concepts of Rules," 24. It should be noted that the summary conception of rules, on Rawls's account, does not coincide with what Searle calls as "regulative rules." (See Searle, *The Construction of Social Reality*, 27f.) Nor are rules under Rawls's account of the practice conception the same as what Searle calls "constitutive rules."

regulative rules insofar as they are logically posterior to the individual actions that fall under them.[35] An action that accords with a regulative rule is, as such, independent of the rule with which it accords, just as an action that manifests a habit is. The constitutive nature of rational capacities, by contrast, entails that they relate to the individual cases that actualize them in just the way that rules, on Rawls's practice conception, relate to the cases that manifest them. Rawls's now-famous example of how rules function on the practice conception draws on the rules of baseball, the status of which he describes as follows:

> Striking out, stealing a base, balking, etc., are all actions which can only happen in a game. No matter what a person did, what he did would not be described as stealing a base or striking out or drawing a walk unless he could also be described as playing baseball, and for him to be doing this presupposes the rule-like practice which constitutes the game. The practice is logically prior to particular cases: unless there is the practice the terms referring to actions specified by it lack a sense.[36]

Rawls characterizes rules on the practice conception by saying that such rules are "logically prior" to the particular cases that actualize the practice those rules articulate. On Rawls's account, the central content of the claim that practices are logically prior to their instances basically comes down to three things. First, it entails that certain concepts lack a sense independently of their reference to the practice. Second, and consequently, certain actions can only exist as instantiations of a practice because the concepts, under which they fall, depend for their

---

What is important for our purposes, however, is just that both these pairs of rules align with our distinction between habits and rational capacities insofar as summary or regulative rules share the same features we've ascribed to habits, just as practice or constitutive rules share those we've ascribed to rational capacities. In the next section, I will go on to highlight how regulative rules differ from mere habits. On this point, see also Searle, *Speech Acts*, 34–35. For more on this distinction, see Cavell, *The Claim of Reason*, 28; and Haugeland, *Having Thought*, 320–321.

[35] Regulative rules, Searle says, "regulate a pre-existing activity, an activity whose existence is logically independent of the rules" (*Speech Acts*, 34).

[36] Rawls, "Two Concepts of Rules," 25. See also Thompson's account in *Life and Action*, 176–177.

sense upon essential reference to the practice in question. And it follows from this, third, that there are certain concepts that can exist only if and insofar as the practice upon which their sense depends also exists. Now this last thought is not, of course, meant to imply that one can employ such concepts only as long as the practices that fund their sense continue to endure. Once the practice of baseball is up and running, we can retain the concepts we deploy to describe it even if (and after) the practice itself dies out. The concepts whose sense is constitutively funded by the practice need not die out just because the practice itself does.

In keeping with our above reflections, we can now say that rational capacities are, in this respect, like rules on Rawls's practice conception of rules: actions that actualize a rational capacity are such as to be identified by concepts that one cannot understand without reference to the capacity they actualize. For they get their particular sense only from the unity of acts whose elements they describe. Actions that actualize a rational capacity involve an essential reference to the unity of various actions that fall under the relevant capacity. Such reference is constitutive of those actions being identified (and identifiable) as actions that manifest the relevant capacity. We might express this by saying that rational capacities, in contrast to habits, are something general that stands in an interpretive relationship to the individual acts that fall under them. When we bring a particular action under a rational capacity, we thereby make reference to what Thompson has termed an "interpretive structure."[37] That is to say, in bringing actions under a rational capacity, e.g., when we claim that Jim is swinging his legs in direction of the turn, we bring to bear an understanding of these actions that entails not only an understanding of Jim's previous actions but also of his next actions. This means that when we look up the slope and judge that Jim is swinging his legs in the direction of the turn, we are always doing much more than simply bringing his behavior under a concept.

---

[37] On the concept of an "interpretive structure," see Thompson, *Life and Action,* 199, where he describes a life form as the most general instance of such an "interpretative structure."

We are bringing to bear an understanding of a unity of concepts to which we give voice in identifying Jim's behavior as an act that exhibits that unity.

Let us briefly take stock. We have now brought out an initial but essential difference between habits and rational capacities. This difference lies in the fact that a rational capacity is a unity of acts that is logically prior to the several acts that collectively make it up. In order now to adduce still further distinctions—and, in so doing, to bring to light the conceptual apparatus we will need in order to understand why the concept of knowledge can rightly be understood as the concept of a rational capacity—we will next turn our attention to two further logical features of rational capacities. The first one they share with regulative rules, and it differentiates them from habits. For rational capacities are like regulative rules in that they stand in a normative relation to the cases that fall under them, whereas habits are not normative in this sense. This has tempted several authors to construe the normative status of knowledge in terms of rules that must regulate the doxastic behavior of the subject in order for her beliefs to enjoy the status of knowledge.[38] The second feature they share with habits, and it differentiates them from regulative rules. For rational capacities are like habits in that they have an explanatory character which regulative rules do not have. This, in turn, has misled many authors to construe knowledge as a mere habit. As we will see, it characterizes rational capacities that they combine both these features. Knowledge, we shall then be able to

---

[38] The idea of a specifically normative epistemology stems from the thought that knowledge is a normative status that results from a subject's successfully following such regulative epistemic rules—rules it is the task of epistemology to identify. Problematic proposals along these lines can be found in, among others, Chisholm, *Theory of Knowledge;* Pollock, "Epistemic Norms"; and Van Cleve, "Foundationalism, Epistemic Principles, and the Cartesian Circle." If knowledge is an act of a rational cognitive capacity, however, it follows that we must reject the idea of a normative epistemology that unites all epistemological positions of moderation we have considered. Epistemology does indeed contain normative concepts at its core; but it misunderstands its own nature and task when it therefore construes the claims it makes about these concepts as normative claims.

argue, is neither an act of habit nor an act that accords with regulative rules. It is an act of a rational capacity for knowledge.

## 3. Habits and Regulative Rules

Regulative rules are, for our purposes, to be understood as rules that prescribe particular actions and that thereby designate one action among other possible actions as the correct one, yet without thereby enjoying a constitutive status vis-à-vis the actions they prescribe.[39] A characteristic example of a regulative rule is the rule (in the United States, Germany, and elsewhere) that one drive on the right side of the road or, alternatively the rule in English golf clubs that men may not bring their female companions into the smoking room. When we say that these rules are regulative, what we are saying is that they are norms for actions, whose identity as the kind of action that falls under these norms is independent of these norms. The identity of the action of driving is independent of whether the United States, Germany, or any other place has a regulation that one is supposed to drive on the right side of the road.[40] The rule that determines which side of the road one is supposed to drive on is not itself constitutive of what it is to drive. One can equally well drive in the absence of any rule saying that one ought to drive on the right. Regulative rules thus have a normative character in the following sense: they say what one ought to do. They have the form of imperatives and thereby set up a standard of correctness with reference to which we can then assess individual behaviors as correct or incorrect. But the fact that there are such rules and standards of correctness is not constitutive for the identity of the actions that we judge as correct or incorrect by reference to those rules and standards. And, hence, the existence of such rules is not constitutive of the existence of actions that fall under the concept of these actions.

---

[39] See Searle, *Construction of Social Reality*, 27.

[40] Thus, Searle writes, "driving can exist prior to the existence of that rule" (*Construction of Social Reality*, 27).

The normativity of regulative rules carries with it the characteristic, *inter alia,* that one can offend against them, violate them. The fact that a rule has the character of an imperative for a subject entails that it is possible for the subject to fail to fulfill that imperative. Kant famously formulates this thought in articulating the deontological status that the moral law has for finite subjects, in contrast to the status it would have for holy wills. According to Kant, the moral law applies to holy wills just as much as it does to us. Yet because it is impossible for holy beings, on account of their holiness, to so much as want to do anything apart from what would agree with the moral law, the latter does not have the status of an imperative for them. For finite subjects, by contrast, who, on account of their sensible nature, can also desire (and even will) actions that are not in accord with the moral law, the latter must therefore have the status of an imperative. The reason the moral law has an imperatival character for finite subjects, according to Kant, is that it is possible for finite subjects to will actions that deviate from the moral law.[41]

This normative character clearly distinguishes regulative rules from habits. For the description of a habit is not the description of an imperative that one might violate. It is instead the description of a general way of doing something, to which neither the idea of correctness nor the idea of incorrectness—nor, correlatively, the idea of a violation—has any application. When we describe a habit, we are admittedly describing a general way of doing things that determines which actions agree with the relevant pattern and which do not. But this agreement or disagreement is not specifically normative as it is in the case of an action that accords with a regulative rule. If, after going jogging and showering one morning, I proceed to eat my toast with cherry jam instead of my usual Nutella, I am indeed deviating from my habit and routine. But this deviation does not have the normative significance of a violation, a mistake, a misdeed. The non-actualization of a habit, as such, has no normative significance.[42] This does not mean that habits cannot be objects of

---

[41] See Kant, *Grundlegung zur Metaphysik der Sitten* [Groundwork of the Metaphysics of Morals], AA 4:413–414.

[42] This does not, of course, mean that there cannot be cases in which deviating from my habit also involves my doing something incorrect or even morally bad. What is deci-

normative evaluation. Perhaps smoking is a bad habit. For our purposes, what it means is that, unlike a regulative rule, a habit does not, as such, stand in a normative relation to the cases that fall under it.

When we bring a particular act under the category of a habit, we do not thereby bring it under a norm. Rather, as we indicated above in our discussion of Aristotle and Hegel, we thereby bring the act under something general that provides a particular sort of explanation of the act in question. Ryle reminds us of the same point. By treating a behavior as habitual, we connect the behavior with a particular form of explanation—namely, one that explains what happened not by appeal to an antecedent event as its cause but rather by locating the cause of what happened in something general. The concept of habit is an explanatory concept. To refer an action to a "habit," as Ryle puts it, is not to refer it to a "peculiar internal event or class of events," but to say that a "specific disposition explains the action."[43] "Why is Peter out there smoking?" One possible answer could be: "Because he's a habitual smoker." Referring to a habit gives us a special sort of answer to the question of why someone is presently doing what she is doing. We are thereby implying that the action is an instance of something that can explain not just this one action but, in principle, indefinitely many actions performed by the same subject. To say that a behavior is habitual is to say not just that it agrees with a general way of doing something but also that this general mode of behavior is, in a certain sense, the "cause" of the present behavior.[44]

---

sive here, however, is that, in such a case, what I am doing is not bad *because* it deviates from my habit but rather for some other reason.

[43] See Ryle, *The Concept of Mind,* 91, also 89–90, 138. If one interprets some bit of behavior as the actualization of a habit, as Ryle puts it, then one equips oneself with a particular form of explanation of that behavior—namely, an explanation that does not appeal to one particular event as the explanans of another but instead one that makes a "lawlike proposition" (89).

[44] For this reason it would be wrong to explain the contrast between habitual behavior and behavior due to a rational capacity in terms of the contrast between regular behavior and rule-following behavior, if one understands regular behavior as behavior that is merely in agreement with a rule and rule-following behavior as behavior that is explained by the rule in question. This is the contrast Haugeland has in view in *Having Thought,* 305–306. Haugeland calls this the contrast between "rule-exhibiting" and "rule-governed" behavior. But even behavior that actualizes a habit is not merely in agreement with a rule: it is also explained by that rule. Wittgenstein comes closer

Let us contrast this with the relation in which a regulative rule stands to the actions that fall under it. Does English golf clubs' rule prohibiting female companions from entering the smoking room straightaway give us an answer to the question of why our friend Denis is presently entering the smoking room without any female companion? By no means. For we might well imagine that Denis only very recently became a member of the golf club and may not be explicitly familiar with all its regulating rules. Or perhaps he has not yet had sufficient opportunity to glean the unspoken validity of such rules by observing the behavior of other members. If Denis has no idea that women are not allowed in the smoking room, then this rule cannot explain why Denis is currently doing precisely what he is supposed to be doing according to the rule in question. It is a necessary condition for a regulative rule to possibly explain the actual performance of some action that the subject performing the action actually be conscious of the rule as a possible reason or ground for doing what she does when she acts in accordance with that rule.

This is not the case with habits. Reference to a habit avails us of an explanation for behavior that is not or does not have to be mediated by any consciousness of the habit on the subject's part as a reason for engaging in the behavior in question. The habit does not explain the behavior by appealing to the subject's conception of her habit as a possible reason for acting in a certain way. Now this does not mean that our habits need not be conscious, in a certain sense, in order for them to explain our behavior. Habits do not just play themselves out behind our backs. A habitual smoker knows that she is a habitual smoker. Otherwise she wouldn't always have a supply of cigarettes with her. But this consciousness that we have of our habits is of a different sort from the kind of consciousness a subject has of a regulative rule when the latter explains what she ends up doing. In performing some habitual action, I need not be conscious of my habit as a reason for so acting in order for

to the contrast between habits and rational capacities when he distinguishes a case in which someone is brought through "drill" to have the association "yellow" upon the presence of yellow objects from a case in which someone is brought through "training" to perform a behavior that agrees with a rule—i.e., a case in which such training involves a process that contains the expression of the relevant rule as an element. See Wittgenstein, *The Blue Book*, 12–13. We will return to this point in Part Four.

that habit to explain my action. The efficacy of the habit in relation to my behavior does not depend on my consciousness of that habit as the ground of my action. By contrast, in order for a regulative rule to explain, for example, the behavior of our friend Denis, he must be conscious of that rule as a possible ground for action. For the rule can be efficacious in his behavior only if he is conscious of it as a possible ground for acting.

But is this sufficient? Let us imagine that our friend Denis is, indeed, aware of the rules of his club but that he doesn't happen to know any woman who would be willing to join him in the smoking room in the first place. If he did know such a woman, perhaps he wouldn't be doing what the rule says he ought to do but would instead take impish delight in her accompanying him into the smoking room. If such a case is possible, however, then we can't explain his behavior's agreement with the rule simply by appealing to his knowledge of the rule. For in such a case, he would have known full well what the rule demanded even as he entered the smoking room with a female companion.

This shows that consciousness of a regulative rule as a possible ground for action is not sufficient to explain a subject's behavior. There is a further condition: namely, that the subject acknowledges the rule as valid and determinative of her action. The club rule that women are not allowed into the smoking room can explain why Denis's behavior is as the rule says it ought to be only if he is not only aware of the rule but also acknowledges it as a determining ground for his behavior. But precisely because Denis must not only know but also acknowledge the rule in question, acknowledgement of the rule as a determining ground for action is also not sufficient to explain why Denis's behavior is as the rule prescribes. We are in a position to explain why Denis does what the rule prescribes only once we know Denis's reasons for acknowledging the rule. One reason might be that he wants to be the next president of the club. And in order to increase his chances of collecting the votes of the more conservative club members, it makes sense for him to avoid irritating them with too much rule breaking. Another reason might be that Denis thinks it is right, in principle, to cleave to rules once they are established, regardless of whether one thinks they are sensible. A further reason might be that Denis thinks it is proper for men to have a place where they can freely discuss important issues that women do not understand. Philippa Foot has characterized this fact by saying that it is in the nature of regulative rules, such as the club's rule about the smoking room, that they do not, merely as such, provide the subject with reasons for action. There is a gap between the subject and the regulative rule that can only be bridged by an act of acknowledgment on the part of the subject.[45] And that is precisely why a regulative rule can never suffice to explain a particular bit of behavior.

Behavior that agrees with a regulative rule is characterized by the fact that it cannot be explained solely by that rule. In order to explain some subject's behavior, we must have recourse to some reason the subject has independently of the rule in question that motivates her to follow the rule. This is precisely what we were producing examples of in the previous paragraph: wanting to be club president, thinking it proper to obey established rules, wanting to be able to converse with other men without any interloping women, etc. All these are reasons for following the club rule about the smoking room. They are reasons that might explain why Denis does what the rule prescribes. But they are reasons that are external to the rule with which his behavior is in agreement, in the sense that these reasons themselves cannot be explained by reference to the regulative rule in question. They are reasons that Denis must have independently of the rule if they are to be capable of explaining his behavior.

## 4. The Normativity of Rational Capacities

In the previous section we laid out some logical features of both habits and regulative rules. Our task now is to develop a twofold contrast that differentiates rational capacities in terms of these logical features. This will enable us to understand why the concept of knowledge is a concept of a rational capacity. Habits, we said, logically differ from regulative rules in two respects: they do not stand in a normative relation to the

[45] Foot, "Morality as a System of Hypothetical Imperatives," 309.

cases falling under them, as regulative rules do, yet they do stand in an explanatory relation to their instances in a way regulative rules do not. I will now argue that it characterizes rational capacities to combine both of these features.

Let us imagine Jim skiing down the slopes. As he does so, he is explosively extending his legs, rapidly pulling up his skis, turning his legs in isolation from his hips, and increasing the pressure on his inner ski. It would not be surprising if, at that moment, we were then to see Jim fall headlong over his skis, pop out of his bindings, and slide several meters down the mountain. For he just made a serious mistake in skiing parallel short turns. After turning his legs, he increased the pressure on his inner ski instead of the outer ski, which is one of the graver errors one can commit while skiing, yet also one that even experienced skiers such as Jim occasionally make, especially when the slope is very steep and uneven. The description makes it clear that by bringing Jim's behavior under the concept of the capacity to ski parallel short turns— namely, by interpreting his individual movements as elements of a constitutive unity of acts—we have thereby brought a standard of correctness to bear on his actions. When Jim puts pressure on his inner ski while preparing to turn, he is making an error. He is doing something that is not in accordance with the norm of the very capacity under which we have subsumed his behavior.

The unity of acts we have implicitly invoked in describing Jim's behavior as an explosive extension of the legs in preparation for a sweeping turn stands in a relation to the individual motions that we see him perform that is not only constitutive but also normative. If we understand what Jim is doing (or attempting to do) as skiing parallel short turns—and not as fooling about in the snow—then he is doing something wrong in putting pressure on his inner ski in preparing to turn. The identification of Jim's behavior as an act that realizes a capacity provides us with a standard for assessing the correctness or incorrectness of his behavior that is itself immanent to that behavior. When we correctly understand what Jim is doing (or attempting to do) as skiing parallel short turns, then what he is doing fixes what behaviors would be correct and which incorrect. It is a mistake to put pressure on the inner ski under those circumstances. Pressure should be put on the outer ski. The rational capacity under which we bring Jim's behavior is not only the source of the identity of that behavior, it is simultaneously the source of the normativity of his behavior.

Rational capacities are constitutive unities of acts that provide a standard of normative assessment for the very acts that actualize them. Ryle gives voice to this normative character of rational capacities by distinguishing between concepts that merely signify the "occurrence" of actions and those that signify the "occurrence" of "suitable or correct actions," or, as he also puts it, that signify "achievements."[46] When we ascribe a rational capacity to someone, we are thereby "signifying that the person described can bring things off, or get things right."[47] To use Ryle's own example, when we say that a child can spell a word, we do not merely mean that she can give "some collection or other of letters, but the right collection in the right order."[48]

This connection we have just brought to light, which reveals that rational capacities are at once the source of the interpretation of a particular activity as well as the source of its normative assessment, can also be brought out by considering things from the opposite direction—namely, when we err in the interpretation of someone's behavior. For example, if Jim were to retort to our criticism that he wasn't trying to ski parallel short turns in the first place but was rather attempting to perform a spectacular fall. If that is what he was doing, then he really wasn't making a mistake in putting pressure on his inner ski prior to the anticipated turn. And we would, accordingly, have to retract our admonition. For our criticism of Jim's behavior has a basis only insofar as it is correct to interpret what he is doing as a manifestation of the capacity to ski parallel short turns. Such criticism can thus only reach as far as our reference to the capacity in question provides a basis for it.

Rational capacities are, in this respect, like regulative rules. They are something that specifies, in a general way, which actions are correct and which incorrect. What crucially distinguishes rational capacities from regulative rules is that, in the case of regulative rules, the identity of the action that is subjected to the standard of the rule is determined

---

[46] Ryle, *The Concept of Mind,* 130.
[47] Ibid., 133.
[48] Ibid., 130.

independently of the application of the rule itself. Rational capacities, by contrast, subject actions to a standard that is constitutive of the identity of those actions. An action that agrees with a rational capacity thereby agrees with a standard of assessment that is intrinsic to the action itself, in the sense that determining the identity of the action presupposes some reference to the capacity that determines whether or not the action is correct. When it comes to behavior that falls under a rational capacity, what one actually does already fixes what a correct performance is (or would be).[49]

Suppose we have understood someone's behavior as an exercise of the capacity to ski parallel short turns. If we then see her put pressure on her outer ski to initiate the turn, then she is doing just what she ought to do in keeping with the capacity in question. Likewise, someone who drives on the right side of the road while in Germany is doing just what she should do, according to the prevailing traffic laws. Yet in the first case, what the subject should do and what makes her performance correct are determined by what she actually does, whereas in the second case, what she should do is not fixed by what she does but by something external to her action.[50]

According to the standard reading of "constitutive rules," it is impossible to connect these two logical features that we have identified as characteristic of rational capacities—namely, the fact that their relation to their instances is both constitutive and normative. How can there be something general that is constitutive of the acts that fall under it even though it is nevertheless possible for the acts that fall under it to diverge or even violate the general principle in question? The standard understanding of constitutive rules therefore denies that they can have a normative character.[51] As we saw above, however, it is precisely such

---

[49] Sebastian Rödl's discussion of a violin maker provides a striking illustration of the intrinsic interconnection between the constitutive and normative character of the sort of generality that pertains to "arts" in the Aristotelian sense. See his "Interne Normen," esp. 183–189. Aristotelian arts are, on our account, just *one* form of rational capacities.

[50] On this distinction between external and internal norms, see ibid., 177–180, 183–184.

[51] For versions of this view see, *inter alia*, Schnädelbach, "Rationalität und Normativität"; Glüer, "Bedeutung zwischen Norm und Naturgesetz." Hans Julius Schneider, by

a combination of constitutive and normative status that is distinctive of rational capacities. As we can see in our example of the capacity to ski, we can grasp the idea of such a connection without any trouble. How is such a connection possible?

What enables us to see how such a connection is possible is the fact that the kind of generality that we are dealing with has the character of a unity of elements. This means that we are dealing with a generality whose actuality in particular cases can be a matter of degree, depending on the extent to which the unity in question is realized. When we bring an action under a rational capacity—e.g., when we understand Jim's behavior as an act of skiing—we are not thereby saying that the action is precisely as it ought to be in light of the capacity under which we have subsumed it. When we bring an action under a rational capacity, we are instead subjecting it to a standard that leaves room for a variety of modes of agreement, ranging from perfect actualizations, on one end of the spectrum, to the most varied forms of failed actualizations, on the other.

## 5. Aristotle's Conception of a *dynamis meta logou*

Up to this point we have said very little about what it means for a particular capacity to be specifically rational. Thus far, we have followed Aristotle in saying that it is a feature of rational capacities that they are acquired in a specific manner—namely, "by previous exercise." But we have not said much to spell out in detail how this is to be understood. In book IX of his *Metaphysics,* Aristotle undertakes to give a characterization of the nature of rational capacities, which we will discuss in this section. In section 6 of this chapter we will take up the account of rational capacities that we have reached so far and give an account of their rational character by focusing on what it is that rational capacities are

contrast, has defended the possibility of understanding constitutive rules as normative, albeit in a different manner from the one I explore here. He connects these features by introducing a distinction between "internal" and "external" perspectives. See Schneider, "Konstitutive Regeln und Normativität."

meant to explain. This will give us a first, preliminary idea of the kind of explanation that rational capacities provide for the acts that fall under them.[52] This focus on the explanatory character of rational capacities has the happy result that it confirms and deepens the Aristotelian understanding of rational capacities.

Aristotle begins his characterization of rational capacities *(dynameis meta logou)* by highlighting the following feature:

> And each of those which are accompanied by reason is alike capable of contrary effects, but one non-rational power produces one effect; e.g., the hot is capable only of heating, but the medical art can produce both disease and health.[53]

Now how are we to understand this? A first pass might be the following. Aristotle wants to say that rational powers or capacities have a larger range of effects than non-rational capacities, namely, a range that includes a given effect as well as its contrary.[54] Rational capacities, on this account, would be characterized by the fact that they can produce not only that which falls under their concept but also the contrary of what falls under their concept. The idea is that rational capacities are the sorts of capacities that cannot only be used but also misused, as the

---

[52] As things stand, one might be tempted to say that talk of rational capacities is in no better explanatory position than is talk of a *virtus dormitivus* to explain why someone who has taken a sleeping pill is currently sleeping. We will see why such an objection is deeply misguided once we have developed an understanding of the form of explanation that rational capacities provide. Jonathan Lear goes so far as to claim that someone who raises such a "virtus dormitiva objection" thereby expresses her incapacity to develop an understanding of the peculiar form of explanation that is fundamental to Aristotle's views—namely, an explanation of something particular through its general form. As he puts it: "It is widely believed that if any explanation has the structure of a virtus dormitiva explanation, it must therefore be circular and non-explanatory. Thus Aristotelian powers are viewed as inevitably suspect. This, I think, is a mistake" (Lear, *Aristotle: The Desire to Understand,* 23–24).

[53] Aristotle, *Metaphysics,* IX.2, 1046b4–7.

[54] Heidegger discusses this interpretation in his *Aristoteles: Metaphysik IX, 1–3,* 132–133. This interpretation has been advanced by, *inter alia,* Freeland, "Aristotle on Possibilities and Capacities," 83–84; and Witt, *Ways of Being: Potentiality and Actuality in Aristotle's Metaphysics,* 65–66.

example of medicine illustrates. To use a capacity would be to employ it in those activities that define the capacity in question. It would be to use, for example, one's medical capacities to heal the sick. To misuse a capacity would then be to employ it in activities contrary to those that define it. For example, to use one's medical capacities in killing, or making ill. But can this interpretation be right? One obvious consideration that speaks against such a reading is that many of the capacities that should be rational, on Aristotle's account, do not seem to admit of misuse. Unlike the case of medicine, when it comes to many rational capacities, it is completely unclear what a misuse would (or could) consist in. What would be the respective contrary of speech? Or of reading? Or of skiing? Or of potting?

In light of such considerations, Anthony Kenny has suggested an alternative interpretation that avoids such problems. According to Kenny, we should understand Aristotle's distinction between non-rational capacities (such as the power of fire to burn) and rational capacities (such as the capacity of a human being to learn Greek) in the following way. Whereas it characterizes non-rational capacities that they are necessarily actualized whenever all the conditions necessary for their actualization obtain, it characterizes rational capacities that all the conditions necessary for their actualization can obtain without the capacity in question being actualized. When it comes to non-rational capacities, according to Kenny, the conditions necessary for their actualization are also jointly sufficient. In the case of rational capacities, by contrast, we must make a distinction between necessary and sufficient conditions, because the actualization of a rational capacity essentially depends upon the will of the subject who possesses it.[55] If the subject of a rational capacity is in a situation where all the necessary conditions for the actualization of her capacity obtain, she can still decide not to actualize her capacity. A gifted German scholar standing before an attentive audience of German

[55] See Kenny, *Will, Freedom, and Power,* 52–53. This reading is shared by Wolf, *Möglichkeit und Notwendigkeit bei Aristoteles und heute,* esp. 26–34, 343–358; Makin, "Aristotle on Modality," esp. 143–149, see also his "Commentary" on bk. Theta of Aristotle's *Metaphysics,* esp. 40–44 and 111f.; and Beere, *Doing and Being. An Interpretation of Aristotle's* Metaphysics *Theta,* 140–145.

speakers might nevertheless, for whatever reason, refrain from saying anything.

On this interpretation, Aristotle's claim that rational capacities can also be directed at their contraries is not to be understood to mean that it is essential to rational capacities that they can be used or misused. Aristotle's point is rather that it is essential to rational capacities that their actualization is a matter of someone's actually choosing to use or to not use them. This is how Kenny connects Aristotle's initial account of rational capacities in terms of contraries with his broader and more central characterization of them as capacities associated with "decision" or "choice" *(prohairesis)*. Aristotle connects these two characterizations in the following way:

> For the non-rational potentialities are all productive of one effect each, but the rational produce contrary effects, so that they would produce contrary effects at the same time; but this is impossible. That which decides, then, must be something else; I mean by this, desire in the sense of choice [*orexis ê prohairesis*]. For whichever of two things the animal desires decisively, it will do, when it is in the circumstances appropriate to the potentiality in question and meets the passive object.[56]

Kenny's thesis is that Aristotle understands rational capacities as "two-way powers" or "voluntary powers." According to Kenny, any capacity whose actualization depends on a decision on the part of the subject who possesses it is a "two-way power."[57] Kenny goes on to object that this understanding of rational capacities is both too broad and too narrow. Let us imagine that Sebastian is in the kitchen and calls

---

[56] Aristotle, *Metaphysics,* IX.5, 1048a5–15. I have slightly altered the Revised Oxford Translation in order to make clear that I read "*ê*" in "*orexis ê prohaeresis*" to express a further explication rather than an alternative. In the second book of the *Nicomachean Ethics,* Aristotle characterizes *prohairesis* as *orexis dianoetike*. Because we seek to understand the exercise of rational capacities, *prohaeiresis* should not be read as an alternative to *orexis* in the present context, but instead as indicating that Aristotle means a particular form of *orexis*. For a defense of this reading, see Liske, "Inwieweit sind Vermögen intrinsische, dispositionelle Eigenschaften?," 283.

[57] Kenny, *Will, Freedom, and Power,* 52–53.

out, "Where is the olive oil?" I am in my study and hear the sentence clearly and distinctly. Is it then somehow dependent on a decision on my part whether or not I understand the sentence? It would seem the opposite is closer to the truth. When I hear someone uttering sentences in a language I have mastered, it is not open to me to simply not understand them. Yet there can be no doubt that understanding language is a rational capacity on Aristotle's account. A similar objection can be made from the opposite direction. Kenny observes that we also ascribe "two-way powers" to animals. When I call my cat, she may come to me if she wants. But she may also continue enjoying the ball of yarn she is currently playing with.[58] And this seems to conflict with Aristotle's thought that it is essential to the bearer of a rational capacity to be human.

Kenny's objection rests on a misunderstanding, however. For he mistakenly thinks that Aristotle understands rational capacities to be "two-way powers" (in Kenny's sense). If one understands Aristotle's account of rational capacities as Kenny does, one can no longer claim that there is a purely formal distinction between rational and non-rational capacities. Yet that is precisely what Aristotle is attempting to capture—even on Kenny's reading. The reason Kenny's "two-way power" interpretation cannot yield a formal distinction between rational and non-rational capacities is that, on Kenny's reading, there is nothing in the so-called element of decision (*orexis* in the sense of *prohairesis*) that would prevent us from simply adding it to the list of necessary conditions that have to be fulfilled in order for the relevant capacities to be actualized. The decision of the subject to exercise her capacities appears, on Kenny's account, as just a further condition that has to be fulfilled in order for the capacity to be actualized. But then it is hard to see why this element of decision does not likewise belong to the class of necessary conditions for the capacity. And that would enable us—quite contrary to Kenny's intent—to analyze a "two-way power" in such a way that it is formally indistinguishable from a non-rational capacity. For the claim "Peter is able to speak" can then be analyzed into the conditional claim: If Peter is awake, and his vocal chords are not damaged, and his mouth is

---

[58] For an analogous example, see ibid., 52, also 124–125.

not obstructed, etc., and he wants (chooses) to speak, then Peter will necessarily speak.[59]

This makes nonsense of Kenny's own account of "two-way powers." For if we can count an act of decision among the necessary conditions for a given capacity, we lose the purportedly formal differentiating criterion that Kenny invoked in order to distinguish "two-way powers" from non-rational capacities: namely, the fact that the necessary conditions for a two-way power are not jointly sufficient for its actualization.

Kenny's error in thinking that Aristotle identifies rational capacities with "two-way powers" (in Kenny's sense) stems from the fact that he accords no significance to Aristotle's explanation (in IX.2) of why rational capacities make reference to their respective contraries. The very fact that rational capacities make such reference to their contraries is something that stands in need of explanation, on Aristotle's view. The differentiating criterion Aristotle then introduces in IX.5 is part of this explanation. It thus has a different content and function from the one Kenny takes it to have. Aristotle introduces this differentiating criterion in IX.5 in order to capture the presupposition of the initial account of rational capacities he gave in IX.2. As we saw above, Aristotle claims in IX.5 that capacities that have a reference to their contraries are possible only on the presupposition that there must be something "which decides." Otherwise such capacities "would produce contrary effects at the same time," which is "impossible." The crucial intermediary step that Kenny skips over in his interpretation is Aristotle's earlier explanation of why rational capacities have this reference to their respective contraries, which comes directly after the passage from IX.2 we are considering. Aristotle writes:

[59] This account of "two-way powers" (as distinct from "rational powers") has actually been put forward by Freeland, "Aristotle on Possibilities and Capacities," 83–84. Freeland's position has also been adopted by Witt (*Ways of Being,* 66). It is also shared by Beere, *Doing and Being,* 144–145, who does not seem to be worried about this consequence. Kenny, by contrast, is quite aware that this analysis has to be avoided; see Kenny, *Will, Freedom, and Power,* 129–130. Yet to avoid this analysis, it is not enough to simply insist that "the locus of wanting is precisely this gap between circumstances and action, the gap left by the unpredictability of action from circumstances" (ibid., 129). One has to give an account of the relevant act of "decision" or "choice" that makes such an analysis impossible.

The reason is that science [sc. as a case of a rational capacity; A. K.] is a *logos,* and the same *logos* explains a thing and its privation, only not in the same way [ . . . ]. Therefore such sciences must deal with contraries, but with one in virtue of their own nature and with the other not in virtue of their nature; for the *logos* applies to one object in virtue of that object's nature, and to the other, in a sense, accidentally. For it is by denial and removal that it explains the contrary; for the contrary is the primary privation, and this is the entire removal of the positive term.[60]

Rational capacities—*dynameis meta logou*—make reference to their respective contraries, Aristotle explains, because they are forms of *logos.* There are basically two readings of *logos* that have been suggested for the above passage. Either we interpret the *logos* that defines rational capacities as a sort of rule, principle, or "rational formula."[61] Or, alternatively, we interpret *logos* as itself a *dynamis:* as the ability to understand, to reflect, to give an explanation (as a "power of reasoning").[62] Because *logos* appears here as a specification of a *dynamis,* I take it to be appropriate to construe *logos* as a *dynamis* in the rest of the passage— namely, as the ability to understand, to reflect and explain. What is crucial for our purposes, however, is the fact that Aristotle's rationale for claiming that rational capacities make reference to their contraries in virtue of the *logos* proper to them is that a *logos* is characterized as something with explanatory force. In particular, *logos* explains both the actualization of the capacity ("the object") that is definitive of that capacity as well as the privative case of that capacity—albeit, as Aristotle notes, "not in the same way."

The characterization of rational capacities that Aristotle arrives at here thus holds that they make reference to their respective contraries

---

[60] Aristotle, *Metaphysics,* IX.2, 1046b7–16.

[61] See Ross's translation of Aristotle's *Metaphysics.*

[62] That is the interpretation defended by Burnyeat, Owen, McDowell, and Heidegger, among others. For Burnyeat's and Owen's position, see Burnyeat, *Notes on Eta and Theta of Aristotle's Metaphysics,* 52–53. For McDowell's reading, see his "Virtue and Reason," 57–59. Heidegger's position is in *Aristoteles: Metaphysik IX, 1–3,* 136–137. I agree with this reading. This contention finds further support in Aristotle's description of *logos* in *Metaphysics,* VII.7.

in virtue of the fact that they are intrinsically connected with the ability to explain the exercises of those capacities. It is in virtue of being able to explain the exercises of the relevant capacity that rational capacities make reference to their contraries. Aristotle wants to say that if possessing a capacity, whatever it may be, involves being able to explain cases that fall under it, then someone who possesses such a capacity can, for that reason, explain two kinds of cases: namely, those that actualize the object that defines the capacity in question as well as some "privative cases." Someone who can explain her acts of skiing in virtue of her capacity to ski can *ipso facto* also explain cases of skiing that Aristotle would designate as privative. For "*logos* applies to both, though not in the same way."[63]

Now how exactly should we understand such talk of "contraries"? In the case of medicine, the contrary is sickness. That much is clear. But as we saw above, the case of medicine does not make it clear what it fundamentally means to speak of "contraries" with reference to rational capacities. We can come a bit closer to understanding what Aristotle means by the "contrary" of a rational capacity by considering the status he accords it and the manner in which it is explained by the capacity. Aristotle characterizes the status of a rational capacity's contrary as a "privation."[64] Rational capacities, as Aristotle understands them, are so constituted that the cases they serve to explain can be divided into two classes that stand in an asymmetrical relationship to one another. One class consists of cases that the *logos* of the relevant capacity explains "in virtue of their own nature." The other class consists of cases that it explains not in virtue of their own nature but "in a sense, accidentally." The former are the *positive* cases in terms of which the relevant capacity is defined. This class of cases contrasts with another class of cases that are differently constituted but that can nevertheless be explained in terms of the *logos* of the capacity in question, "though not in the same way" as the positive cases are.

---

[63] Aristotle, *Metaphysics,* IX.2, 1046b20.
[64] Compare Aristotle's fourfold distinction between meanings of "contrary," of which one is the "positive/privative" distinction. *Categories* 10, 11b15f.

These "privative" cases are all in some way deviant and the capacity in question therefore explains them "in a sense, accidentally"—namely, "by denial and removal" of something that is present in the positive case. Examples of such privative cases would include a skier who crashes while slaloming, a literate person who misreads something, an accountant who miscalculates something, an architect who builds a house that collapses when the front door is opened, or a fluent speaker who misunderstands what her friend says to her. Or, finally, a doctor who does not make her patients healthy but instead does them in with a poisonous drug cocktail. In explaining a privative case, one makes reference to the positive case and singles out an element of the latter that is lacking in the former. Consider the question "Why did Jim crash while skiing?" "Because he put pressure on his inner ski." Or "Why didn't Peter hear the telephone?" "Because he was sleeping."

We can express Aristotle's general point by saying: someone who possesses a rational capacity is thereby in a position to explain two distinct kinds of case, albeit "not in the same way." This account of rational capacities is presupposed by the concept of decision that Aristotle introduces in IX.5 as a further characterization of rational capacities. For this further characterization, as we saw above, aims to answer a difficulty that the initial characterization seems to raise—namely, the difficulty expressed in the phrase "but this is impossible." Hence, in order to accurately capture the notion of decision that is relevant to Aristotle's account of rational capacities, we must first develop a more precise understanding of the distinction between the respective forms of explanation proper to the two kinds of case that rational capacities are meant to explain. A first step toward understanding this distinction involves looking at the manner in which non-rational capacities explain the cases that manifest them, i.e., capacities that do not themselves contain the capacity to give an explanation. Consider, for example, the ability of wood to burn. Aristotle's general account of this ability is that wood necessarily burns when one tosses it into a fire. Now let us imagine that the wood is tossed into a fire and that it does indeed burn. What explains the present burning of the wood, *hic et nunc,* is its combustibility. This is not, of course, an explanation that the wood itself can give. That the wood has the capacity to burn does not entail that it can give an explanation of its acts of burning in terms of this capacity. The capacity to burn is not a rational capacity. We, however, can provide such an explanation in virtue of the fact that we possess an understanding of this capacity of wood to burn.

Now one is perhaps tempted to object at this point that what explains the present burning of the wood is that someone tossed it in the fire, that the fire was sufficiently large, that the wood was dry, that there isn't a gale blowing, that the wood wasn't wrapped in aluminum foil, etc. The sum of all these conditions—so the objection goes—is what *really* explains the burning of the wood. Aristotle does not dispute this. His claim rather is that to say all this is nothing other than to articulate what it means for wood to be combustible. The circumstances that must obtain in order for the wood's capacity to burn to be actualized are not something that is external to our understanding of the capacity in question. They are part of our understanding of the burning of the wood as a manifestation of the wood's capacity to burn. Hence, it is absurd, on Aristotle's account, to say that a capacity is actualized only if nothing "interferes."[65] The exclusion of "interferences" is already contained in our understanding of something as a capacity, and therefore it is not something that could possibly be added to such an understanding. We will dwell on this point more extensively in Chapter VII of this part. For the moment it suffices to observe that, for Aristotle, in a case where what happens is precisely what the capacity is a capacity for, that occurrence is explained by nothing other than the capacity itself.

Now it may well happen that some wood is tossed into a sufficiently strong fire and yet fails to burn. How should we explain such a case? We can explain such a case by establishing that the circumstances under which wood's ability to burn would be actualized do not obtain. Thus, whereas we explain the case in which the wood burns by reference to its ability to burn, to explain the wood's failure to burn, we have to single out a particular circumstance that explains why its ability to

---

[65] Aristotle puts forward this thesis in *Metaphysics*, IX.5, 1048a15–20. I will discuss this intrinsic connection between capacities and the circumstances of their actualization at greater length in Chapter VIII, section 2, below.

burn was not actualized. This particular circumstance is only contingently related to the capacity in the sense that it is not contained in our understanding of the wood's ability to burn.

When Aristotle says that the *logos* explains the contrary case of a capacity in a different manner from how it explains cases of the capacity's successful actualization, what he means is this: Whereas the *logos* explains the so-called positive cases through the capacity itself, it explains the contrary cases only derivatively, by reference to particular and contingent circumstances that explain why the actualization of the capacity was hindered. This asymmetrical structure of explanation holds for rational and non-rational capacities alike. What is peculiar to rational capacities is that they are defined in terms of acts that entail acts of explanation—unlike, say, the capacity of wood to burn, where the *logos* is only externally connected with the capacity. Bearers of rational capacities are therefore capable of themselves explaining the acts that fall under those capacities through those very capacities. In particular, the bearer of a rational capacity is, in virtue of bearing that capacity, capable of explaining positive cases through the capacity in question and capable of explaining negative cases derivatively by appeal to particular and contingent circumstances that explain why the actualization of the capacity in question was hindered. To return to our skiing example, Jim can explain why he is explosively extending his legs by referring to the capacity to ski. But he cannot explain the privative case in the same manner. Jim cannot simply explain why he crashed by invoking his capacity to ski. He might blame the fall on a rock, or on his lack of concentration, etc.

We are now in a position to ask what content the concept of "decision" or "choice" must have, in light of the considerations Aristotle introduces into his account of rational capacities in IX.5. What does Aristotle mean when he says that a *prohairesis* must be "that which decides" in the case of rational capacities? As we saw above, the introduction of the concept of *prohairesis* is meant to capture the presupposition involved in the idea that rational capacities are capacities to "produce contrary effects." Rational capacities have this feature in virtue of being capacities that entail that someone who possesses such a capacity, just in virtue of possessing it, is able to explain two classes of cases—namely, those that agree with the capacity in question and those that diverge from it in some respect. For it follows from this that someone who possesses a rational capacity is able, just in virtue of possessing it, not only to bring about cases that actualize the capacity but also to bring about privative cases. For someone whose capacity to ski entails that he is capable of explaining privative cases of skiing—e.g., who is capable of explaining why he crashed while he was skiing—is also, just in virtue of that capacity, capable of bringing about such privative cases. For bringing about such privative cases only requires that the bearer of the capacity does something that effectively denies, hinders, or otherwise removes the actualization of the capacity in question ("by denial and removal"). Someone who is able to ski can also, in virtue of her capacity to explain her acts of skiing through her capacity to ski, do something on the slopes that causes her to fall—she need only shift her weight onto her inner ski instead of her outer while turning at sufficiently high speed.

The problem that Aristotle raises in IX.5 can thus be reformulated as follows. The idea of a capacity that involves the capacity to give an explanation for the acts falling under is not yet intelligible. For the capacity to give an explanation seems to make it the case that any capacity that contains it would have to be characterized as a capacity for bringing about two mutually contrary cases "at the same time." And that is nonsensical. There must, therefore, be a feature of such capacities, the function of which is to determine which of the two alternatives obtains in the prevailing circumstances: that is, a feature that determines whether the capacity is actualized or whether its actualization—in whatever form—is "denied." The role of the notion of decision here is to describe this determining act. Without this determining element, the idea of a capacity that involves a capacity for explanation would make no sense. The notion of decision that is characteristic of a rational capacity is thus characterized from the very outset in a particular manner: *prohairesis* is a decision about what to do in the prevailing circumstances with a view to the capacity in question.

It follows from this, however, that Aristotle is not, as Kenny assumes, deploying the concept of decision in order to denote an act that is independent of the idea of a rational capacity in the sense that it might just as well be an act of a creature that has no such rational capacity. He is instead using it to describe an act that one cannot understand independently of a rational capacity—namely, independently of the fact that the subject of such an act is *conscious of her capacity* as something through which she can determine her action. Only a subject of a rational capacity is in a position to make the sort of decision in terms of which Aristotle elucidates the idea of a rational capacity. And this makes it clear why Aristotle denies rational capacities of precisely the same creatures—namely, animals and small children—that he denies *prohairesis* of.[66]

Yet the concept of *prohairesis* is still more determinate. Let us imagine someone who can ski. In virtue of her capacity to ski, she knows what it means to ski—e.g., she knows that one must explosively extend one's legs when one makes a turn. But let us imagine that our skier decides just then not to explosively extend her legs for some reason—perhaps because she thinks it would simply be too exhausting at the moment—even as she still hopes to make the turn. She is doing something that she knows, on account of her understanding of skiing, is not an act in accordance with her capacity to ski. Nevertheless, what she is doing is the manifestation of a decision about what to do in which she is conscious of her capacity. And this seems to raise a problem. For the fundamental characterization of rational capacities has it that rational capacities explain their so-called positive cases "in virtue of their nature." They explain cases of their privation, by contrast, "in a sense, accidentally"—that is, they explain privative cases only derivatively, by reference to a contingent and particular element that explains why the capacity is hindered from being perfectly actualized. Now in the case we just described, we have an action that is a privation of the capacity to ski but nevertheless is the manifestation of a decision, which has the capacity to ski in view. Because, on Aristotle's account, a defective case

---

[66] See Aristotle, *Nicomachean Ethics,* 1111b7–10. This is likewise how Christoph Rapp understands the concept of *prohairesis* to function in the *Nicomachean Ethics.* See Rapp, "Freiwilligkeit, Entscheidung, Verantwortlichkeit." See also Irwin, "Reason and Responsibility in Aristotle." As we will shortly see, however, this account of the concept is also deficient. For it does not suffice to completely capture the content of the concept of decision that is essential to rational capacities.

cannot figure among the cases that the capacity, just as such, explains, it follows that the idea of decision that goes with a rational capacity, must be the idea of an act that rules out such a case. Not just any reflective decision can count as the sort of *prohairesis* that characterizes a rational capacity. To rule out cases like the one above, Aristotle must understand *prohairesis* as a decision specifically about what is correct to do under the prevailing circumstances according to the capacity in light of which one acts.[67] To make the sort of decision in terms of which we understand what a rational capacity is doesn't mean coming to some decision or other. It instead means coming to a decision about what would be right to do under the prevailing circumstances according to the capacity.

The act of decision that Aristotle invokes to characterize rational capacities is thus an act whose performance cannot be understood independently of the capacity in question. Someone who performs such an act of decision does not perform an act that is logically prior to an exercise of the very capacity whose exercise is in question. To decide to do what it is right to do under the prevailing circumstances in light of the relevant capacity means exercising that capacity in the way that is paradigmatic of it *qua* rational capacity: namely, exercising it in such a way that one is thereby *guided by* the capacity in question. That is to say, it is to exercise the capacity in such a way that one's act is a manifestation of one's understanding of what, under the prevailing circumstances, it is in accordance with the capacity to do. Imagine that Jim is up on the slopes skiing parallel short turns and that he proceeds to explosively extend his legs because he decided to do what, in light of his capacity to ski, was the proper thing to do under the prevailing circumstances. It would be wrong to think that what is going on here involves two distinct acts—an act of decision and an act of explosively extending his legs—each of which falls under a different capacity. Rather, what we

[67] On this interpretation of *prohairesis* in Aristotle, see McDowell, "The Role of Eudaimonia in Aristotle's Ethics," 6. McDowell characterizes the concept of *prohairesis* in connection with moral deliberation in an analogous way—namely, so that it is more contentful than the notion of "deliberative desire" insofar as it has a reference to the good, the right. This is in line with the interpretation put forward by Heidegger, *Aristoteles: Metaphysik IX. 1–3*, 152.

have here is a single act, which has its cause in the rational capacity to ski and which exercises that capacity in the way paradigmatic of that capacity.

It is thus part of the notion of decision Aristotle deploys in his account of rational capacities that it describes an act that cannot be counted among the list of all those conditions that must be fulfilled in order for the capacity to be actualized. For it describes not a condition of the actu-alization of a rational capacity but rather the paradigmatic actualization of a rational capacity. It follows from this that rational capacities, on Aris-totle's account, are neither "voluntary powers" in Kenny's sense nor ca-pacities whose exercise can be understood through the idea of an act that manifests just any kind of "reflective decision." They are instead capaci-ties whose paradigmatic exercise consists in an act that manifests a deci-sion about what would be right to do according to the relevant capacity under the prevailing circumstances.

This reading of the relevant concept of decision provides us with an answer to the observation we considered above—the observation, namely, that when someone says something intelligible to me in a lan-guage I have mastered, it is not open to me to simply not understand him or to understand him to have said something else. We can now see that this observation does not pose any objection to the Aristotelian concep-tion of rational capacities. When I understand what someone says to me, I am doing precisely what is correct or appropriate in light of the capacity I thereby exercise—namely, my capacity to understand the language she is speaking. The fact that my understanding of the other's words is the manifestation of a decision does not mean that there is some act of de-cision I perform that precedes and produces my understanding of the utterance. It rather means that my understanding of what the other person says is guided by my capacity to understand the language in question. My understanding is thus guided in the sense that it is a manifestation of my understanding of what is in accordance with this capacity.

Therefore a situation where I understand another person immedi-ately—in the sense of being not mediated by further acts of deliberation—is every bit as exemplary of a rational capacity as are cases in which my eventual understanding is mediated by further reflections on how to understand what the other said—e.g., because what was said was un-clear, or indistinct, or complicated.[68] When someone who can under-stand a given language is spoken to intelligibly in that language, she does not need to engage in a mediating process of reflection on how to understand the words uttered—wondering whether to understand them this way or that—in order to come to understand them at all. And someone who can ski doesn't need to engage in a mediating pro-cess of reflection on how to ski by wondering whether to put weight on the inner ski rather than the outer ski or whether to explosively extend her legs in order to make a turn. On Aristotle's account, someone who is practiced in something does not need to engage in such a mediating process of reflection on what she is doing; she does not need to consider alternative possibilities of its exercise and then come to a decision about which one to pursue.[69] If the fundamental account of a rational act is that rational acts spring from rational ca-pacities, then the paradigmatic case of a rational act is not one that requires a mediating process of reflection. What is required is, in-stead, that the subject has a reflective consciousness of her capacity such that her acting in accordance with the capacity is a manifesta-tion of that consciousness.

## 6. Rational Capacities as Self-Conscious, Normative Explanations

In what follows, we will take up the account of rational capacities as we developed it so far and explore the feature that makes a capacity spe-cifically rational by considering what it is that such capacities purport to explain—namely, acts that are rational in the sense we introduced at the outset of this book. We will then be in a position to ask what features a rational capacity must have if it is to explain such acts. It will turn out that the account of rational capacities that we will reach at the end of

---

[68] On this point, see Anscombe, "Thought and Action in Aristotle."
[69] See Aristotle, *Nicomachean Ethics*, 1113a1–2.

this section is in line with the Aristotelian account given in the previous section.

In Part One we introduced a rational act as one that involves the use of concepts—i.e., general representations whose paradigmatic use is in judgments. The idea of such an act, we argued, goes hand in hand with the idea of a particular form of explanation, namely, a normative explanation that the subject herself is, in principle, in a position to give. We then characterized the acts that are subject to such a form of explanation as acts that someone performs for a reason or as acts in which one responds to a reason. We then went on to ask how we can make sense of the possibility of such acts.

Thus far, our abstract account of how to explain the possibility of such acts is that we should understand them as exercises of a rational capacity. Habits explain habitual behaviors. Rational capacities explain rational acts. Our task now is to work out what a rational capacity must be in order to be capable of explaining acts that meet this formal characterization—namely, acts that can occur only if the subject herself is in a position to give a normative explanation of them. If a rational capacity is to explain acts of this form, it must be part of a rational capacity to have a specific mode of exercise. That is to say, rational capacities can have the required "explanatory standing" with respect to the acts in which they are manifested only if it is part of what a rational capacity is that it be exercised in a specific way. It must be part of the concept of a rational capacity that the efficacy of the capacity in the acts that agree with it is dependent on the subject's being conscious of that efficacy in the acts she performs in accord with the capacity in question. A rational capacity must be one whose exercises, in the paradigmatic case, entail that the subject is conscious of the efficaciousness of her capacity in the act in which it is manifested.

Let us call this form of efficacy "self-conscious efficacy" and let's accordingly term the correlative capacity a "self-conscious capacity." A rational capacity must be a self-conscious capacity, in this sense. That is, it must be a capacity whose acts, in the paradigmatic case, would not occur if the subject were not conscious of them as exercises of that very capacity. Only a capacity of this sort can be the "cause" of acts that meet our formal characterization—namely, that the subject herself, just in virtue of being the subject of such an act, is in a position to trace the act back to the relevant "cause." A capacity that the subject must be conscious of, in order to possess and exercise it, thereby puts the subject in a position to explain an act that manifests that capacity by invoking that very capacity. It follows from such a capacity that the act of explanation in which the subject invokes her capacity to explain her manifestation of that capacity would itself be a manifestation of that very capacity, namely, a manifestation of the subject's consciousness of that capacity. When an act that falls under a rational capacity is justified through that capacity by the subject who performs the act in question—e.g., when a skier says, "I am putting pressure on the outer ski during the turn because that's how one skis short turns"—then, in giving such an explanation, the subject is exercising the very same capacity she is adverting to in that explanation. Moreover, in so doing, she is thereby performing the very act that her capacity enables her to explain in that manner.

The fact that a subject who possesses a rational capacity is conscious of the capacity in question and understands what it means to possess and to exercise that capacity is no accidental or merely desirable quality that we happen to find in subjects of rational capacities. It is part of what it is to possess a rational capacity in the first place. That is to say, we are dealing with a rational capacity only if and insofar as it is manifested in acts that make reference to the capacity in question in such forms of explanation. A rational capacity, merely as such, must be manifested in the employment of such forms of explanation whereby one explains one's behavior by reference to the capacity in question and, in particular, by representing it as in accordance with that capacity—i.e., by representing one's behavior as a manifestation of the capacity.[70]

With this, we arrive at an understanding of rational capacities that confirms the Aristotelian account we developed in the previous section. A rational capacity is self-conscious because only a subject who is conscious of her capacity as a norm for her behavior is so much as capable of performing an act that not only falls under this norm but falls under it in such a way that she is guided by that norm and is thus in a

---

[70] Compare Thompson's account of practices in *Life and Action,* 198.

position to explain her act by reference to it. When Jim is skiing up on the slopes and proceeds to increase the pressure on his outer ski while turning, he is doing precisely what it is correct to do in light of what it means to ski. Now if it is intrinsic to the capacity to ski, insofar as it is a rational capacity, that it is self-conscious, then Jim, too, will be guided in his behavior by a representation of how one skis. And someone who is thus guided in his behavior by a representation of how one skis is therefore in a position to give a normative explanation of what he is doing by representing it as an act that is as it is supposed to be according to the norm that is guiding his behavior.

A subject who exercises a rational capacity accordingly performs acts that she can normatively explain precisely by portraying them as acts of the rational capacity she is exercising: e.g., as acts of skiing, or calculating, etc. If Jim has the rational capacity to ski parallel short turns and is currently doing so, his capacity provides him, *inter alia,* with a reason for putting pressure on his outer ski as he begin each turn.[71] Thus, what enables Jim to explain his current action of increasing pressure on his outer ski is something that serves as a reason not just for that action here and now but as a reason for, in principle, indefinitely many such actions. When a subject gives a normative explanation for acts that manifest a rational capacity of hers, she is not exercising a different capacity from the one she manifests in the acts for which she gives that explanation. Rather, she articulates her consciousness of what it is to possess and exercise that capacity—a consciousness that is constitutive for the performance of such acts in the first place.

It is thus important to flag the following misunderstanding. When we say that someone who possesses a rational capacity enjoys a consciousness of the capacity under which her behavior falls, this does not mean that she has to be familiar with the expressions that one would find, for example, in a ski manual. By no means. Her consciousness of her capacity need not be articulated in the manner of a textbook account.

---

[71] Naturally, I only have such a reason if I am not currently suffering a heart attack, in which case I should immediately lie down, or if someone is not about to ski right in front of me, in which case I should perform a parallel stop, etc. We will address the problem of exceptions in Chapter VIII, sections 1 and 2.

Very few skiers have that sort of articulated consciousness of their capacity. Nor does it have to be articulated in any other specific way. That someone is indeed self-conscious of the capacity that explains her behavior can come out in a wide variety of ways. It can express itself, for instance, in her capacity to adduce examples of exercises of the capacity in question, or in her capacity to demonstrate the relevant behavior, or to point out instances of it. A subject faced with the question of what parallel short turns are can accordingly demonstrate her consciousness of the capacity by answering, "It's what I'm doing right now," or "It's what Jim is doing up there." The reflective consciousness that is constitutive of a rational capacity is not the sort of highly articulated consciousness that is required for writing a ski manual, or an instruction book for chess, etc. The opposite is true: Textbooks are an essentially posterior form of articulation of the sort of consciousness that everyone who possesses the capacity has, albeit in a far less articulated form. The sort of consciousness that is intrinsic to rational capacities has its fundamental locus not in textbooks but in paradigmatic exercises of the respective capacities: in skiing, dancing, swimming, etc.[72]

We are now in a position to return to the question we formulated above: namely, in what sense do rational capacities explain the occurrence of the acts that fall under them? Our more detailed account of what a rational capacity is has made it clear that the sort of explanation they make possible has a particular form. Our reference to a rational capacity in explaining an action is not an appeal to a psychological event that causes the action we are interested in explaining. Nor does such an explanation appeal to a non-psychological event. The explanation of the performance in question doesn't involve appealing to an antecedent event of any sort. It explains the action by appeal to something general—something to which the subject herself makes reference, in

---

[72] If one fails to appreciate the idea of a rational capacity but instead identifies the idea of rationality with the idea of acts that are guided by rules, then any insistence on the rational character of acts must appear as an "intellectualistic" misconception of human experience and action. Lack of the idea of a rational capacity is the source of the misunderstanding that drives, for example, Dreyfus in his criticism of McDowell. See Dreyfus, "Overcoming the Myth of the Mental" and "The Return of the Myth of the Mental" as well as McDowell's response in "What Myth?"

the paradigmatic case, and that she invokes in a normative explanation of her action. That is to say, the sort of explanation that rational capacities provide is essentially one that could never be discovered through what we might call an empirical investigation. A rational capacity is rather a "cause" of particular actions in the sense that it accords those actions a normative explanation—but one that is available only insofar the subject performing the action can herself give that explanation of her behavior and give expression to it in specific acts.

# VII

# Rational Capacities for Knowledge

## 1. Knowledge as Rational Capacity

The category of a rational capacity, as we have developed it so far, is the concept of something general bearing the following four features. (1) It is constitutive: acts that fall under this general item depend on it for their identity. (2) It is normative: acts that fall under it can be judged with reference to it to be correct or incorrect, good or bad, successful or unsuccessful. (3) It is explanatory: acts that fall under it are explained by it in a particular sense. (4) It is self-conscious: a subject who possesses a rational capacity is conscious of her capacity, which consciousness manifests itself in her use of concepts and her employment of forms of explanation that are dependent on the very capacity that is manifested in her acts. These features are jointly sufficient to enable us to understand and vindicate the thought from which we began: namely, that the concept of knowledge is the concept of a rational capacity. If the concept of knowledge is the concept of a rational capacity, a number of things follow.

First, the content of the concepts we invoke in our account of knowledge are dependent on the concept of knowledge. And that means that the concepts of belief, truth, and grounds for belief do not denote acts or properties of acts that are self-standing—i.e., intelligible indepen-

182

dently of their connection with the concept of knowledge.[73] Rather, the acts or properties of acts denoted by these concepts are intelligible in virtue of the unity they form in the description of knowledge. It follows from this, furthermore, that it is impossible to apply the concepts of belief, truth, and grounds for belief to someone without thereby understanding her as possessing a rational capacity for knowledge.

Second, if the concept of knowledge is the concept of a rational capacity, then the elements we invoke in elucidating the concept of knowledge make up a unity that has the status of a norm vis-à-vis those elements. The elements of knowledge are, in virtue of being elements of such a unity, intrinsically subject to evaluation with respect to whether or not they accord with this norm. Cases of someone's holding a false belief or someone's lacking truth-guaranteeing grounds for her belief are, accordingly, deficient cases of belief: in these cases, the subject holds a belief that does not accord with the norm that is constitutive for holding beliefs. For in these cases, the subject does not have knowledge.

A third consequence is that the elements in terms of which we comprehend knowledge make up a unity that explains the occurrence of each of those elements in a particular normative sense—i.e., in a way that renders the occurrence of each element intelligible by representing it as being, or as approximately being, in accordance with that unity.

Finally, a fourth consequence of understanding knowledge as a rational capacity is that the unity of acts that constitute knowing can only obtain if this unity is manifested in the employment of concepts whose very content depends on this capacity—that is, if it is manifested in the employment of concepts those that of belief and truth, and in the employment of forms of explanations that are available to those who

---

[73] This would give us a positive account of the irreducibility of the concept, which is, where it is noticed, mostly misunderstood (see the introduction to Part III, Chapter VI). It is even misunderstood in cases where the significance of the concept of a capacity within epistemology is acknowledged. See, for instance, Alan Millar, "Knowledge and Recognition," 99–110, 120–137. See also his "What Is It That Cognitive Abilities Are Abilities to Do?" By contrast, McDowell's appeal to the idea of a capacity within epistemology appears to be the flipside of his disjunctivist account of sensory experience, and hence to be understood as a step toward a positive account of the irreducibility claim. See McDowell, *Perception as a Capacity for Knowledge*.

possess and exercise that very capacity. That is to say, if we construe knowledge as a rational capacity, we thereby understand the knowing subject to be in a position to give a normative explanation of what she is doing whenever what she is doing belongs to the constitutive unity of acts involved in knowing. The elements invoked in the concept of knowledge are elements of a self-conscious unity.

In the following chapters we will show in a step-by-step fashion what it means to say that the concept of knowledge designates a unity of elements that is constitutive for the concepts we use to denote the elements of that unity. In particular, we are going to show that the concept of sensory experience, the concept of causality, the concept of justification, the concept of truth, and the concept of an empirical fact as well as the concept of the objectivity of such facts are all dependent on the concept of knowledge. At present, however, we have already established the following conditional: If the concept of knowledge is the concept of a rational capacity, then we can retrospectively understand the skeptic's position as one that enables us to recognize, in a negative manner, the constitutive character of the concept of knowledge. Skepticism then emerges as the result of any attempt to give an account of how someone can have knowledge that does not appeal to the idea that the being in question possesses a rational capacity for knowledge. If we follow such an attempt through to its end, we turn out to lose our grip on how the subject in question could even have any grounds for beliefs, and hence, any beliefs at all. That is what our transcendental reflections demonstrated. And this is precisely what we should expect if the concept of knowledge is the concept of a rational capacity. For if the concept of knowledge is the concept of a rational capacity, then, it must indeed be impossible to make sense of the idea that someone has a particular belief independent of some reference to a rational capacity of hers, in virtue of which she can, in principle, acquire knowledge. In the absence of such a reference, talk of "belief" is as empty as talk of a "traversing stance" or "outer ski pressure" outside the context of a description of the capacity to ski.[74]

---

[74] It is interesting to note (and calls for an explanation) why this tends to be overlooked when it comes to the capacity for knowledge, whereas in the case of capacities like

Now let us imagine that we had just one rational capacity for knowledge. In such a case, it would be unnecessary to ask someone who claimed to know something *how* she knows it. It would be unnecessary to inquire into the source of her knowledge, for there would be only one possible answer to this question. Our use of the question "How do you know this?" addressed to someone who purports to know something indicates that we understand ourselves to have more than one rational capacity for knowledge. Moreover, we already encountered an argument to the effect that the idea of *objective* knowledge that is our concern here contains the idea that it must be a capacity for knowledge that is *receptive* to how things are. A capacity for perceptual knowledge, we can now argue, would be such a receptive capacity for knowledge. A capacity for knowledge by hearsay would be another such capacity. Yet in the latter case it is clear that this capacity cannot be a self-standing source of receptive knowledge because it presupposes that someone else has acquired receptive knowledge in a different manner from hearsay for it to be intelligible as receptive knowledge of how things are. This is not to say that a capacity for knowledge by hearsay is not a source of knowledge. Rather, it is to say that a capacity for knowledge by hearsay is a source of knowledge for the individual subject who, in actualizing that capacity, is epistemically dependent on another subject's having acquired receptive knowledge through a capacity that accounts for the possibility of acquiring receptive knowledge in the first place.

If that is so, then we arrive at the following general account: Someone knows something just in case her belief is a perfect exercise of a particular rational capacity for knowledge. The point of saying that she exercises a "particular" rational capacity for knowledge is to indicate that her knowledgeable acts can be sorted into a variety of kinds that reflect formal distinctions between the respective rational capacities for knowledge from which the relevant acts spring. Yet, given our transcendental considerations, we have to privilege one of these capacities for knowledge in our account of objective knowledge: namely, a capacity for perceptual

skiing, swimming, dancing, etc. probably no one would ever think of their paradig-·matic acts without reference to the idea of a capacity.

knowledge. To understand perceptual knowledge in terms of a rational capacity must be our primary concern.

With this, we are in a position to answer the question we raised at the end of Part One: namely, how we are to understand the meaning of statements such as "S perceives that p"? For we now have entitled ourselves to the thought that such statements describe acts of a particular rational capacity for knowledge. They describe someone as actualizing her rational capacity for perceptual knowledge. This is also the place to recall the result of Part Two. Our conclusion there was that we must understand statements such as "S perceives that p" to have an irreducibly factive sense. The reason for this, as we can see now, lies in the fact that the role of such a statement is to describe an act of a constitutive unity of acts—i.e., of a unity of acts that are not more fundamental than the unity to which they belong.

This account of knowledge deepens and adds a further dimension to our understanding of the insight we gained in Chapter V. We saw there that a disjunctive understanding of sensory experiences constitutes the flipside of the irreducibility of statements of this form. We have to understand the concept of sensory experience as describing either a case of perception—and hence a truth-guaranteeing ground for belief— or a case in which one only seems to perceive and hence only seems to have a truth-guaranteeing ground for belief. We now have a deeper appreciation of what makes this disjunctive understanding of sense experience compulsory. We must understand sense experience disjunctively because such an experience must consist either in an act that perfectly actualizes the capacity in question or in an act that fails to be a perfect actualization of the capacity.[75]

---

[75] The inner connection between the idea of a capacity for perceptual knowledge and a disjunctive conception of sense experience is not recognized in most disjunctivist accounts. "Disjunctivism" is usually treated as an independent epistemic or ontological doctrine. Williamson's criticism of disjunctive conceptions in *Knowledge and Its Limits* is partly due to this failure in many disjunctivist accounts. McDowell is an exception, although he is not explicit about it. Haddock's disjunctive conception in terms of "cases of seeing" can also be seen as an attempt to appreciate that inner connection. See his "Knowledge and Action," esp. 220–223.

## 2. Knowledge of the Explanation of Knowledge

One implication of this conception of knowledge as a rational capacity is that the sense experiences that enable us to understand how a subject can form empirical beliefs must have conceptual content. For the role of the concept of a sensory experience, as it is employed in describing a rational capacity for knowledge is, as we saw above, either to describe a sense experience that perfectly actualizes this capacity or to describe an experience in which the perfect actualization of this capacity fails or misfires. Now, both of these sensory experiences fall under a rational capacity for perceptual knowledge. It is accordingly part of what it is to enjoy them that the subject can adduce such experiences in order to explain why it is correct for her to believe (or not to believe) a particular conceptual content. It follows from this that these sensory experiences—regardless of whether or not they perfectly actualize the capacity in question—have a conceptual content in virtue of which the subjects who enjoy them are able to refer to those experiences in explaining why it is correct for them to endorse (or to refrain from endorsing) a particular conceptual content.

Note, however, that this capacity account of knowledge is not to be understood as claiming that it is simply an empirical fact that the sensory experiences enjoyed by creatures capable of forming beliefs always happen to have a conceptual content.[76] It instead claims that it is part of the sense of the concept of a sensory experience, as it applies to creatures capable of forming empirical beliefs that are responsive to reasons, to describe the act of a rational capacity for knowledge.[77]

---

[76] Hence, the capacity account of knowledge does not rest on the thought that we must distinguish two forms of sensory experiences that rational creatures enjoy—namely, conceptual impressions and nonconceptual impressions, where the latter are understood to be more fundamental than the former. That is the position made prominent by Dretske in *Seeing and Knowing*. It has also been advocated by Künne, "Sehen: Eine sprachanalytische Betrachtung."

[77] Marcus Willaschek, who likewise argues that human sensory experience has conceptual content, bases his position on the negative point that we do not need to assume any nonconceptual sense experiences in order to explain the possibility of perceptual knowledge. He leaves it open whether he thinks that conceptual content belongs to the nature of human sense experience. See Willaschek, *Der mentale Zugang zur Welt*,

Consequently, the very meaning of the claim that some creature has a sensory experience is dependent upon whether or not that creature is capable of forming beliefs in the relevant sense. If the creature can form beliefs in the relevant sense, then we are dealing with an employment of the concept of a sensory experience, the role of which is to describe acts that fall under a rational capacity for perceptual knowledge and, hence, to describe something that a subject can recognize as a ground for belief.

This makes it appear that the capacity account of knowledge must fall prey to a common phenomenological objection. For it seems unable to account for the fact that our sensory experience "makes" differentiations that are far more fine-grained than those we can make using available empirical concepts.[78] In the case of colors, the objection runs, it is manifest that we can sensibly distinguish far more colors than we can express through our repertoire of color concepts. The fineness of grain of these color differentiations, which our sensory experiences enable us to make, cannot be captured by our color concepts. Rather, our color concepts must constantly abstract from this fineness of grain manifested in sensory experience. If we do not wish to deny the obvious richness of detail exhibited by sensory experience, the objection goes, then we must either understand the content of sensory experience to be wholly nonconceptual,[79] or at least acknowledge that it contains nonconceptual elements.[80] Because the capacity account of knowledge disputes precisely these points—insofar as it claims that

266–271. One of the strengths of the capacity account of knowledge is that it enables us to understand that, and why, it is an intrinsic feature of sensory experiences of rational creatures to have conceptual content.

[78] For versions of this objection, see *inter alia* Evans, *The Varieties of Reference,* 229; Schildknecht, "Anschauungen ohne Begriffe?," 467.

[79] This is Evans's thesis in *The Varieties of Reference,* 229. Concepts, for Evans, are necessary only for our cognitive access to the content of our sense experiences; they are not a necessary part of the very content of such experiences.

[80] For a representative example of this position, see Christopher Peacocke, *A Study of Concepts* and "Nonconceptual Content Defended." The view that the content of sensory experience is essentially nonconceptual has been further developed by a variety of contemporary authors, including Crane, "The Nonconceptual Content of Experience"; and Martin, "Perception, Concepts, and Memory."

creatures capable of judgment enjoy sensory experiences whose content is defined by its possibility to serve as the content of judgments—the capacity account of knowledge cannot be correct. So the objection goes.

The capacity account of knowledge would be unacceptable if it were incapable of accounting for this phenomenological observation about the fineness of grain of sensory experience. But it is not actually a problem for the capacity conception that our sense experience of colors and other phenomena is finely grained in a sense that our repertoire of color concepts is not. In order to account for the fact that, in viewing a particular rose, say, we enjoy a sensory experience of a red hue the particularity of which we cannot fully capture through any of the color concepts available to us, we do not have to fall back on the idea that our sense experience of the rose has a nonconceptual content. As John Mc-Dowell, among others, has argued, we can easily do justice to the fine-grained character of our sensory experience of colors if we disentangle the idea that our sensory experience of color has conceptual content from the idea that "we must have ready, in advance of the course our colour experience actually takes, as many colour concepts as there are shades of colour that we can sensibly discriminate."[81]

To do to justice to the fine-grained character of our sensory experience of color, we need only equip the subject with the concept "shade of color," which then enables her to have as many color concepts as there are shades of color that she can sensibly discriminate. For then she need only accompany this concept "shade of color" with a demonstrative to coin a demonstrative color concept. Demonstrative concepts are concepts in which one connects a predicate with a demonstrative expression. Their content is thus intrinsically determined by the constitution of the object to which we use them to refer in concrete situations (in phrases such as "this red hue").[82] Hence, they have a content only insofar as there is an object that determines the content of the predicate. And because their content is intrinsically determined by the constitution of the objects to which we use them to refer, they are concepts that

---

[81] McDowell, *Mind and World,* 58.
[82] See ibid., 56–58.

one can understand in the first place only if one actually perceives the object to which we are referring by means of the concept in question.

The very possibility of such concepts shows that there is no reason to think that the content of our sensory experience must be different, in principle, from the sort of content our judgments have. In order to understand the fineness of grain of sense experience, we do not need to ascribe it some nonconceptual content; we need only understand its conceptual content to be demonstrative.

The fact that this phenomenological objection can be answered so easily indicates, to my mind, that it does not capture the actual motivation driving the authors who insist that the sensory experience of creatures capable of judgment must have a nonconceptual content. For nearly all these authors (Gareth Evans is, as far as I can tell, the only exception), the phenomenological object has its roots in a deeper methodological objection. The objection contends that one cannot give a non-circular explanation of how we can even have empirical concepts if one denies nonconceptual content to the sense experiences that are supposed to explain the empirical contents of our judgments. The challenge is to explain our possession of concepts whose content is dependent on sensory experience. And the objection holds that a conceptualist cannot do this. For in characterizing the content of sensory experience, upon which such concepts depend, conceptualists must appeal to precisely the sort of concepts whose possibility they were supposed to be explaining.[83]

A certain kind of circularity is indeed a feature of the capacity conception of knowledge. For the capacity conception of perceptual knowledge explains how it is possible for someone to make a judgment with a particular empirical content by appealing to a sensory experience, the content of which is partly determined by precisely those concepts that make up the content of that judgment. Now imagine we were to demand that an explanation of the empirical content of a judgment must trace that judgment back to sensory experiences that have a nonconceptual content. This would mean insisting that the only sort of

---

[83] For a version of this point, see Peacocke, *A Study of Concepts,* 9; see also Schildknecht, "Anschauungen ohne Begriffe?," 468.

explanation of these judgments that would be legitimate would be one that the subject making the judgment could not, as a matter of principle, herself be in a position to actually give. It would be to demand an explanation that involves an empirical, perhaps neurophysiological, investigation. It would be to claim that the ground that "really" explains how it is possible for a subject to form an empirical judgment—e.g., the judgment that this rose here is red—is one that is, in principle, different from the sort that the subject is in a position to adduce for her claim. For any ground the subject can herself adduce must have a conceptual content—e.g., that she sees that this rose is red. But this ground, the objection maintains, cannot be what "really" explains why the subject makes the judgment she does.[84]

If one claims that we need that sort of explanation of how it is possible for a subject to make a judgment with empirical content, then one is thereby denying that the concept of a sensory experience and the concept of an empirical judgment each describe acts of one and the same rational capacity for knowledge and, hence, denying that they describe acts that are logically interdependent. But to deny this is nothing other than to deny that perceptual knowledge is an act of a rational capacity. It isn't just that the sort of explanation demanded here is one that we don't yet know we will ever be able to provide. Rather, the demand for such an explanation expresses a misunderstanding of what perceptual knowledge is. If the fundamental meaning of the concept of a sensory experience—as it applies to creatures capable of judgment—is to describe an act that actualizes a rational capacity for perceptual knowledge, then it follows that a sensory experience is something that provides an explanation for a judgment that the judging subject herself, just in virtue of enjoying such an experience, can give. A subject who explains her judgment by adducing a perception as her ground for so judging is not thereby providing something that is available to her independently of her making the judgment. She is instead specifying the capacity from which her judgment springs: she is portraying her judgment as a manifestation of her rational capacity for perceptual

---

[84] For a critique of this non-circularity requirement, see also McDowell, *Mind and World,* 166–167.

knowledge. The point of adducing her perception as a ground for her judgment is to present her judgment as an act that is as it is supposed to be in light of the rational capacity for perceptual knowledge she is exercising—and that thereby, by being presented in that way, exercises the capacity for perceptual knowledge in just the perfect manner it is presented to exercise.

## 3. Knowledge as Self-Conscious Act

According to our fundamental account of knowledge, someone who knows something has a belief that is a perfect exercise of her rational capacity for knowledge. To have a belief that is a perfect exercise of one's rational capacity for knowledge is to believe something on the basis of a truth-guaranteeing ground. We can understand the possibility of a subject believing something on the basis of a truth-guaranteeing ground, we argued, if we understand beliefs, as well as the grounds on which they are based, to be actualizations of a rational capacity for knowledge. This does not imply that every ground a subject has for believing something guarantees the truth of what she believes. But it does mean that the fundamental case of a ground is one that guarantees the truth of what it grounds.

It further means that the fundamental case of a ground is one that the subject recognizes as a truth-guaranteeing ground of her belief. That she recognizes her truth-guaranteeing ground means, in the case of perceptual knowledge, that she recognizes her sensory experience as a perfect manifestation of her capacity for perceptual knowledge and, in so doing, perfectly exercises the very capacity whose perfect manifestation she recognizes. Thus, as we made clear above, the recognition of a truth-guaranteeing ground as a truth-guaranteeing ground is not to be understood as an act that is logically prior to the corresponding belief. Rather, it is *one and the same act*. For one cannot recognize something as a truth-guaranteeing ground for a particular belief without thereby forming the corresponding belief, and forming it on this ground. The fact that a subject forms her belief that p in this manner—namely, in responding to a truth-guaranteeing ground whose recognition she manifests in that response—thus means that she knows that p in such a way that she is aware of her ground for knowing that p. If knowledge is an act of a rational capacity for knowledge, then knowing that p and knowing that one has a ground for knowing that p are not two distinct acts. They are two aspects of one and the same act of a self-conscious capacity for knowledge—namely, two aspects of an act in which one exercises this capacity perfectly.

Let's return once more to one of our examples. Let's imagine someone who knows that there is apple juice in the fridge on the basis of her perception that there is apple juice in the fridge. She has a truth-guaranteeing ground to believe that there is apple juice in the fridge. That she perceives that there is apple juice in the fridge means that she performs an act that manifests her capacity for perceptual knowledge. Because this capacity is a self-conscious capacity, this means that her ground is efficacious in her belief that there is apple juice in the fridge in virtue of the fact that she is conscious of it *as* a ground for that belief. Yet being conscious of one's perception as a truth-guaranteeing ground entails that one believes what one thus has a ground to believe. In being conscious that I perceive that there is still apple juice in the fridge, I believe that there is apple juice in the fridge.

It follows from this that, on the capacity account of knowledge, whether or not I have a truth-guaranteeing ground for knowledge and whether or not I have a true belief are not two separate questions. They are two aspects of one and the same question. If a ground for knowledge is an act of a rational capacity for knowledge, then grounds for knowledge are something that one cannot possess independently of the truth of the belief they ground. We might express this by saying that consciousness of a truth-guaranteeing ground as a truth-guaranteeing ground is not an act that is prior to the exercise of the relevant rational capacity for knowledge. Nor is it an act that springs from a different capacity as the truth-guaranteeing ground from which it springs. Rather, it is an act in which one actualizes the capacity that is the source of one's truth-guaranteeing ground (e.g., of one's perception) in the specific manner that is distinctive of rational capacities: namely, self-consciously. Moreover, one actualizes one's capacity not only self-consciously but in such a way that its self-conscious exercise is an act of knowledge.

We already made the general point above that the grounded character of acts—i.e., the fact that we perform certain acts on grounds or
for reasons—is not a property of those acts that stems from a capacity
distinct from the capacity from which those acts themselves arise.
Their grounded character instead reflects the specific manner in which
rational capacities are actualized: namely, in such a way that their subjects are conscious of their acts as manifestations of the relevant capacities. If knowledge is an act of a rational capacity for knowledge, it
therefore follows that recognizing a perception as a ground for a particular belief is not to be understood as an act that springs from a capacity
distinct from the one from which the perception itself springs. It is instead a specific manner of actualizing the very capacity that is the
source of perception that is paradigmatic of that capacity *qua* rational
capacity.

## 4. Knowledge and Non-Accidentality

The thought that someone who knows something holds a belief that she
formed by exercising a rational capacity for knowledge is connected
with the idea that knowledge is non-accidental in two ways. First, a
belief that is formed in this way is non-accidentally true. Second, it
is no accident that a belief thus formed is non-accidentally in accord
with the concept of knowledge—namely, true and sufficiently justified.
While the first point is one that, as we have seen, cannot be sustained
within the framework of contemporary epistemology, the second point
cannot so much as come into view within that framework. The central
point of our account of knowledge consists in showing the unity of both
aspects.

Let us consider the non-accidental truth of beliefs a bit more closely.
If someone has a belief, which she arrived at by perfectly exercising her
rational capacity for knowledge, this entails that she based her belief
on a ground that could not have led her to form that belief unless things
were the way her belief represented them as being. For if things had
been otherwise, then she would not have been able to actualize her rational capacity for knowledge in the manner that provides her with a

truth-guaranteeing ground for believing what she believes—e.g., with a perception of the relevant fact. A belief that rests on such a ground is non-accidentally true precisely because it is formed on the basis of such a ground.

It is helpful to contrast this understanding of non-accidental truth with one formulated by Strawson. According to Strawson, what explains why a belief based on a perception is non-accidentally true is the causality of the perception—i.e., the fact that a perception is a mental act that is caused by the fact that makes up its conceptual content.[85] It is this causality of perception, on Strawson's account, that explains why it is no accident that beliefs based on perceptions are true. John Hyman has argued, however, that this cannot be right.[86] His argument appeals to the familiar example that Alvin Goldman posed as a problem for any causal analysis of perception. Imagine that Henry arrives in a village that is scattered with facades of barns that are so realistic that they are indistinguishable from real barns to the naked eye. But suppose there is a single genuine barn in the area. And suppose that Henry happens to be standing directly before it. The visual impression of a barn that he thereby enjoys results, in this case, from the fact that there is, in fact, a barn before him. Nevertheless, Goldman rightly concludes, we would not want to say that Henry knows that it is a barn, because it is a sheer accident that the belief he holds is true.[87]

Now Hyman argues that such examples demonstrate that the causality of perception cannot be what explains why perceptual beliefs are non-accidentally true. But the example does not in fact show this. What the example shows is that the causality of perception cannot explain the non-accidental truth of such beliefs if we understand this causality in the way Strawson, Hyman, and Goldman do: namely, as a kind of causality that one can make sense of without reference to a rational

---

[85] Strawson, "Causation in Perception," 71.

[86] See Hyman, "The Evidence of our Senses," 250. Hyman mistakenly concludes from this objection (just as we have seen Snowdon do, above) that causality is not an essential element of perception. The proper conclusion is rather that this sort of causality is irreducibly normative.

[87] See Goldman, "Discrimination and Perceptual Knowledge."

capacity for perceptual knowledge.[88] On the capacity account of perceptual knowledge, however, such an explanation is impossible. For it conceives of the causality of perception as something one cannot describe without describing the perception as a manifestation of a rational capacity for perceptual knowledge, whose paradigmatic exercise consists in an act that the subject herself, just by enjoying it, recognizes as a paradigmatic manifestation of her capacity for perceptual knowledge. This means that one can be a perceiver, in this sense, only if one can, simply by enjoying a sensory experience, recognize it as a paradigmatic manifestation of one's capacity for perceptual knowledge.

But this is precisely impossible in the village of barn facades—even if the subject is standing in front of the lone real barn. In the village of barn facades, it is, as a matter of principle, impossible for a subject that stands in front of what happens to be the only genuine barn in the area to recognize her sensory experience of a barn as a paradigmatic manifestation of her capacity to gain perceptual knowledge. For, to be recognizable as a paradigmatic manifestation of such a capacity, one's sensory experience of a barn would have to be a manifestation of something which must not be, as matter of principle, providing a ground for perceptual knowledge on indefinitely many occasions. However, this is precisely what is ruled out in the barn facades case. For in the village of barn facades, it isn't simply that there are many facades around. Rather, the village is specifically constructed so that there is only one genuine barn. To that extent, in this village it is *ruled out in advance*, as a matter of principle, that a sensory experience of a barn can be a manifestation of a capacity for perceptual knowledge, because it is ruled out in advance that it manifests something that can provide a ground for perceptual knowledge on indefinitely many occasions. For a sensory experience of a barn to be a case of perceiving that there is a barn, and hence for it to be something that is recognizable as a paradigmatic exercise of a capacity for perceptual knowledge, it must not be ruled out in advance that the subject might perform such an act on indefinitely many occasions. Because this is precisely what is ruled out in the barn-

[88] Hence, Hyman's objection is valid against Strawson; but it is only conditionally correct.

facades case, the subject's sensory experience of a barn cannot be (described as) a case of perception, and *a fortiori*, it cannot be a case of perceptual knowledge.

We said above that the idea that knowledge is the actualization of a rational capacity for knowledge is connected with the idea that knowledge is non-accidental in two ways. This second connection has to do with the fact that a subject who knows something holds a belief that is non-accidentally in accordance with the concept of knowledge—namely, a belief that is both non-accidentally true and also non-accidentally sufficiently justified. This stems from the fact that a rational capacity has a specific mode of actualization—namely, a self-conscious actualization. This means that the acts that are explained through the relevant capacity are such that their very occurrence is dependent on the subject's consciousness of the efficacy of her capacity in the very act that she performs. The acts that spring from this capacity—and that are explained by it—cannot, therefore, occur at all unless the subject is conscious of the capacity as efficacious in her acts. To exercise a capacity whose acts contain a consciousness of themselves as actualizations of that capacity is thus to perform acts whose occurrence, as such, implies that the subject performing them can justify her act by presenting it as being (or approximately being) as it ought to be in light of the capacity in question. For by justifying her act in this way—i.e., by presenting it as an act that manifests the relevant capacity—the subject just renders explicit the self-conscious manner in which the act was performed.

It is thus no accident that acts stemming from such a capacity are such that the subject herself can justify them by pointing to the capacity in question. For the subject is in a position to do this precisely *in virtue of* possessing the capacity that such acts manifest. Accordingly, a paradigmatic actualization of a rational capacity for knowledge involves a belief that is not only non-accidentally true but also non-accidentally justified.

# VIII

# Rational Capacities and Circumstances

## 1. The Asymmetry of Knowledge and Error

Our result thus far is that the concept of knowledge, as it applies to creatures capable of forming beliefs, has its fundamental sense in the fact that it describes a rational capacity. "'Know'," as Ryle puts it, "is a capacity verb, and a capacity verb of that special sort that is used for signifying that the person described can bring things off, or get things right."[89] Or, as he also puts it, "to know is to be equipped to get something right [...]."[90] Thus, in a certain sense, it is correct to describe a knowing subject as having "achieved" something.[91] But the idea that knowledge involves "success" and is hence an "achievement" does not mean that acquiring knowledge is strenuous or requires special effort. It means that the acquisition of knowledge consists in the exercise of a capacity at which it is, in principle, possible for the subject to fail. Ryle expresses this point by saying that it is an "important fact" that when someone can spell or calculate, "it must also be possible for him

---

[89] Ryle, *The Concept of Mind*, 133.
[90] Ibid., 134.
[91] Compare ibid., 130, 149–150.

---

Is this similar to the 'at eat us' or 'avian' model or the knowing possibility if knowledge simultaneously not know?

to misspell and miscalculate."[92] We might reformulate this thought by saying that it is an "important fact" that the claim "she can calculate" is connected with the claim "she can miscalculate" and that the claim "she can spell" is linked to the claim "she can misspell." In precisely the same manner, the claim "she is capable of knowledge" is inextricably linked with the claim "she is liable to err." In seeking greater clarity about this "important fact," our next task is to inquire how exactly these claims are connected.

On the strength of what we have worked out thus far, we can already see that the second claim can be true only if the first is. Only someone who can calculate can miscalculate. Yet these two claims do not stand on the same level. One depends on the other. It follows that the sense of 'can' must be different in each claim. While the 'can' in "she can calculate" is the 'can' of a capacity, the 'can' in "she can miscalculate" is, as Ryle puts it, not a capacity but a "liability."[93] It is a liability that afflicts everyone who possesses the corresponding capacity.

Let's now bring this insight to bear on the skeptic's position. The skeptic is unsettled by the thought that the claim "she is liable to err" is dependent on the claim "she is capable of knowing something." For this dependence means that the claim "she is liable to err," which constitutes the central premise of the skeptic's argument, itself depends on a claim that negates the skeptic's conclusion. Wittgenstein occasionally undertakes to refute the skeptic's argument by pointing to just this relation of dependence.[94] It is not wrong to undermine the skeptic's argumentation in this manner. But it is philosophically ineffective. It is ineffective because this insight into the logical dependence relation has clearly already been distorted for someone who would deny it. So the

---

[92] Ibid., 130.

[93] Ibid., 131.

[94] See, for example, the following passage, in which Wittgenstein suggestively compares the problem of knowledge with the problem of calculating a sum: "This surely means: the possibility of a *mistake* can be eliminated in certain (numerous) cases.—And one does eliminate mistakes in calculation in this way. For when a calculation has been checked over and over again one cannot then say 'Its rightness is still only *very probable*—for an error may always still have slipped in.' For suppose it did seem for once as if an error had been discovered—why shouldn't we suspect an error *here?*" (*On Certainty,* §650).

import of this formulation of the dependence relation can only be to serve as an indication of a deeper insight that we have yet to develop. For the skeptic is precisely concerned to deny that the proposition "she is liable to err" actually is dependent on the proposition "she is capable of knowing something."

So let us ask ourselves how it is possible to believe that one could deny such dependence. In order to believe that such dependence is dubitable, one must believe that the 'can' in the proposition "she can err" is not to be understood as a liability afflicting those who possess a rational capacity to acquire knowledge about how things are. One must instead understand it as a logical possibility that pertains to those who possess an apparently more fundamental capacity—"more fundamental" in the sense that one need not employ the concept of knowledge in describing it. Let us call this apparently "more fundamental" capacity the capacity to form beliefs. We can accordingly understand the skeptical position—and, with it, all epistemological positions of moderation—as denying that the concept of knowledge is a concept of a genuine capacity and as instead maintaining that knowledge should be understood in terms of a capacity whose acts do not, as such, fall under the norm of knowledge. The skeptic then seeks to understand how a subject who possesses this apparently more fundamental capacity can enjoy knowledge. We can then formulate the skeptic's conclusion as the insight that it is unintelligible how such a basis could enable a subject to attain knowledge. The skeptic then draws a negative conclusion from this—namely, that knowledge is unintelligible.

What we have come to see, by contrast, is that knowledge cannot be reconstructed out of some more fundamental capacity. Rather, the concept of knowledge describes itself as a fundamental capacity. This has weighty consequences for the significance of the possibility of error. For on the capacity account of knowledge, it is likewise the case that the claim "she can err" describes a logical possibility. Yet we have to conceive of it as a possibility that can obtain only for someone who possesses the capacity to know something. And that means that this possibility has the status of a liability: a liability to perform acts that are not as they ought to be, according to the capacity that is constitutive of the identity of these acts. In saying that the possibility of error has the status of a liability, what we are saying is that cases of error stand in an *asymmetrical* relation to cases of knowledge.

Let us get clearer about the character of this asymmetry between knowledge and error. When we claim that there is an asymmetry between knowledge and error, we are not making a claim about their relative statistical frequency. We are not saying that knowledge occurs more often than error. The asymmetry is *logical*. It consists in the fact that the description of a case of error is possible only with reference to the concept of knowledge—namely, as a case in which something is lacking or one that negates what takes place when knowledge is present. The fact that someone errs means that she holds a belief that is deprived of knowledge. Yet the converse does not hold. In the case of rational capacities, this logical asymmetry is, as we have seen, connected with an *explanatory* asymmetry. Knowledge represents the case that is explained through the capacity, that is, without any further reference to particular circumstances that are contingent with respect to the capacity in question. By contrast, the privative case of a capacity is one that is not like the sort of case that is explained through the capacity but one that can only be explained by reference to particular circumstances, the role of which is correlatively to explain why the actualization of the capacity was hindered in the present case. When Sebastian is drunk and believes he sees a pink elephant, or when he stands in the glaring desert sun and believes he sees an oasis, he finds himself in circumstances that might hinder—and in these cases really do hinder—the actualization of his capacity for perceptual knowledge. And because in rational capacities this logical asymmetry between the positive and negative cases is connected with a normative asymmetry, we can accordingly describe the relation between knowledge and error in the following way. Someone who knows something thereby performs an act that realizes precisely the norm that is constitutive of that act's identity. Someone who errs thereby fails—as a result of particular circumstances—to realize the norm that is constitutive of her act.

The skeptic, by contrast, thinks that the 'can' in the proposition "she can err" does not have the status of a liability. The skeptic instead thinks it describes one of two possibilities, which stand in a symmetrical relation to one another. In precisely the same sense that one can err, one can likewise come to form a true belief. In keeping with this line of thought, the 'can' in the proposition "she can know something" has the same meaning as the 'can' in the proposition "she can err." On this view, error and knowledge are alike in the sense that neither is explained just by reference to the capacity that is supposed to make it intelligible how a subject can have beliefs at all. For the capacity that the skeptic introduces in order to make it intelligible how a subject can so much as hold beliefs does not, as such, provide either an explanation of cases of error or an explanation of cases of knowledge. In both cases—cases of error as well as cases of knowledge—we must have recourse to something external to the capacity in question, some additional element. Or so the thought goes. We must, in particular, appeal to how things are. If things are as I believe them to be, then I have knowledge. If not, then I don't.

Our transcendental considerations in Part Two, by contrast, have shown that one cannot detach the concept of belief from the concept of knowledge. The concept of knowledge, we therefore concluded, must itself be a fundamental concept. This insight led us to the thought that the concept of knowledge belongs to the category of concepts for rational capacities.

## 2. Favorable and Unfavorable Circumstances

The previous section makes it clear what status error must have if the concept of knowledge is the concept of a rational capacity. Error represents a case in which there is a failure in the exercise of one's capacity for knowledge. Error accordingly cannot be explained merely through the relevant capacity that is constitutive of the acts in question. Rather, its explanation must appeal to particular and contingent circumstances that explain why someone who possesses the relevant capacity to know something has failed to perfectly exercise that capacity. In what follows, we will call circumstances that explain the failure or defective exercise of a capacity "unfavorable circumstances." Conversely (and trivially), this means that someone who perfectly exercises a particular capacity finds herself in circumstances that are favorable for the exercise of that capacity. Accordingly, it is possible for someone to perfectly exercise a particular rational capacity only if the prevailing circumstances are favorable for the exercise of that capacity. To exercise a rational capacity—e.g., the capacity to gain perceptual knowledge of how things are—is consequently to execute an act whose performance is dependent on the presence of favorable circumstances—e.g., that it is not dark or foggy, or that she is not drunk or dog tired.

In what follows, we want to understand this dependence upon favorable circumstances, which is characteristic of the sorts of acts we are interested in here. We will thereby gain a deeper understanding of the insight we brought into view in the previous section, according to which knowledge and error stand in an asymmetrical relationship to one another. There are essentially two ways to understand this dependence on favorable circumstances. On one reading, this dependence is a feature of the acts in question that is superadded to their dependence on the capacity. According to this account, the prevailing circumstances are understood as explanatory factors that, together with other factors, serve to explain these acts. On another reading, the dependence on favorable circumstances is a formal feature of the capacities we are concerned with. It is an aspect of their explanatory character. We might also express this by saying that it is a formal feature of the capacities we are concerned with that they are fallible. I will argue that the first reading rests on a widespread misunderstanding of the explanatory character of capacities. The possibility of error, as we will see in section 3, below, is grounded in nothing other than the fact that someone who knows something exercises a fallible capacity. Error is accordingly a possibility that is intrinsically connected with the concept of knowledge because it is the concept of a fallible rational capacity.

In order to get clear about the relation between a rational capacity for perceptual knowledge and the circumstances of its actualization, let's first take a look at the relation between simple dispositions and the circumstances of their actualization—e.g., the disposition of sugar to dissolve in water, or the disposition of wood to catch fire. For whatever it is that distinguishes a rational capacity from a disposition, a rational capacity is, as we have seen, like a disposition in that both are something general that can be actualized, in principle, in indefinitely many states or actions. When we make dispositional claims—such as the claim that sugar is soluble in water—we are not describing a particular state that obtains in a concrete piece of sugar *hic et nunc*. We are instead making a timeless and general claim about sugar. Ryle characterizes such claims as assertions about how sugar behaves under particular conditions.[95] Ryle writes:

> A statement ascribing a dispositional property to a thing has much, though not everything, in common with a statement subsuming the thing under a law. To possess a dispositional property is not to be in a particular state, or to undergo a particular change; it is to be bound or liable to be in a particular state, or to undergo a particular change, when a particular condition is realized.[96]

Ryle's general thought here is that dispositional statements are to be analyzed in terms of a particular form of conditional proposition. For example, the claim "matches are combustible" may receive an analysis of the form, "if one scratches a match, then it lights." Nelson Goodman, however, has objected that such an analysis is not possible.[97] His argument runs as follows. If one claims that such dispositional statements can be analyzed into conditionals of this form, then one is claiming that the proposition "'That match lights' can be inferred from [the proposition] 'That match is scratched'."[98] Goodman's insight is that no such inference is possible. The truth of the proposition "this match lights"

---

[95] See Ryle, *The Concept of Mind,* 43.

[96] Ibid.

[97] See Goodman's classic article "The Problem of Counterfactual Conditionals," as well as his "The Passing of the Possible."

[98] See Goodman, "The Problem of Counterfactual Conditionals," 7–8. At this point I set aside the question whether it is correct to take one's orientation from the counterfactual formulation of this conditional or whether it makes more sense to take a non-material condition as one's lodestar—a conditional that would then, depending on the particular case, take either the indicative, or the potential conjunctive, or the *irrealis* conjunctive mood. Such subtleties are not relevant to our present considerations. On this point, see also Wolf, *Möglichkeit und Notwendigkeit bei Aristoteles und heute,* 305; Mackie, *Truth, Probability, and Paradox,* 125; and Ayers, *The Refutation of Determinism,* 72.

cannot be inferred from the proposition "this match is scratched," because there are conditions under which the latter is true but the former is false—for example, when the match is wet, or when no oxygen is present. But what does this mean? On Goodman's interpretation of the point, there is a difference in meaning between the conditional "if one scratches a match, then it lights" and the dispositional statement "matches are combustible." According to Goodman, whereas the conditional is falsified by the fact that there are cases in which a match is scratched but does not light—e.g., when it is wet—the dispositional statement need not be falsified by such cases.

Goodman concludes from this that conditional propositions describing dispositions could amount to a complete analysis of the disposition only if they contained in their antecedents a complete description of all the conditions that have to be met for the disposition to be actualized. Thus, in the case of the combustible matches we would have to include further conditions such as "if the match is dry," "if sufficient oxygen is present," etc. Hence, if we want to give an analysis of dispositional claims in terms of conditional propositions, these conditionals will have to be "abnormally weak," as Goodman puts it.[99] For our conditional will take the form: "if matches are scratched and all conditions are favorable, they light."[100] But if one realizes that the idea of favorable circumstances is identical to the idea of circumstances under which the disposition is actualized, one would have to say that these conditionals will be not only weak but empty. That is, they would not explain anything at all.

Why, then, does Goodman think that conditionals describing dispositions must always include a clause such as "if all conditions are favorable"? This characterization presupposes that the conditional, which describes the disposition, has the role of enabling us to infer the happening that actualizes the disposition. Yet this interpretation of the situation, which Goodman uncritically accepts, is by no means self-evident. Before we ask whether this interpretation can be correct, we should first consider one of its consequences. If one holds that the relation

---

[99] Goodman, "The Passing of the Possible," 39.
[100] Compare Goodman's example in ibid., 39–40.

between a certain disposition that is described in a conditional and the happening that actualizes it is a relation of inference, then it follows that one has a complete description of the disposition only if the antecedent of the conditional subsumes all the circumstances that, taken together, enable one to derive the relevant happening in a given situation. And in describing these circumstances and conditions, one is accordingly making a *contentful* claim about the disposition. The more of these conditions we can identify and enumerate, the more complete is our description of the disposition. A complete description of the disposition would thus require us to have a complete list of all those circumstances, whose presence enables us, in a given situation, to infer that the relevant happening obtains.

There is, however, another way of interpreting the fact that there are cases where the antecedent of a conditional that describes a disposition is fulfilled and yet the described disposition is not actualized. This fact might be read as an indication that it is wrong to think that the point of such a conditional is to specify the premises of an inference that enables us to derive the happening that actualizes the disposition in question. It might be an indication that the point of these conditionals is to mark out an irreducible form of explanation. Let us ask, therefore: What precondition must one accept in construing such conditionals as describing premises of an inference in which the actualization of the disposition is derived? To understand such conditionals in this manner, one has to believe it is possible to identify and characterize the circumstances that are favorable and unfavorable for the actualization of a certain disposition, without thereby representing any happening as an actualization of that disposition. Otherwise one would have to already make use of precisely the form of explanation that one is trying to avoid in such an account—viz., an explanation that appeals to the disposition itself, as it is exhibited, for example, when to the question "Why does this match light?" one responds something like "Because matches are combustible." In analyzing dispositions in terms of a conditional whose point is to specify the premises of an inference, one is seeking to avoid an account of dispositions according to which they constitute a form of explanation, in which one explains what happens when a disposition is actualized through the disposition itself. In what follows, I will argue

that it is, in fact, impossible to give such an independent characterization of the circumstances that are favorable and unfavorable for a
disposition.

Goodman and others want to say that a match we mean to strike
must not be wet; that the sugar we drop into water must not be wrapped
in aluminum foil and that the water not be saturated with sugar. Yet
what enables us to describe a case in which we scratch the match and
it does not light by saying that the specific reason it did not light was
that the prevailing circumstances were unfavorable for the actualization of the disposition? What enables us to give this sort of explanation
is the fact that we compare the present case to a case that actualizes the
disposition—a case in which, *per definitionem,* all the circumstances are
favorable for the actualization of the disposition. And we make this
comparison in order to then be able to recognize, in light of that "positive case," which circumstances have been "removed" or "denied" in the
case where the disposition does not fire. For it is only by making reference to such a "positive case" that we can describe a given situation as
one in which a particular disposition is present even as we maintain
that it is not actualized because the circumstances are unfavorable for
its actualization.

Suppose that we had, as yet, no understanding of the matches' disposition to light when struck. Now imagine that we scratch a match and it
does not light. If we do not bring anything further into play apart from
what we actually observe in this situation—namely, that the match was
scratched and did not light—it is impossible to describe this as a case of
the non-actualization of a disposition that the matches nonetheless
possess. Without making reference to a case in which the disposition
really is actualized, we do not have the slightest reason to judge that
the match has a disposition to light when struck. But if that is so, then
the very idea of a disposition already entails the idea of so-called favorable and unfavorable conditions for its actualization. In the absence of
the idea of a "positive case" in which the disposition is actualized, it is
simply impossible to even frame the concept of favorable and unfavorable conditions.

It follows from this that one cannot understand the description of a
disposition as the description of something that provides the premises

for an inference that enables one to derive its actualization. For in order to understand the conditional that purports to describe the disposition along these lines—an understanding of which Goodman provides an exemplary case—one must already appeal to a case that undermines precisely this understanding of a disposition. One must appeal to an event that is explained through the disposition itself.[101] The upshot of this insight is that we must conceive of a disposition as something that stands in an explanatory relation to the cases that fall under it—a relation that is non-inferential. We must conceive of a disposition as something that, as such, explains, in a certain sense, the events in which it is actualized. If that is so, then the proviso "if circumstances are favorable," which is involved in the description of a disposition, cannot have the sense Goodman assumes. Its sense cannot be to describe a further premise for an inference. Its sense rather must consist in making explicit a *formal* feature of the kind of explanation a disposition provides: namely, that its explanation is circumstance-dependent.

This is a good place to recall what Aristotle says in his analysis of *dynamis:* "To add the qualification 'if nothing external prevents it' is not further necessary." For a match, say, "has the potentiality in so far as this is a potentiality of acting, and it is this not in all circumstances but on certain conditions, among which will be the exclusion of external hindrances."[102] What Aristotle is saying here is that these supplementary provisos—e.g., that matches light only when no unfavorable circumstances obtain—are not "necessary" because they are already implied in the very idea of the *dynamis* in question.[103] Reference to a particular disposition's dependence on circumstances does not embody a contentful claim about the disposition. It does not describe a further explanatory factor, over and above the disposition, that has to be incorporated into the explanation of the relevant act.

---

[101] This is also the upshot of C. B. Martin's argument against any reductive analysis of dispositions in terms of conditionals. See his "Dispositions and Conditionals," 6.

[102] Aristotle, *Metaphysics,* IX.5, 1048a.

[103] For this exposition of Aristotle's position, see also Burnyeat, *Notes on Eta and Theta of Aristotle's Metaphysics,* 130; Jansen, *Tun und Können: Ein systematischer Kommentar zu Aristoteles' Theorie der Vermögen im neunten Buch der "Metaphysik,"* 182; as well as Moline, "Provided Nothing External Interferes," esp. 249, 253.

Now if this is correct—if the description of a disposition is to be understood as the description of a circumstance-dependent form of explanation—then any list of favorable circumstances, which we purportedly require in order to complete our description of the disposition in question, is not just uncompletable. Our argument rather shows that it is a misunderstanding to suppose we should even have to begin such a list in order to arrive at an understanding of the disposition.[104] For any list of circumstances we might generate already rests on precisely the sort of understanding of a positive case of the disposition that this list is supposed to provide: namely, an understanding of a case as something that is explained through the disposition in question.[105]

The point of these reflections on dispositions and the circumstances of their actualization is to get clear about the meaning of the supplementary phrase "if the circumstances are favorable." For this phrase is common to the description of rational capacities as well. What we have shown is that it involves a fundamental misunderstanding to think that such a supplement makes a contentful claim about the capacity in question. If we say, "Lisa can swim," this claim about Lisa already involves the thought that what explains Lisa's behavior when she manifests her capacity for swimming is something that, as such, is dependent on particular circumstances. If we toss Lisa into the water and she steps on a crocodile, we will not be surprised if she then proceeds to frantically struggle and thrash about in the water. We would not then be moved to claim that she cannot swim after all. We would rather say that she is struggling and thrashing about in the water because she stepped on a crocodile, which hindered her swimming. Thus, when we say that someone who is presently swimming is performing an act that is dependent on particular circumstances, we are not making a statement about her capacity to swim that goes beyond what is already

---

[104] Here I concur with Anscombe in "Causality and Determination," esp. 138.

[105] For an analogous critique of the empiricist's understanding of laws of nature, see Von Wright, "Laws of Nature," 142. Compare also the penetrating discussions of laws of nature in Rödl, *Categories of the Temporal,* chap. 6. A line of thought analogous to the one we have formulated above leads Rödl to the conclusion that the idea of an exceptionless law of nature is incoherent. The same holds *a fortiori* for all lawlike statements about living things, as Rödl argues in "Natur und Norm."

contained in the concept of her capacity to swim. Rather, we are making explicit a formal feature of this capacity—that swimming is an act of a capacity, whose perfect exercise can be hindered by unfavorable circumstances. We characterize such capacities as fallible in order to indicate precisely that feature: That the explanation that such a capacity provides is circumstance-dependent.

Our reflections reveal references to dispositions and capacities to be a *sui generis* form of explanation in that they provide a circumstance-dependent, non-inferential explanation for particular acts through something general. The customary interpretation of dispositions and capacities, by contrast, is based on the tacit assumption that the sort of explanation they deliver is merely an instantiation of the general explanatory schema according to which we explain the actuality of a particular event or act by inferring it from something general. So long as one thinks that the relation between swimming *qua* capacity and particular acts of swimming is one of inference,[106] one will not be able to appreciate that the dependence of actualizations of the disposition or capacity upon favorable circumstances expresses a formal feature of that case—that is, a feature that is expressive of the manner in which a certain capacity or disposition explains the case in which it is actualized. To conceive of capacities in this way is to conceive of Lisa's capacity to swim as something that, as such, can explain why Lisa behaves as she behaves in a given situation, e.g., why she is stretching her arms and legs. Or of Jim's capacity to ski as something that, as such, can explain why Jim behaves as he behaves in a given situation, e.g., why he is putting weight on the outer ski and then rapidly lifting his legs. Capacities and dispositions either explain what they explain in a genuine way or they do not explain anything at all—which would amount to denying that they exist.

---

[106] Even Sellars does not abandon this presupposition in his attempt to improve on Goodman's account. This is why Sellars, too, falls prey to objections like those posed by Von Wright. See Sellars, "Counterfactuals, Dispositions, and the Causal Modalities." Nor does Woolhouse recognize this premise as the actual source of the problem in his own attempt to improve on Sellars's modified account. See Woolhouse, "Counterfactuals, Dispositions, and Capacities."

## 3. Fallible Capacities and Knowledge

When we apply our above reflections on the capacity we are concerned with here, namely a rational capacity for perceptual knowledge, this allows us to understand the fallibility of perceptual knowledge in a specific way: namely, as a formal feature of the capacity for perceptual knowledge. To say that perceptual knowledge is fallible, according to this account, is to say that dependence on favorable circumstances is a formal feature of the kind of explanation that a capacity for perceptual knowledge provides. Thus, it is not simply that no amount of effort, training, or dedication will enable a subject to so perfect her capacity for perceptual knowledge that some day she will no longer have to rely on favorable circumstances in order to actualize it. Regardless of how much she practices, it is impossible, in principle, that she will eventually have a capacity for perceptual knowledge that is no longer susceptible to failure in its actualizations. To have such a capacity is not simply unattainable. If it is a formal feature of a rational capacity for perceptual knowledge to be fallible, it is logically impossible, despite any amount of tireless practice and perfectionistic effort. The best she can hope to achieve are exercises of her capacity that are *de facto* flawless.

It follows from this that someone who attains perceptual knowledge by exercising a fallible capacity cannot possibly eliminate her liability to err—yet not simply out of weakness or a failure to sufficiently perfect her capacity so that her judgments are, in principle, no longer liable to be false. For anyone who acquires knowledge by actualizing a fallible capacity, it is conceptually impossible to eliminate this liability to err. The best one can ever hope for is to go one's whole life without actually erring.

With this understanding of fallibility in hand, we can now see that the misunderstanding of the nature of knowledge, under which the skeptic's position labors, has its complement in a misunderstanding of the nature of the fallibility of knowledge. Once one realizes that the idea of a capacity is the idea of a *sui generis* form of explanation, then one can see that the fallibility characteristic of knowledge has its fundamental locus not in the description of an act but rather in the description of the capacity from which knowledge springs. At the fundamental level, what is fallible—i.e., liable to error—is the *capacity* to acquire knowledge and not the particular acts of knowing that spring from such a capacity.

The capacity account of knowledge allows us, therefore, to understand two things. First, we can understand what it means to say that it is a fundamental feature of human knowledge that it is liable to error. This means that human knowledge springs from a fallible capacity, which entails, as such, that it is possible for circumstances to arise in which the capacity cannot be perfectly exercised and in which no knowledge can be acquired. Second, we can understand that and why knowledge, when it is attained in a particular act, is something that excludes the possibility of error. For what we would have in such a case is an act that perfectly accords with the capacity from which it springs—a capacity that is nevertheless, for its part, fallible.

Let's now apply these considerations to our understanding of what it means for someone to have a sensory experience. We have seen that the concept of a sensory experience—as it applies to creatures capable of enjoying empirical beliefs—owes its fundamental sense to the role it has in the description of a rational capacity for knowledge. It is a consequence of the above considerations that it is part of the description of something that is intrinsically fallible. On the one hand, this means that a sensory experience that fails to be a case of perception is intelligible only because we understand what it is for a sensory experience to actually be a case of perception. The concept of a case in which one has a sensory experience that does not amount to a perception is logically derivative from the concept of a case in which one perceives something. On the other hand, this means that one can have a correct understanding of what it means to perceive something only if one simultaneously has the concept of a sensory experience that does not amount to a perception: i.e., the concept of the sort of sensory experience one has in unfavorable circumstances. That is to say, someone has the rational capacity to acquire knowledge through sensory experience in the full sense only if she understands, *inter alia,* that it is possible for there to be circumstances that are unfavorable for the exercise of that capacity. Someone who has a fallible rational capacity but (as yet) lacks knowledge of the possibility of circumstances unfavorable for its exercise has only partial knowledge of what it is to have and exercise the capacity in question. Yet, because a rational capacity is self-consciously possessed, this means that someone who lacks this kind of knowledge is not yet fully in possession of the capacity in question. To be fully in possession of a fallible rational capacity, one must have knowledge of it as liable to fail in particular exercises.

If perceptual knowledge is an act of a self-conscious, fallible capacity, then our consciousness of ourselves as fallible is not something that is superadded to our consciousness of ourselves as capable of perceptual knowledge. It is instead contained in every act of perceptual knowledge. To understand oneself as capable of perceptual knowledge is to form beliefs on the basis of grounds that actualize a fallible, self-conscious capacity for perceptual knowledge, that is, a capacity one knows to be liable to encounter circumstances in which it will not provide a ground for knowledge but, at worst, something that only seems to one to constitute a ground for knowledge.[107]

On this account of knowledge, a perception is not available as a ground for knowledge independently of the truth of the belief formed on its basis. This might raise the question why, on this account, enjoying a perception is not identical to having knowledge. In other words, why is it not the case that, on this account, for someone to perceive that things are thus and so is just for her to know that things are thus and so? When we say that perceiving is not identical to knowing, this entails that it is possible for someone to have a ground for belief that actually would guarantee the truth of her belief even though she does not form the belief for which she has this ground. Or equivalently, it is to say that

---

[107] In "Wissen vom 'Standpunkte eines Menschen'" I suggest reading the philosophy of deconstruction as a way to conceptualize our fallibility in precisely the manner that we suggest above. I.e., as an argument that aims to show that the possibility to fail to achieve the ideal described by a given normative concept has to be understood as an intrinsic element of our understanding of what it is to fulfill that ideal. Derrida is occasionally accused of making unnecessarily much out of this ubiquitously acknowledged phenomenon of our fallibility. Yet our reflections suggest that he is entirely right in insisting that everything hangs on how one understands this fallibility. And our conclusion is that the majority of the tradition of epistemology is not in a position to see this fallibility as an *intrinsic* feature of acts that fall under concepts that designate an ideal.

it is possible for someone to have a ground that actually would guarantee the truth of a particular belief and for her to actually form that belief, yet not for the truth-guaranteeing ground she has but for some other less-than-truth-guaranteeing ground.

On the capacity account of knowledge, the acquisition of perceptual knowledge is dependent on the condition the perception one enjoys is the ground on which one believes what one believes. To say that perceptual knowledge is dependent on this condition means that it is possible for someone to be in an epistemic position to acquire knowledge yet without actually acquiring knowledge. How do we have to understand this condition on which the acquisition of perceptual knowledge depends?

Let us consider an example. Someone can have a perception of a green necktie lying before her without believing what she perceives—namely, that the necktie is green—because, for example, she believes that the prevailing artificial light distorts the color of the tie, though in fact it does not.[108] What explains her withholding the belief that the necktie is green is her belief that the prevailing artificial light distorts the color of the tie. Her belief that the light distorts the color is a circumstance in the presence of which she cannot believe what she perceives. Yet given that a perception, according to our account, is an act of a self-conscious capacity for knowledge, this raises the question of what entitles us to say that the subject has a perception of a green necktie. Wouldn't we rather have to say that the subject, in such a case, does not have a perception but merely has a sensory experience of a green necktie, which she could also enjoy if there were no green necktie lying visibly before her? For as we argued above, when someone knows that p on the basis of her perception that p, then this means that she believes that p on the basis of a perception that is not available to her independently of the truth of her belief that p. This might seem to entail that someone who does not truly believe that p cannot be described as perceiving that p.

---

[108] For this well-known example, which I make use of in a specific variation, see Sellars, *Empiricism and the Philosophy of Mind,* §14.

However, this objection rests on a misunderstanding of what it is to have and to exercise a rational capacity for perceptual knowledge.[109] According to the capacity account of perceptual knowledge, there can be cases of perception that the subject does not recognize as such, for there may be circumstances that prevent the subject from recognizing her perception. In the above case, this circumstance is her false belief that the light is distorting the color of the necktie. Thus, according to the capacity account of knowledge, a perception that is not recognized as such is not a self-standing act that constitutes the common core of an act of perceptual knowledge as well as of an act of withholding judgment or of error. Instead, it is a *deficient exercise* of one's capacity for perceptual knowledge. It is deficient insofar as the perception is not recognized by the subject as it would be if the capacity were exercised perfectly. And this deficient act, as any deficient act of a capacity, can be explained, not through the capacity alone, as a perfect act would be, but only by invoking prevailing circumstances that explain why the perfect exercise of the capacity has been hindered. In the given case, the circumstance that hinders the subject from forming the relevant belief is her (mistaken) belief that the light distorts the color of the tie.

The possibility of such a case stems from the fact that perceptual knowledge is an act of a self-conscious fallible capacity that is, as such, dependent on the absence of circumstances that hinder its exercise. This makes room for the possibility that a subject may find herself in circumstances under which she believes (rightly or wrongly) that circumstances unfavorable for the exercise of her capacity for perceptual knowledge obtain. To believe that such circumstances obtain itself constitutes a circumstance that hinders its perfect exercise. Only a self-conscious capacity can be hindered in this way—namely, by beliefs about the circumstances of its exercise.

Hence, what allows us to say that the subject in such a case does have a perception, although she does not have perceptual knowledge, is that the perfect actualization of a rational capacity is dependent on the absence of circumstances that hinder it, including beliefs about the

[109] For this objection, see, for example, Stroud "Sense-Experience and the Grounding of Thought," 84.

circumstances of its exercise. We might call the latter sort "reflectively unfavorable circumstances" to highlight the fact that the circumstance that hinders the perfect exercise of the capacity in question is a belief whose content are the circumstances of the exercise of the capacity in question.

Our account of perceptual knowledge thus allows us to say that someone may see something without believing what she sees and, hence, without believing that she sees something. Advocates of non-conceptualism, who argue that we have to reconstruct the case in which someone sees something on the basis of acts that lack conceptual content, occasionally argue that this is the only way to explain the independence of perception from belief. But as we have seen, this objection rests on a view of the theoretical alternatives that undercuts and leaves no room for the capacity account of knowledge. The alternative we purportedly face is that we must describe someone who sees that p either as the subject of a conceptual act that implies that she believes that p, or as the subject of a nonconceptual act that she somehow connects with the belief that p. If this were a complete description of the available alternatives, then rejecting the second option would entail that it is impossible that someone can perceive that p without believing what she perceives. But the capacity account of knowledge precisely denies both alternatives. For the upshot of the capacity account is that it understands the nature of perception in a way that explains both why someone can perceive something without believing what she perceives and why perceptions are nevertheless intrinsically connected with beliefs.

The above example sheds light on the nature of the relation between perception and belief by looking at a deficient case of the exercise of the capacity for perceptual knowledge that explains both acts. Let's now look at the relation between perception and belief in a case in which someone perfectly exercises this capacity—a case in which she actually acquires knowledge on the basis of her perception. In a case where things go well, the subject enjoys a perception that she recognizes as such. And this entails that she believes what she perceives. According to the capacity account of knowledge, her perception that things are thus and so and her recognition of her perception as a perception have to be conceived of not as two acts stemming from two different capacities but as two aspects of a perfect exercise of her capacity for perceptual knowledge in two acts. Whereas the first aspect describes the perpetual character of the capacity for knowledge in question, the second aspect describes the rational, self-conscious character of this very capacity. It follows from this account that the perception one enjoys when one is hindered in recognizing one's perception as such and the perception one enjoys when one is not so hindered are, in a certain respect, not the same. For in the case where one is hindered in recognizing one's perception, one's perception is not an aspect of a perfect exercise of one's capacity for perceptual knowledge. Rather, it is a deficient act.

In this way we come to understand what it means to say, according to the capacity account of knowledge, that perception and perceptual knowledge are not the same. Perception is not identical to knowledge, yet intrinsically linked to it because the perfect exercise of a rational capacity for perceptual knowledge contains two aspects that can come apart, not because they spring from different capacities but because the capacity in question is liable to be hindered from being perfectly actualized.

## 4. Doxastic Responsibility and Knowledge

In characterizing beliefs as acts that actively exercise a rational capacity for knowledge, we are describing them as acts for which we are responsible. Yet what exactly does it mean to characterize beliefs as acts we are responsible for performing? What does it mean to be "doxastically responsible"? In what follows, we will unpack the meaning and the role that the notion of doxastic responsibility has within the framework of the capacity account of knowledge. In order to do this, we will contrast it with the different import that this notion assumes under all conceptions of knowledge that do not conceive of the concept of knowledge as the concept of a rational capacity.

As we have shown, the shared presupposition of all conceptions of knowledge that attempt to eschew the category of a rational capacity lies in the thought that perceptual knowledge is a mental state that must be reconstructed on the basis of a sort of sensory experience that is common to both the case in which someone knows something on its basis and the case in which she does not. If we seek to give an account of perceptual knowledge that takes this notion of perceptual experience as its starting point, then the concept of doxastic responsibility serves to describe rules that regulate one's transition from a perceptual experience to a belief with the purpose to raise the probability that the subject forms a true belief. A subject's behavior then counts as doxastically responsible just in case she follows these rules. Let's call such a conception a regulative conception of doxastic responsibility.[110]

Now it is part of the very idea of such a regulative conception of doxastic responsibility that the various conceptions of doxastic rules put forward by proponents of such a position can be arrayed along a spectrum stretching from those that demand the least of a subject to those that demand the most of a subject in order for her to count as doxastically responsible. The conception that demands the least of a subject would appear to be the "default-and-challenge conception of knowledge." On this conception, a subject is doxastically responsible so long as she adheres to the rule that she form a belief on the basis of an experience only if she *de facto* does not harbor any consideration that would awaken doubt about the truth of that belief. This is the minimal conception because it does not demand that the subject actively engages in acquiring further information relevant to the truth of her belief, nor does it require that she actively reflects on things that are or might be relevant to the truth of her belief. It merely requires the absence of actual considerations that raise doubts about the truth of the belief. From the perspective of the "default-and-challenge conception," all other accounts of knowledge, which demand more of the knowing subject, place too high a standard on knowledge.

---

[110] See, *inter alia*, Williams, *Problems of Knowledge*, 21–37; Fogelin, *Pyrrhonian Reflections*, 26–29, 88–89; Brandom, *Making It Explicit*, chaps. 3 and 4. Programmatic accounts can also be found in Firth, "Are Epistemic Concepts Reducible to Ethical Concepts?"; Alston, "Concepts of Epistemic Justification"; Feldman and Conee, "Evidentialism"; Heil, "Doxastic Agency"; and Kornblith, "Justified Belief and Epistemically Responsible Action."

It is part of the very idea of such a conception of doxastic responsibility that there are other accounts that demand more of the knowing
subject. Given that the purpose of these regulative rules is to raise
the probability that the subject forms true beliefs, it follows that the
more ambitious the rule for doxastic responsibility behavior becomes,
the less likely it becomes that false beliefs result from one's adherence
to that rule. Thus, the more likely it becomes that such beliefs have the
status of knowledge. It follows that the ideal rule would be one that
reduces to zero the probability that appropriately formed beliefs are
false. This would be the maximal conception of doxastic responsibility.

The skeptic maintains that we must adopt just such a maximal rule
in order to have knowledge, yet simultaneously holds that there is no
such rule for a subject for whom it is possible to err. According to the
skeptic, both of these requirements are necessary elements of knowledge: maximal doxastic responsibility, on the one hand, and the possibility of error, on the other. Yet the skeptic further contends that these
elements are incompatible with one another. It follows from this that
any conception that formulates a weaker regulative rule for what it
means to be doxastically responsible must characterize a subject's behavior as always capable of improvement from the perspective of that
subject. No matter what rule the subject follows, so long as it is weaker
than what the maximal conception would demand, it must always
seem to the subject that she could have acted even more responsibly
than she just did, in point of fact, even if what she just did satisfies
everything the prevailing rule demands of her. She could always have
gathered more relevant information and thereby further reduced the
probability that her belief was false. There is always room to do more
than doxastic responsibility demands of one.

By contrast, let us consider what sense the concept of doxastic responsibility takes on within the framework of the capacity account of
knowledge. In the paradigmatic case, the concept of doxastic responsibility describes the behavior of a subject who forms a belief on the
basis of a truth-guaranteeing ground that she recognizes, in believing
what she believes, as a perfect manifestation of her capacity for knowledge. To believe something on the basis of such a ground entails that
one has an understanding (however rudimentary) of what it means to

exercise the relevant capacity for knowledge. And that means, among other things, that one understands that perfect exercises of one's capacity are dependent on favorable circumstances, in the absence of which the perfect exercise of one's capacity is not possible. Let us call a situation where there are no circumstances that would hinder the perfect actualization of the relevant capacity an "opportunity."[111] That is to say, someone who possesses a rational capacity for knowledge understands, as such, that the perfect exercise of her capacity is opportunity-dependent. This entails that she is aware of the possibility of circumstances in which it would be impossible to exercise the capacity in question. Just as it is impossible to ski without snow or to swim without water, it is impossible, in the pitch dark, to know something by seeing it.

It follows that someone who has a rational capacity for knowledge is, simply in virtue of possessing that capacity, receptive to considerations that pertain to the circumstances under which the capacity is to be realized. This does not mean that someone who has a rational capacity for knowledge always takes account of such considerations in a perfectly rational manner. For as we emphasized, her capacity is fallible. But it does mean that, in virtue of possessing such a capacity, her doxastic behavior is, as such, either a perfect or imperfect manifestation of that capacity. Thus, if we take the concept of doxastic responsibility not as describing a regulative rule for behavior to maximize the truth of one's belief but instead as describing an aspect of the manner in which one exercises a self-consciously possessed capacity for knowledge, then we need no longer regard it as a paradoxical ideal that we can only approach but never attain. For then it describes something that is manifested in the subject's behavior whenever she actualizes the capacity in question and that can be and, indeed, sometimes is, perfectly realized: namely, whenever the subject comes to know how things stand.

The contrast between the regulative conception of doxastic responsibility and the capacity conception is nowhere clearer than in cases

---

[111] See the characterization Kenny gives of this concept, which is, as far as it goes, quite right: "Opportunities are circumstances which permit the exercises of abilities. If I am to have an opportunity to do something there must be no external impediment to my doing it." Kenny, *The Metaphysics of Mind*, 68.

where the capacity conception enables us to explain how someone was actually prevented from knowing something precisely because she knew too much. Consider the following case. Imagine a little boy who, for whatever reason, has been regularly running into his parents' room shouting, "Fire, fire, fire!," even though nothing in the vicinity was actually burning on any of these occasions. Now let us suppose that a small fire begins burning outside the window of our little boy's room. He sees it and runs into his parents' room shouting, as always, "Fire, fire, fire!"[112] In such a case, the knowledge his parents have about the little boy, which suggests that it is highly unlikely that he is crying "Fire!" because there is actually a fire, hinders them from recognizing the boy's cry as what it is: namely, a ground for believing that something is aflame. From the parents' perspective, it would not be doxastically responsible to believe that there is a fire in the vicinity on the basis of what the child says to them. On the basis of what they know about their son, they are prevented from acquiring knowledge through his report. Let us now supplement our situation by adding an aunt, who differs from the parents in that she is unaware of the boy's previous false alarms, because she only comes to visit every few years. Because she does not have this knowledge of his past behavior, there is nothing that hinders her from being doxastically responsible in recognizing the boy's cry as a ground for believing that there is a fire. Unlike the parents, she is in a position to gain from the boy's reports the knowledge that something is on fire.

The capacity account of knowledge enables us to describe a particular situation as one that is identical for two different subjects in that it constitutes an opportunity for both of them to exercise their capacity for knowledge. But they differ in that only one of them can take this opportunity to acquire knowledge. In the above example, only the aunt is in a position to do so precisely because she lacks specific information that would hinder her from making the judgment that there is a fire somewhere in the vicinity in a responsible manner. In this case, the information the parents have about their son represents a circumstance that explains why they cannot exercise their capacity for knowledge in

---

[112] For further discussion of such a case, see McDowell, "Knowledge by Hearsay," 436–437.

such a manner that it would result in knowledge. They are hindered from doing so because there are reflectively unfavorable circumstances—namely, the mistaken belief that the circumstances for the exercise of that capacity are unfavorable. Having a false belief about the circumstances itself constitutes a hindrance against taking an opportunity to acquire knowledge that one could otherwise have taken.

By contrast, if one takes the concept of doxastic responsibility to describe a regulative rule, one will describe a situation where someone is attempting to acquire knowledge as one in which it is, in principle, always possible for her to behave even more responsibly: e.g., by gathering further information about the prevailing circumstances.[113] On the capacity account of knowledge, by contrast, this does not make sense. The idea of ever more responsible behavior and, hence, of an endless approach toward an unattainable ideal of responsibility is inapplicable from the very outset. For when someone sees that there is a glass of water in front of her, there is nothing whatsoever she can do to improve her cognitive situation, nothing she can do to act more doxastically responsible. For she is in a situation where she can perfectly actualize her capacity for perceptual knowledge, and hence fulfill the ideal of doxastic responsibility: she can believe something on the basis of a ground that rules out that her belief might be false. The capacity account of knowledge renders the idea of an infinite improvability of one's cognitive situation through gathering more and more information nonsensical. It instead allows for cases in which a subject is cognitively worse off than she would be if she knew less than she happens to.

Hence, for a subject who possesses a rational capacity for perceptual knowledge, there are three possible cases of privation in which a sensory experience fails to be a case of knowledge:

(1) Someone has a sensory experience that p without perceiving that p and hence without having a ground for knowing that p.
(2) Someone believes that p on the basis of a sensory experience that p without knowing that p.
(3) Someone perceives that p without knowing that p.

[113] This is, for example, Fogelin's view in *Pyrrhonian Reflections*, 31–32.

In all three cases one's capacity for perceptual knowledge is not perfectly exercised. Whereas the first case describes a case of privation in which a sensory experience is deprived of being a perception, the second describes a case in which a perceptual belief is deprived of being knowledge, and the third describes a case in which a perception is deprived of being knowledge. To explain each of these cases, we cannot look solely to the capacity that is manifested in them. We have to additionally refer to prevailing circumstances that explain why the capacity is *hindered* from being perfectly exercised. In the first case, such a circumstance could be distorting light conditions under which things appear different from how they are. The description of such a case leaves it open whether it is a case of error. For if the subject knows that these circumstances obtain, she will not believe that p on the basis of her sensory experience that p and, hence, will not err. In order for it to be a case of error, one has to assume that the subject believes that she perceives that p without actually doing so. This is what happens in the second case. If the subject does not know that the prevailing circumstances are unfavorable for the exercise of her capacity for perceptual knowledge, then case (1) will turn into case (2). In the third case, the circumstance to which we have to refer in order to explain the subject's lack of knowledge is her belief about the circumstances in which she finds herself. Perceiving that p without knowing that p is only possible if one believes that there obtain unfavorable circumstances that hinder one's capacity for perceptual knowledge from being perfectly exercised. So one's belief about the prevailing circumstances being unfavorable, then, itself constitutes an unfavorable circumstance for the exercise of one's capacity.

What is common to all three cases is that their explanation requires more explanatory factors than the explanation of a case of perceptual knowledge. To explain such cases, one has to look not only at the capacity for perceptual knowledge but also to particular circumstances that one's knowledge of the capacity in question allows one to identify as unfavorable for the exercise of that capacity. Thus, the capacity account of knowledge brings to light that a case of error, instead of being a case that one can just presuppose, requires an explanation that is more demanding than a case of knowledge. So the capacity account of knowledge inverts the explanatory order between knowledge and error that is generally taken for granted. Usually the intelligibility of error is taken for granted and knowledge is taken to be a mental state that is difficult to understand. The capacity account of knowledge shows that the intelligibility of error depends on the intelligibility of knowledge. Whereas a case of perceptual knowledge is explained through the capacity itself, a case of error requires further explanatory factors, for it requires an explanation of why the capacity has been hindered from being perfectly exercised.

This explanatory asymmetry, which goes hand in hand with the idea of a rational capacity, makes it intelligible why someone who cites her perception as a ground for her belief is not simply making a further unsupported assertion, the truth of which she still needs to guarantee. That is the objection we encountered at the end of Part Two. The objection claims that someone who cites her perception as the ground for a belief is making a claim—namely, that her sensory experience is a case of perception and not merely the appearance of a perception—the truth of which she still needs to establish, just as she needs to establish the truth of the belief she attempts to ground. What we have now seen is that one cannot even formulate this objection unless one denies that someone who sees that there is still apple juice in the fridge is thereby actualizing a rational capacity for perceptual knowledge. If one denies this, then it must indeed seem as though someone who, without further justification, justifies her belief by saying that she sees what she believes, is doing nothing more than putting forward another undefended claim.

At the conclusion of Part Two we announced in anticipation that (i) the explanation of how it is possible to know that there is still apple juice in the fridge on the basis of a visual experience and (ii) the explanation of how it is possible to know that one sees that there is still apple juice in the fridge must be one and the same. This is something we could only anticipate at the end of Part Two. For we could not yet see what this explanation was. The account we have now given enables us to see this. It explains the possibility of both acts of knowledge—knowledge of the world around us on the basis of our perceptions as well as knowledge of our perceptions—by conceiving them as two aspects of one and the same perfect exercise of a rational capacity for perceptual knowledge.

# PART FOUR

## *The Teleology of Knowledge*

IN PART ONE WE INTRODUCED BELIEFS AS ACTS IN THE PERFOR-
mance of which the subject is guided by the norm of truth. Someone
who believes something claims to believe something true. On this understanding, beliefs are not just any normative acts. They are self-
consciously normative acts. Our reflections have now shown us that we
can be entitled to this understanding of beliefs only if we understand
beliefs as acts that, in the fundamental case, exercise a rational capacity
for knowledge that is receptive to how things are. A rational capacity for
perceptual knowledge, we argued, is such a capacity. In describing beliefs as acts of a rational capacity for knowledge, we are describing
these acts in a manner from which epistemology has long abstracted—
particularly in the last century. We are, namely, describing beliefs as
acts whose performance is determined by an end—and, moreover, an
end that the subject of such acts represents to herself. Believing is an
act that, when it is knowledge, realizes an end that the subject performing it is conscious of. For rational capacities, on any account of
them, have a "teleological" structure.[1] That which rational capacities
are capacities for, has the character of an end that one aims to realize.

In what follows, we will deepen our account of what it is to possess a
rational capacity for perceptual knowledge by unfolding its teleological structure and hence the teleology of the mind that goes with it. In
doing this, we will address at a deeper level the sort of causality that we
have been invoking in our characterization of rational capacities. A rational capacity for knowledge, as I will argue, is to be understood as a
form of causality that I will, in following Kant, characterize as "teleological causality." That is to say, this sort of causality is *sui generis* when
compared with another sort of causality, which I will again follow Kant
in terming "mechanical causality."

As will become clear in what follows, that a rational capacity for
knowledge has a "teleological" structure means that creatures who possess such a capacity stand in an irreducibly twofold relation to knowledge. First, knowledge is, for them, an *actuality*. It is the actuality of a

[1] See Sosa, "Knowledge and Intellectual Virtue," 226–227.

capacity. At the same time, knowledge is for them an *ideal*. It is the ideal of acts that guides the bearers of such a capacity whenever they actualize it. Both these characterizations of knowledge—as the actuality of a capacity and as the ideal of its actualizations—will prove to be two aspects of a single account. For it will turn out that the first characterization of knowledge—viz., knowledge as the actuality of a capacity—can apply to a creature only insofar as the other characterization—viz., knowledge as an ideal governing her acts—applies as well, and *vice versa*. That is, it turns out that only someone who is guided by the ideal of knowledge can have the capacity to acquire knowledge by being so guided, and conversely, only someone who has the capacity to acquire knowledge can be guided by the ideal of knowledge.

# IX

# The Teleology of Rational Capacities

## 1. Virtue Epistemology and "Epistemic Capacities": A Critique

In describing beliefs as acts of a rational capacity for knowledge, we represent them as acts that, when they are knowledge, realize an end that the believing subject is conscious of. In recent decades, the literature on epistemology has come to rediscover this fundamental teleology of the mind. That is, the literature has regained a consciousness of the fact that the theoretical life of the mind is, in a certain sense, a teleological activity. The growing trend in "virtue epistemology" finds its distinctive contribution in this rediscovery. Any answer to the question of what knowledge is and how it is possible requires that we grasp the acts we are seeking to understand as acts that realize a *telos*, an end. Recent debates about intellectual virtues, by authors such as Zagzebski and Montmarquet, as well as alternative language about epistemic capacities, which authors such as Sosa and Greco prefer, stem from this common motive—namely, to register that the idea of virtues and rational capacities is the idea of something that makes reference to an end. The conception of capacities and virtues that is relevant to epistemology, Sosa tells us, is a "teleological conception," according to which rational capacities and virtues have a teleological structure.[2] Someone who has a virtue, Zagzebski tells us, is so constituted that her act's relation to its respective end ensures that she is reliable "in bringing about that end."[3]

We can characterize the shared insight of so-called virtue epistemology through the following three claims:

(1) Believing is an activity, whose end is the truth.
(2) Capacities are general properties of subjects that explain the occurrence of acts that fulfill the end in terms of which the capacity is defined.
(3) Therefore, capacities that are defined as having the truth as their end make it intelligible how there can be beliefs that are non-accidentally true, i.e., that constitute knowledge.

With this general insight, virtue epistemology takes itself to be in a position to address the problem that, as we have shown in the previous chapters, structures all discussions in epistemology: viz., the problem of non-accidental truth, which is definitive of the concept of knowledge. We concur with virtue epistemologists that this problem has gone unresolved in contemporary epistemology, insofar as it seeks to do without the idea of virtues or capacities. The intelligibility of the concept of knowledge, however, stands or falls with the solution to this problem. What ultimately makes virtue epistemology distinctive is its claim that the key to solving the accidentality-problem of which the so called Gettier-cases have reminded us is to introduce notions of intellectual virtues or epistemic capacities as fundamental epistemological concepts.

Reference to intellectual virtues or epistemic capacities is motivated by the insight that, in introducing such things, we are dealing with a kind of "cause" that explains why acts that are directed at a particular end—"performances" that have an "essential aim" or "an aim inherent in [them]," as Sosa puts it—are such as to "attain" the end at which they

[2] Ibid.
[3] Zagzebski, *Virtues of the Mind,* 137.

are directed.[4] Virtues and capacities, in the sense relevant here, have to be understood, according to virtue epistemology, as the sorts of "causes" of particular acts that serve to explain why those acts accord with the end at which they are directed. Just as the capacity to play baseball describes a kind of cause that explains why someone who has this capacity performs acts that accord with the end of playing baseball, we can likewise explain knowledge as an act whose "cause" is an epistemic capacity that explains why the act is so constituted that it accords with its end—namely, to be an act of knowledge. And just as we can say that playing baseball consists in the exercise of a kind of "agency," which characterizes a subject that has the capacity to play baseball, so too can we describe knowledge as the exercise of a kind of "agency," which characterizes a subject who has a certain "epistemic capacity."[5]

Let us call this the distinctive insight of virtue epistemology: we employ the concept of intellectual virtues or epistemic capacities in our analysis of knowledge because they provide an explanation for the agreement of an act with an end that is intrinsic to it *qua* act, or, as Sosa puts it, for its agreement with "an aim inherent in it". In order to understand the idea of non-accidentally true belief that our concept of knowledge carries with it, the suggestion goes, we have to understand knowledge as an act of a capacity whose end is truth. This insight enables us to view the normativity of knowledge as a special case of a more general, everyday, and familiar form of normativity, which has application whenever someone succeeds in doing something by exercising the relevant capacity for doing such things. When we say that someone knows something, what we are saying, on this view, is that she has succeeded in forming a true belief precisely in virtue of exercising an epistemic capacity in forming that belief. Knowledge is, in this respect, like playing baseball or skiing. John Greco expresses the view as follows:

> [K]nowledge is a kind of success from ability. Put another way, knowledge is a kind of achievement, or a kind of success for which the

[4] Sosa, *Knowing Full Well,* 14–15.
[5] Ibid., 19.

knower deserves credit. And in general, success from ability (i.e., achievement) has special value and deserves a special sort of credit. This is a ubiquitous and perfectly familiar sort of normativity. Thus we credit people for their athletic achievements, for their artistic achievements, and for their moral achievements. We also credit people for their intellectual achievements. Epistemic normativity is an instance of a more general, familiar kind.[6]

In what follows, our aim is to understand the teleological structure that characterizes a rational capacity, as it is exhibited in such ordinary activities as playing baseball or skiing, in order to then develop an account of the teleological structure of a capacity for knowledge. I will argue that virtue epistemology fails to do justice to what I have called its distinctive insight because it labors under a false conception of the kind of causality that characterizes a capacity for knowledge.

Sosa introduces the idea of capacities in the following way: A shot at a target can hit the bull's-eye without such success manifesting any competence on the part of the shooter. When that happens, we say that the outcome is just an accident, the result of pure chance. But it can also happen that a shot hits the bull's-eye because of the competence of the marksman. A competent marksman doesn't hit the bull's-eye just by accident. In such a case, we have an explanation for her success. It is her competence in shooting that explains why she hits the bull's-eye. The idea here is that we can evaluate beliefs in just this fashion. A belief may be true simply by accident—namely, when it isn't the manifestation of any relevant competence. But a belief can also be true on account of the subject's capacity. What accounts for the fact that the belief is non-accidentally true, in the relevant sense, is a particular competence that explains the occurrence of a true belief.[7]

Sosa accordingly defines knowledge as follows: "Belief amounts to knowledge when [...] its correctness is attributable to a competence exercised in appropriate conditions."[8] John Greco similarly claims:

---

[6] Greco, *Achieving Knowledge*, 7.
[7] Ibid., 23.
[8] Ibid., 92.

"*S* knows that *p if and only if S* believes the truth (with respect to *p*) because *S*'s belief that *p* is produced by intellectual ability."[9]

Sosa defines a "competence" as follows: "[A] competence is a disposition, one with a basis resident in the competent agent, one that would in appropriately normal conditions ensure (or make highly likely) the success of any relevant performance issued by it."[10] Thus, according to Sosa, a capacity can be analyzed into two components: a disposition to bring about certain acts and a high rate of "successful" acts under "appropriately normal" circumstances, i.e., a high rate of acts that realize the end of the competence in question. Sosa accordingly describes the requisite criterion of success by saying that a disposition can have the status of a "competence" or a "capacity" if and only if the disposition in question "is sufficiently reliable, at least in its distinctively appropriate conditions."[11] That is to say, a certain disposition counts as a competence of the relevant sort if and only if it is sufficiently reliable, under appropriate conditions, in bringing about acts that are in accordance with the end that defines the competence in question.[12]

According to this account, a capacity, such as the competence to bring about y-acts, can be analyzed into the following two components:

(1) the disposition to bring about x-acts

and

(2) a high rate of acts resulting from (1) that are in accordance with the concept of y-acts, under the conditions that are appropriate for such acts.

Sosa then brings this general characterization of capacities to bear on the idea of an epistemic competence and analyzes the latter in terms of:

[9] Ibid., 71.
[10] Sosa, *A Virtue Epistemology*, 29.
[11] Ibid.
[12] Ibid.

(1) the disposition to form beliefs on the basis of "intellectual
    appearances"

and

(2) a high rate of acts that spring from (1) that are in accordance
    with the concept of a true belief, under circumstances that
    are appropriate for such accord, i.e., a high rate of true beliefs
    that are formed on the basis of "intellectual appearances."

The concept of "intellectual appearances" is meant to signify, for Sosa, a
particular type of conceptual representation, which arises from sensible
affection and which thereby forms a potential reasons for belief—such
as the state of a subject who is enjoying the visual appearance that p.

Let us ask, then, what exactly it is, on this analysis, that qualifies a
mere disposition to form beliefs on the basis of so-called "intellectual
appearances" as an epistemic competence. Clearly such a disposition
would need to provide an explanation for the success of certain acts.
But what kind of explanation? One way to bring to light the upshot of
this analysis is to note what is not required for a disposition to qualify
as an epistemic competence, according to Sosa. For a disposition to
qualify as an epistemic competence, it need not be such as to explain a
belief in a way that rules out that a belief that is explained in that way
could be false and hence, not knowledge. According to Sosa, the criterion of success that is definitive of competences is rather that someone
who possesses an epistemic competence and actualizes it under appropriate circumstances meets, with sufficient frequency, with the sort of
success that is definitive of that competence. This means that, on Sosa's
account, it is perfectly intelligible for someone to possess the relevant
competence and exercise it under conditions that are appropriate for
its exercise and yet fail to exercise it successfully. Such a case is intelligible because the idea of someone possessing a competence doesn't
mean that she is in possession of something that forecloses the possibility that an exercise, in the appropriate circumstances, can fail to be
successful. It only means that she possesses something whose exercise,
in the appropriate circumstances, is successful for the most part. Under

these so-called appropriate circumstances, two outcomes are logically possible: the exercise of the competence succeeds, or it does not.

However, this means that whenever the competence is exercised in the appropriate circumstances, its success or failure must be a matter of luck—a chance occurrence. The reason for this is that, given Sosa's description of the successful case, it is logically possible that there can be an unsuccessful case that is in no way different from the successful one, so that there is nothing we can appeal to in order to explain why the one case was successful and the other was not. Nor can we explain the successful case simply by appealing to the competence itself. For the competence is defined solely by the fact that its exercise mostly meets with success in the appropriate circumstances. So the competence, just as such, cannot provide an explanation for the successful case. Nor can we explain the successful case by pointing to specific circumstances that explain why the exercise met with success on this occasion. For, by definition, the same circumstances can also obtain in a case where the exercise of the competence fails. And if we cannot explain the success of the case either in terms of the competence or in terms of the prevailing circumstances, then its success can only be a matter of chance, a matter of luck. If that is so, however, the idea of epistemic competences or capacities, thus conceived, cannot solve the accidentality problem for which it was introduced.[13]

So far, we can glean the following general insight from this failure: Any epistemology that cannot construe an epistemic capacity as an explanation of acts of knowing that rules it out that something that is explained in that manner is not knowledge will inevitably fail to resolve the accidentality problem. That is to say, any epistemology that understands epistemic capacities as general characteristics of a subject

---

[13] Duncan Pritchard pursues a quite different argumentative route to arrive at the same verdict, namely that virtue epistemology cannot solve the accidentality problem. See Pritchard, "Virtue Epistemology and Epistemic Luck." But Pritchard is wrong to conclude from this failure that there is no reason to endorse an epistemology that treats the concept of epistemic capacities as fundamental. Virtue epistemology fails not because it treats epistemic capacities as fundamental but because it misunderstands the very idea of such capacities. For a more detailed critique of virtue epistemology, see my essay "Knowledge as a Fallible Capacity."

that do not explain a belief in a way that rules it out that a belief thus explained could be false, will not be able to solve the accidentality problem. An epistemic capacity must be a general characteristic of a subject that *guarantees* truth. That is, it must be a characteristic that rules out the formation of a false belief in the circumstances that are appropriate for its exercise.

At this point an obvious objection comes to mind—and it is presumably an objection along these lines that explains why virtue epistemology doesn't even consider the idea of a truth-guaranteeing capacity of a subject as a possible option. The objection is that it is unreasonable to demand of someone who possesses an epistemic capacity that the beliefs produced through the exercise of that capacity are *always* true. That simply demands too much of the cognizing subject. It seems more reasonable to demand that, in the appropriate circumstances, an epistemically competent person will *often* form a true belief, not that she will always form true beliefs. To demand the latter would be to demand epistemic infallibility. For it would mean that someone has the capacity to acquire knowledge only if her capacity rules out, as a matter of principle, that she can be mistaken. And that is a conception of knowledge that cannot sensibly be attributed to human beings. The thought that human beings are capable of knowledge cannot reasonably be cashed out in a way that would require us to be epistemically infallible.

Yet if we consider this objection more closely, it is easy to see that it rests on a misunderstanding. The objection mistakenly equates two thoughts that must be held apart. Namely:

(1) The idea of an epistemic capacity implies that beliefs formed through exercises of that capacity in the appropriate circumstances are always true.
(2) Bearers of an epistemic capacity are epistemically infallible.

How does one come to assimilate these two thoughts? For there is quite obviously another way of doing justice to the fallibility of beliefs without at all disputing thought (1)—a way that we have already developed in Part Three. It will be helpful to briefly revisit this alternative understanding of fallibility in the context of a capacity familiar to us all: the capacity for speech. According to thought (1), if someone has the capacity for speech, then whenever the circumstances are appropriate for the exercise of that capacity, it is impossible for an exercise of the capacity to fail. Of course, it can happen that the appropriate circumstances obtain but the bearer of the capacity chooses not to exercise it. Thought (1) only rules out cases in which the capacity is exercised in the appropriate conditions and yet the exercise goes awry. But the thought that someone is able to speak is quite obviously not the same as the thought that it is impossible for her to make mistakes in speaking. Someone who can speak can also misspeak—she can make a grammatical error, misuse a word, and so on. So how do these thoughts go together? It is at least clear how we shouldn't interpret such cases—namely, as cases in which the appropriate circumstances obtain and yet the exercise of the capacity misfires. And this itself indicates how we ought to understand such cases: namely, as cases in which the exercise of the capacity misfires in some respect precisely because the circumstances appropriate for its exercise do not obtain. More precisely: because circumstances obtain that hinder or restrict the successful exercise of the capacity.

Once we construe cases of success and failure in this manner, we can satisfy the demand elaborated above, according to which we require a conception of an epistemic capacity as something truth-guaranteeing. This conception doesn't preclude but instead ensures that there can be conditions under which someone will be hindered from exercising her epistemic capacity "correctly," or "properly," or "successfully."

With this understanding of capacities in hand, we can easily reconcile the possibility of error with the idea of truth-guaranteeing capacity. If an epistemic capacity is a truth-guaranteeing capacity, then it explains a successful case in a manner that rules it out that a case that is explained in that manner could not have been successful. By contrast, any case that is not successful, but instead is defective in some way or other, can be explained only by invoking (in addition to the relevant capacity) unfavorable prevailing circumstances that explain why the exercise of the capacity failed in one way or another. We called such a capacity a fallible capacity. A fallible capacity is one that cannot be successfully exercised under all possible circumstances. It is one whose successful exercise depends on the presence of favorable circumstances. Yet, to

say that a capacity is fallible is not, as Sosa thinks, to say that its successful exercise under favorable circumstances is only very likely. It is
to say that the favorable circumstances on which its successful exercise
depends are part of what it means to exercise it successfully.

## 2. Rational Capacities as a Species
## of Teleological Causality: A Kantian Approach

In section 1 of this chapter, I claimed that the concept of epistemic capacities, as it has been invoked in recent virtue epistemology, is incapable of resolving the problem it is meant to address because it is blind
to the idea of a truth-guaranteeing capacity. Why is contemporary
virtue epistemology blind to the idea of a truth-guaranteeing capacity?

Virtue epistemology seeks to claim that the relevant concept of
capacities that we require in epistemology contains the idea of an
end. The conception of virtues and capacities that is relevant to epistemology, to quote Sosa again, is a "teleological conception." It is striking,
however, that contemporary virtue epistemology gives us no indication
of what it takes an end to be. This is no arbitrary omission. For as we
will see in what follows, virtue epistemologists do not feel the need to
elucidate the concept of an end because their account of epistemic capacities hinges on the implicit presupposition that describing an epistemic capacity as the "cause" of an act involves a kind of causality that
is independent of the end that defines this capacity. That the concept of
an epistemic capacity is a concept that contains the idea of an end does
not mean, on the contemporary conception, that it is the concept of
something that has a special form of causality, distinct from the form of
causality proper to those things whose concept does not contain the
idea of an end. Now my aim in what follows is not to provide a general
refutation of this conception of capacities. For we have already seen
that this conception of capacities refutes itself when applied to the case
of knowledge. My aim instead is to contrast this conception of capacities with the conception of capacities we have developed in Part Three,
by unfolding the different understanding of the causality of capacities
that this conception entails. That is, our task now is to make explicit the
idea of causality that has been implicitly at work in our understanding

of capacities. We will do this by first looking at an alternative approach to capacities, which brings into focus the idea that the relevant concept of a capacity is a "teleological" concept, and which takes its point of departure from a reflection on precisely that feature of the relevant concept of capacities.

A paradigm example of such an alternative conception of capacities can be found, *inter alia,* in the work of Kant. Kant is particularly helpful in addressing our question, for two reasons. First, Kant argues that the idea of a "teleological causality" is a sort of causality that is *sui generis.* That is to say, Kant develops an account of the idea of a "teleological causality" by arguing that it contrasts—formally—with another kind of causality, which he calls "mechanical causality." His highly abstract conception of "teleological causality" will provide our basis for understanding the teleological structure of capacities and, more narrowly, the teleological structure of a capacity for knowledge. This will allow us to conceive of the failure of contemporary virtue epistemology as the consequence of a misunderstanding about the kind of causality that is exhibited by capacities. Virtue epistemology conceives of capacities as instances of mechanical causality rather than as instances of teleological causality. The second reason Kant is helpful here is that the concept of a capacity for knowledge lies at the very center of Kant's metaphysics of mind in a way that is true of few other philosophical systems. Though Kant does not himself explicitly develop the concept of a capacity for knowledge as the concept of a teleological kind of causality, this teleological understanding is implicit throughout Kant's work. Moreover, some crucial aspects of his account of knowledge, as I will argue in what follows, can be made intelligible on the basis of this teleological conception and will likewise help us to deepen our account of knowledge in terms of a rational capacity we have developed so far.

It is a telling feature of the literature on Kant that, thus far, very little work has been done on Kant's notion of a rational capacity, despite the fact that even a superficial reading of the text reveals it to be one of his key terms.[14] In what follows I will therefore provide some basic elements

---

[14] See, for example, the collection of papers in Perler, ed., *Faculties,* which give an historical overview of the role of the notion of faculties through the philosophical tradition. In his contribution "Faculties in Kant and German Idealism," Johannes Haag

of a Kantian account of the idea of a capacity for knowledge by first considering Kant's abstract notion of an end or "telos". I will then apply this account of ends to the idea of a capacity that is defined by the end of knowledge.

In the third Critique, Kant first introduces the concept of an end in its most abstract sense. An end, he tells us, is "the object of a concept insofar as the latter is considered the cause (the real ground of the possibility) of the former."[15] The concept of an end is, accordingly, "the concept of an object, insofar as it [the concept] contains the ground of the possibility of that object."[16] When we characterize an object as an end, we are thus determining an object through a concept that serves to explain the reality of that object, in a particular sense.

To get an initial grip on this highly abstract definition, it is helpful to bring it into contact with other formulations where Kant elucidates the concept of an end by employing causal terminology. In §64 of the third Critique, for example, Kant elucidates the concept of an end by saying that to characterize an object as an end is to understand it as the effect of a cause "whose efficacy [Vermögen zu wirken] is determined through concepts."[17] What we need to understand in order to comprehend the

nicely brings out the widespread conception of the role that "faculties" play in Kant's account of knowledge. Kant's "transcendental approach"—as opposed to, for example, a psychologistic approach—brings with it, Haag argues, the assumption that the "metaphysical status of the faculties invoked in this type of reasoning no longer carries any importance" (199). This opposition between a "transcendental approach" and a "metaphysical project," however, is unfortunate, for it seems to suggest that the point of Kant's so-called transcendental approach is to merely justify the "introduction of a particular faculty" into our philosophical account without itself providing an understanding of what that thing is that is thus introduced. Kant's "transcendental approach" is an attempt to answer the question of how it is possible to have representations with objective purport. This brings him to "introduce" the idea of sensibility and understanding as the two stems of a receptive capacity for knowledge whose very idea he then seeks to unfold in the course of his inquiry. Now, if one thinks that the metaphysical status of this capacity "no longer carries any importance," one fails to appreciate the very task that Kant sets himself in the course of his inquiry, especially in the Transcendental Deduction: namely, to give an account of what a receptive capacity for knowledge is by showing us how we have to conceive of it in order for this idea to be so much as intelligible.

[15] Kant, *Kritik der Urteilskraft* [Power of Judgment], §10, AA 5:220.
[16] Ibid., introduction, §IV, AA 5:180.
[17] Ibid., §65, AA 5:369.

idea of an end, Kant tells us, is the idea of a special kind of cause: namely, a cause "whose efficacy is determined through concepts." According to Kant, this means that we must distinguish between two irreducibly different kinds of causal connection. On the one hand, we can think of a causal connection among elements that involves a one-sided dependence of one element on another—i.e., a connection in which the element that is regarded as the effect cannot also serve as the cause of the element whose effect it is. We typically call this sort of causal connection "that of efficient causes," or *nexus effectivus*.[18] Following Kant and traditional usage, we can also describe such a form of causality as "mechanical causality." In addition to this kind of causal connection, however, we can also conceive of a further sort, which involves a reciprocal dependency between the relevant elements. This would be a causal connection "in which the thing which is at one point designated the effect nevertheless deserves [ . . . ] to be called the cause of the very thing whose effect it is."[19] We can call this kind of causal connection "teleological causality," or *nexus finalis*.

It is telling that Kant gives such an abstract explanation of what it means to represent something as an end. Obviously Kant understands this to be a purely formal characterization, which, as such, contains no indication of the sort of objects that can enter into such a causal connection as elements.

So let us consider Kant's most prominent illustration of this account in the practical realm, while bearing in mind that we should understand it as an exemplary case of a more general phenomenon. The example has to do with building a house. Kant writes: "In practice (namely, in art) it is easy to find such connections, in which, for example, a house is the cause of the money that can be taken in as rent, while it is also the case that, conversely, the representation of this possible income was the cause of the house's being built."[20] Now in what sense does the thing that at one point is designated the effect also deserve to be called a cause? In this sort of causal connection—between the house and the income from rent—the thing that is at one point designated an effect

---

[18] Ibid., §65, AA 5:372.
[19] Ibid.
[20] Ibid.

(the rent) also deserves to be called a cause (of the house) in the sense that the representation of that effect is what explains the presence of the thing that is the cause of that very effect. The representation of the effect is what explains the existence of the house, in the sense that a rational creature who has this representation of a house is determined, through that representation, to perform precisely those actions that lead to the existence of a house. To give a complete account of the cause of the rental income, in this example, we would have to include some reference to a rational being who has a certain conceptual representation of the effect of the house, which representation leads her to build the house.

Thus, it is clear that when Kant describes a teleological causal connection as a cause "whose efficacy is determined through concepts," what he has in mind, in this context, is a rational subject capable of intentional action. A rational agent embodies a cause whose efficacy is determined through concepts in the sense that such a being produces things precisely by acting in accordance with a conceptual representation of the things she produces (or is going to produce). The things that rational agents produce in this manner—namely, in accordance with a concept of the thing in question—accordingly stand in a special relation to that concept on account of the special manner in which they were produced. In particular, their agreement with the concepts that represent them is no mere accident but a matter of necessity. We can therefore say that an object that exists as an end is one that necessarily agrees with the concept of that end. This enables us to understand what Kant means by saying that an end is the object of a concept insofar as the concept contains the ground of the actuality of the object. On this Kantian conception of an end, it is logically ruled out that an object that exists as an end is merely accidentally in agreement with the concept of that end.

We can therefore express Kant's formal characterization of the idea of teleological causality in the following minimal way: It is the idea of a causal connection in which the thing that is represented as the cause is logically dependent on the thing that is represented as the effect. Let's now apply this account of the idea of a teleological causality to the idea of a capacity that is defined by the end of knowledge. We want thereby to take into account that the capacity we are interested in cannot be exercised under all possible circumstances—that is, that there is a distinction between circumstances that are appropriate for its exercise and circumstances that are less than appropriate for its exercise. This gives us the following, preliminary understanding of the kind of cause that a capacity for knowledge is: *A capacity for knowledge is a cause that is logically dependent on its effect (viz., knowledge) in the sense that exercises of that capacity, as such, fall under the concept of knowledge as being in either perfect or imperfect agreement with the concept of knowledge.*

As we proceed we will develop a more determinate account that specifies the idea of teleological causality—in terms of a logical dependency of cause on effect—as it applies to a capacity for knowledge. Yet our preliminary characterization of the kind of cause that a capacity for knowledge is already provides a basis for getting clear about the contrast between this teleological conception of a capacity for knowledge and the conception of capacities presupposed by contemporary virtue epistemology. For contemporary virtue epistemology is defined by a conception of capacities that conflicts with the above characterization. In particular, it understands knowledge as the effect of a cause— namely, an epistemic capacity—that is logically independent of the end at which it is directed. The capacity *qua* cause is logically independent of its end (knowledge) in the sense that a state of knowledge is understood as the effect of a cause whose causality can be fully described without any employment of the concept of the thing at which its activity is directed *qua* end.

Recall that the fundamental characterization of an epistemic capacity that we find in contemporary virtue epistemology consists of two elements: (1) the disposition to produce beliefs on the basis of intellectual appearances, and (2) a high rate of agreement, under appropriate circumstances, between beliefs produced on the basis of intellectual appearances, and the concept of a true belief. While (1) describes the causality of this capacity as involving the production of beliefs, (2) describes the accord of beliefs thus explained with the end of that capacity, which Sosa characterizes in terms of true beliefs. The central feature of this account of an epistemic capacity lies in the fact that the first element of the account is logically independent of the second element. The sort of causality that explains the occurrence of beliefs does not, as such, explain the agreement of these beliefs with the concept of a true belief. It follows that it is logically excluded, from the very outset, that one can explain an instance of a true belief just by appealing to the relevant sort of causality, i.e., the capacity.

We have followed Kant in calling such a form of causality "mechanical causality." It is part of Kant's central argument that an account that conceives of the causality of the relevant capacity as a form of mechanical causality is unable, for logical reasons, to understand the agreement between a particular act and the concept that designates the end of the capacity as a necessary agreement. Thus, any line of thought that seeks to understand a capacity for knowledge as analyzable into two logically independent elements—one that describes the causality of the capacity and another that describes the agreement of its acts with the end of the capacity—will be unable to lay claim to the idea of knowledge as non-accidentally true belief. The idea of a non-accidentally true belief remains unintelligible on such an account because it is impossible, in the context of such an analysis, to explain the truth of a belief through the causality of the capacity in question.

To get a clearer view of what it means to have a mechanistic conception of the causality of the relevant kind of capacities and how such a conception differs from a teleological conception, let's look at how virtue epistemology analyzes the idea of a case that is successful, not just in one respect or other, but, as Sosa puts it, on all "levels of success."[21] Consider, once again, the capacity for y-acts. On this view, a successful exercise of this capacity for y-ing consists in meeting the following three conditions:

(1) The act agrees with the end of the capacity to y.
(2) The act is a manifestation of the capacity to y.
(3) (1) is true because (2) is true—i.e., the act agrees with the end of the capacity to y because the act is a manifestation of the capacity to y.

---

[21] Compare Sosa, *Knowing Full Well*, 1.

If an act fulfills condition (1), Sosa calls it "accurate." If it fulfills condition (2), Sosa calls it "adroit." And when it fulfills condition (3)—which implies the fulfillment of (1) and (2)—it is a successful exercise of the capacity, which Sosa would call "apt."[22] It is thus an essential feature of this conception of a capacity that it is possible for two acts to be identical insofar as both fulfill (1) and (2) but for only one of them to fulfill (1) specifically *because* it fulfills (2). Thus, virtue epistemology holds that it is possible for an act to constitute a manifestation of an epistemic capacity *in the very same sense* that an act of knowing does, yet without itself being an act of knowing. This might be because it does not fulfill the end of the capacity, in which case the act is competent in the sense of being "adroit" but not "accurate," or it might be because the act does fulfill the end of the capacity but not in virtue of its competence, in which case the act is "accurate" and "adroit" but not "accurate" because "adroit."

This analysis of a successful exercise of a capacity illustrates that and how the causal efficacy of a capacity is, on this conception, logically independent of the end of that capacity. For on this conception, the causal aspects of our notion of a capacity—which we exploit in speaking of "manifestations," "actualizations," or "exercises"—can be understood quite independently of the question of whether a particular act agrees with the end of the capacity. The question whether an act is a manifestation of the capacity to y can be settled independently of determining whether it fulfills the end of that capacity. According to virtue epistemology, claims (1) and (2) are logically independent of one another. This is why claim (3) must be separately added to the account.

Now if we instead understand a capacity for knowledge as a form of teleological causality, we precisely deny this logical independence. For we then represent the causal efficacy of a capacity as logically dependent on its end. Whereas a mechanistic conception of capacities takes it to be possible to describe what it is for an act to constitute a manifestation of a capacity without thereby making reference to the telos of the capacity in question, a teleological conception of capacities demands

[22] Ibid.

that one refer to the telos of the capacity in order to so much as describe a given act as a manifestation of the capacity in question. It follows that characterizations of acts as manifestations of capacities that cannot be exercised under all possible circumstances must, accordingly, be understood disjunctively: namely, either as perfect manifestations of the capacity, which would then be identical with the perfect realization of its telos, or as manifestations of the capacity that are faulty in one way or another, which would amount to an imperfect realization of the capacity's telos. If a capacity for knowledge exhibits a teleological form of causality, then judging that a given act constitutes a manifestation of that capacity entails a judgment about the act's agreement with the concept of knowledge under which we bring it in characterizing it as a manifestation of a capacity for knowledge.

### 3. Kant's Refutation of the Idea of an "Implanted Subjective Disposition"

We argued that we need a teleological conception of capacities in order to adequately account for the idea of knowledge. A mechanistic conception of capacities will not do. However, a teleological conception of a capacity for knowledge is faced with a question that might threaten its very intelligibility. For the above account of a capacity for knowledge must explain how we can understand the possibility of a "cause" whose efficacy depends on the employment of the concept of knowledge. How can we account for such a "cause"? How, we have to ask, is such a "cause" even possible?

I will develop an answer to this question by taking as my starting point Kant's discussion of the same issue. Kant's most straightforward answer to this question can be found in §27 of the *Critique of Pure Reason,* where he summarizes the argument he has just given in the so-called Transcendental Deduction. For our purposes we do not have to worry about the details of the Deduction but only need to consider its most general ambition, as Kant presents it. The task of the Transcendental Deduction is to demonstrate the "objective validity" of the "pure concepts" that correspond to the forms of judgment. Kant takes himself to have completed this task by the end of §26. One way to characterize his result, which brings it into contact with the question we now face, is as follows. By the end of §26, Kant takes himself to have shown that the idea of a subject capable of forming judgments about sensibly given objects is identical to the idea of a subject who possesses a capacity for knowledge about sensibly given objects. For the very concepts a subject must possess in order to make judgments about sensibly given objects—the "pure concepts"—are demonstrably valid, *a priori,* of any sensibly given object. However, this characterization of the result of the Transcendental Deduction seems to elicit a worry about the very possibility of such a capacity. Up to this point one might think Kant has managed to show that, and why a sensible being who possesses the concepts constitutive of the unity of a judgment is thereby in possession of a capacity for knowledge of objects of experience. But it is tempting to think that he has not yet addressed the question of how a capacity for knowledge of objects of experience itself is possible. How, one might ask, can there even be such a thing as a capacity for knowledge of objects of experience?

This question rests on the assumption that demonstrating the objective status of the "pure concepts" does not yet provide an answer to this question. The discussion in §27 is meant to show that a proper understanding of the status of the "pure concepts" already contains an answer to this question. Thus, §27 aims to ensure that the idea of "pure concepts" is understood in the right way. It does so by arguing that a certain account of the "cause" of a capacity for knowledge of objects of experience is incompatible with a proper understanding of such a capacity and that there is, in fact, only one way to adequately conceive of it.

The account that Kant wants to rule out as incompatible with a proper understanding of a capacity for knowledge of objects of experience is one that tries to answer the question we raised above in the following way. We can understand a capacity for experiential knowledge in an analogous way to how we understand artifacts. According to this argument, the idea of a capacity for experiential knowledge is a species of a genus of teleological causality whose fundamental understanding is provided by the idea of artifacts. Kant's concern is to rule out this (mis)interpretation. In so doing, he brings into view an alternative understanding of the kind of teleological causality that is exhibited by a capacity for knowledge, one that is, in a crucial respect, different from that exhibited by artifacts.

Let us therefore take a look at the case of artifacts and how to account for the kind of teleological causality they exhibit. One of Kant's paradigmatic examples of an artifact in the third Critique is a clock. The defining characteristic of a clock is its ability to tell time. We can express this by saying that, like a capacity for knowledge, a clock is a cause whose efficacy is dependent on the concept of its distinctive effect—namely, telling the time. For it is no accident that the clock has this ability. Rather, the concept of the clock's distinctive effect—namely, telling the time—is, in a certain sense, the cause of its being constituted in the particular way that it is. The concept of its effect is the cause of the clock in the sense that the concept of telling the time becomes efficacious in the actions of a rational subject by determining her actions "in the production and combination of [its] parts" through a conceptual representation of this effect.[23] The fundamental cause of the clock is thus a rational subject—the clockmaker—who produces the clock in accordance with a conceptual representation of its distinctive effect. And a clock that is thus produced in accordance with a concept of this effect is constituted precisely so as to generate this effect. Thus, an object that is produced in such a way will do things that necessarily agree with the concept of telling time.

Kant considers the question of whether a capacity for knowledge of objects of experience, which we want to know how it is possible to possess, can also be understood in this manner. He invites us to think of our cognitive faculty as a "subjective disposition for thinking implanted in us with our very existence [ . . . ] which is so ordered by our creator that its use is in precise agreement with the laws of nature in accordance with which experience proceeds (a sort of preformation system of pure reason)."[24]

Kant's proposal here is that we should try to understand our capacity for knowledge of objects of experience in just the same way that we understand a clock's capacity to tell time. We should, accordingly,

---

[23] Kant, *Kritik der Urteilskraft*, §65, AA 5:373.
[24] Kant, *Kritik der reinen Vernunft*, B167.

imagine that some creator has implanted in us a subjective capacity for thought and that this creator has instituted this capacity for thought in such a way that it agrees "with the laws of nature in accordance with which experience proceeds." The idea that this subjective faculty for thought is ordered precisely so as to agree with the "laws of nature in accordance with which experience proceeds" means that our creator has equipped this faculty with precisely those concepts whose employment in thought leads to judgments that agree with objects of experience.

Kant formulates several objections to the mooted hypothesis, though he takes only one of them to be "decisive."[25] The crucial objection is supposed to demonstrate that the mooted proposal is actually incompatible with the concept of knowledge. The objection is that this suggestion can only make sense of the "subjective necessity" of employing the concepts "implanted" in us but cannot account for their "objective necessity." Kant's argument runs as follows. The hypothesis can admittedly explain why we cannot help but make judgments about objects of experience by bringing them under one or another of the concepts that have been "implanted" in us. But if the employment of these concepts represents nothing more than "an arbitrary subjective necessity implanted in us" for "combining representations in accordance with such a rule governing their relations," then it is impossible for us ever to make a judgment in which we are conscious that our judgment necessarily agrees with the object of experience.[26] In such a case, Kant says, one can only ever say: "I am so constituted that I cannot think these representations otherwise than as thus connected."[27] And this outcome, Kant writes, "is precisely what the skeptic most desires. For then all our insight through the supposed objective validity of our judgments is nothing but sheer illusion, and there would be no shortage of people who would not admit this subjective necessity (which can only be felt) in their own case."[28]

What Kant is saying here is that the idea of a creator who installs in us a faculty of thought in accordance with a concept of the agreement

---

[25] Ibid., B168.
[26] Ibid.
[27] Ibid.
[28] Ibid.

between its judgments and the objects of experience is incompatible
with the idea of knowledge. His argument is that, according to the hypothesis, we are unable to perform acts in which we combine concepts
into the kind of unity that involves a consciousness of the "objective necessity" of this combination, i.e., the sort of unity that involves consciousness of the necessity of combining these concepts to a unity that is *in the
object* and not just in us.[29] Yet performing a judgment of the form "a is F,"
Kant argues, involves doing just that: namely, combining concepts into a
kind of unity that involves a consciousness of the necessity of this combination as one that resides in the object—one that is therefore and in that
sense represented as in necessary agreement with the object.

On the creator hypothesis, performing a judgment of the form "a is F"
would simply be impossible. For it is conceivable, on this hypothesis,
that there could have been, in fact, no agreement between our faculty
of thought and the objects of our experience. This rules out the possibility to combine concepts in a way that involves a consciousness of
their necessary agreement with the objects we experience. Thus, if this
hypothesis were true, it would be impossible to perform judgments
that exhibit this form.

Kant's refutation of the idea that a capacity for knowledge of objects
of experience might be considered an "implanted subjective disposition" entails a denial of the idea that the teleological causality exhibited by a capacity for knowledge of objects of experience is of the same
sort as that exhibited in an artifact. In order to get clearer about this
distinction between two different species of a teleological causality
that is entailed in Kant's argument, let us compare, once more, a capacity for knowledge with a clock's capacity to tell time. In the latter
case we can understand quite well how a thing can have a capacity
whose causal efficacy is determined by a concept (of its proper effect):
namely, by positing a creator, distinct from the thing in question, who
has the rational capacity for producing things in accordance with a
concept of their effects. The idea of a creator, distinct from the thing in
question, who has the rational capacity for producing things in accordance with a concept of their effects, is not only not incompatible with

---

[29] Ibid., B167.

the thing's capacity. Rather, it constitutes its very explanation. By contrast, this mode of explanation, Kant wants to say, is unavailable to us in the case of a capacity for knowledge of objects of experience. Kant's argument, as we seen above, focuses on the possibility of a judgment in which one is conscious of one's judgment as being in necessary agreement with the object of experience. Now, being conscious of one's judgment as being in necessary agreement with the object of experience means being conscious of one's judgment as non-accidentally true. Yet if knowledge consists in non-accidentally true judgment, then being conscious of one's judgment as non-accidentally true means that one is conscious of one's judgment as in agreement with the concept of knowledge. That is, the idea of judgment Kant is concerned with is the idea of judgment as a self-conscious exercise of one's capacity for knowledge.

Thus, when Kant claims that the idea of an "implanted subjective disposition" undermines the very intelligibility of an act of judgment, his argument is not based on the idea that the concept of knowledge is distinct from the concept of telling time, in terms of its content. Rather, it is distinct in form. In contrast to the concept of telling time, Kant argues, the concept of knowledge is the concept of a *self-conscious* teleological cause. What fundamentally distinguishes a capacity for knowledge from a clock's capacity to tell time is that the activities of a clock, which manifest its capacity to tell time, are logically distinct from the acts that determine those activities as manifestations of the capacity to tell time. The clock tells the time—but it does not itself make judgments about its present activities as acts of telling the time. To be sure, the clock would not have the capacity to tell the time in the first place if there had never been a judgment that asserted an agreement between its activities and the concept of telling time. But a judgment that asserts an agreement between the clock's activities and the concept of telling time is a manifestation of a capacity that is different from the one manifested in the clock's own activities. Hence, in the case of an artifact there are two distinct capacities in play. On the one hand, there is the capacity for judgments about the agreement between certain acts and the telos of a certain capacity, e.g., telling the time. On the other hand, there is another capacity, distinct from the first, which the clock manifests when it tells the time. The clock's capacity to tell time is characterized by the fact that its manifestations are logically distinct from actualizations of the first capacity. We can express this by saying that the clock's capacity is a non-self-conscious teleological cause.

Knowledge is different from telling time, Kant argues, in that it is a self-conscious telos. That is, unlike the clock's capacity, a capacity for knowledge is not simply one whose exercises consist in acts that fall under the concept of that capacity from some perspective or other. A capacity for knowledge is one whose exercises fall under the concept of this capacity from the perspective of the subject whose capacity it is. It is a capacity whose exercises consist in an employment of the concept of that capacity by the subject who possesses it. In the case of a capacity for knowledge, an act that manifests this capacity contains a representation of that act as being in (perfect or imperfect) agreement with the concept of the capacity. The representation of an act as being in agreement with the concept of the relevant capacity and the exercise of that capacity itself are not two acts stemming from different capacities but two aspects of one and the same act.

We have thus come to the following characterization of the kind of cause that a capacity for knowledge is: *A capacity for knowledge is a cause that is dependent on the concept of knowledge in the sense that exercises of the capacity are dependent on a subject's representing her act as being in agreement (whether perfect or imperfect) with the concept of knowledge.*

Kant's argument is thus that the hypothesis that a creator implanted in us a subjective capacity for thought—a capacity constituted in such a way that its acts agree with objects of experience—can offer no answer to the question of how a capacity for knowledge, in the above sense, is possible. Rather, the creator hypothesis is incompatible with self-conscious acts of knowledge. The sort of explanation that the mooted hypothesis offers renders impossible the very thing it is trying to explain.

It is worth noting that the idea of a creator, taken in its logical form, can come under various headings, all of which would still be subject to the same Kantian argument. For example, the creator hypothesis might come in the guise of the idea of "inborn capacities," i.e., in the guise of the idea that we happen to have a capacity for knowledge of objects of experience as part of our natural endowment as a matter of luck. Or it might come in the guise of the idea that we happen to have such a capacity as part of our natural endowment, not as a matter of luck but as the result of evolution, given that only those beings who happened to possess a capacity for knowledge managed to survive various ecological pressures. By now it should be obvious that, when applied to the idea of knowledge as a self-conscious teleological cause, the evolutionary story operates in the very same logical framework as the deistic story. For the evolutionary account—just like the deistic hypothesis—explains the agreement between our judgments and their objects in a way that is external to the judgments thus explained. The one hypothesis attributes such agreement to an intelligent creator, the other attributes it to an evolutionary process. By "external" I mean that these accounts conceive of the capacity they want to explain as one whose exercise does not, as such, entail a judgment about its agreement with the object to which it refers. If the agreement is thus represented as external to exercises of the capacity, however, then what is explained is not a capacity for knowledge in the sense of a capacity that is self-consciously exercised in judgments. The most that we could explain in such a manner would be a subjective disposition to combine certain representations in a certain way. This disposition might be so strong that one cannot help but actualize it. But it would not be a capacity for combining concepts into the unity of a judgment that represents that combination as grounded in the object.

Any explanation that represents a capacity for knowledge as something whose agreement with the objects is external to it, in the above sense, undermines the very capacity it seeks to explain in the attempt to explain it. We should therefore understand Kant's discussion of the creator hypothesis as a vivid example of a much more general class of explanations that are, logically speaking, in the same boat.

## 4. Knowledge as a Self-Constituting Capacity

We asked how we can understand the possibility of a capacity for knowledge, e.g., the capacity for knowledge of objects of experience. Our result, so far, is negative. We have established how it cannot be understood: we cannot conceive of it as a subjective disposition implanted in us "with our existence"—whether by a creator, or by evolution, or by luck—a disposition in virtue of which it just happens to be the case that our thoughts agree with the objects of our experience. How then are we to understand it?

Kant discusses the creator hypothesis as a tempting apparent "middle path" between what he describes as the "only two ways" of understanding the possibility of a necessary agreement between "experience and the concepts of its objects" we employ in judging about them, and thus to understand the possibility of knowledge. Kant writes:

> Now there are only two ways in which we can conceive [denken] of a necessary agreement between experience and the concepts of its objects: either experience makes these concepts possible, or these concepts make experience possible.[30]

Now, it is clear that the first way of conceiving the necessary agreement between experience and the concepts of its objects—namely, by thinking of the experience of the object as making the concept of the object possible—is not available to us here. For the present issue is to understand how there can so much as be a capacity whose concepts of objects are in necessary agreement with its experiences of objects. And one cannot explain how there can be such a capacity by supposing that experiences of objects make the concepts of those objects possible. Experiences of objects that make concepts of those objects possible can explain how there can be concepts whose use in judgments would be a manifestation of a capacity for experiential knowledge. But they cannot explain how there can be a capacity for experiential knowledge in the first place—i.e., how the capacity presupposed by this explanation is itself possible.

Kant therefore concludes that a capacity for knowledge of objects of experience must be conceived of in the second of the "only two ways."

---

[30] Ibid., B166, see also B124–125.

We have to conceive of a capacity for knowledge of objects of experience as a capacity that contains concepts of objects that, in a certain sense, bring about the objects of experiential knowledge—and hence experiential knowledge itself. Such concepts do not bring about the objects of experiential knowledge in the sense that they generate the existence of the objects, "since," as Kant emphasizes, "representation unto itself does not produce its object with respect to its existence."[31] Instead, such concepts give rise to its objects *as* objects of possible experiential knowledge. To employ such concepts, Kant argues, means to have general representations of objects that necessarily agree with the objects of experiential knowledge, for they make the objects of experiential knowledge, as such, possible. Having such general representations of objects thus means to have a kind of *knowledge* of these objects. What kind of knowledge is this? Kant calls it "a priori knowledge." It is *a priori* knowledge in a sense that contrasts with experiential knowledge. It is a kind of knowledge that cannot be acquired through an exercise of a rational capacity for experiential knowledge, for it is knowledge that explains how a rational capacity for experiential knowledge is possible in the first place. Now, given that this kind of knowledge consists in representations that make the objects of experiential knowledge, as such, possible, it is a kind of knowledge of objects that would be manifested in any act of experiential knowledge as that which explains any such act. Because it is not knowledge of this or that particular object, but knowledge of something general that characterizes any object of experiential knowledge, as such, it is a kind of *general* knowledge of objects of experience. Yet the idea of a capacity that contains general knowledge of objects of experience that would be manifested in any act of experiential knowledge as that which explains the possibility of any such act is nothing other than the idea of a capacity for experiential knowledge that contains *a priori* knowledge of itself as a capacity for experiential knowledge.

Kant's answer to the question of how a rational capacity for experiential knowledge is possible thus is the following: What makes a rational capacity for experiential knowledge possible is a certain kind of knowledge—namely, *a priori* knowledge of itself as a capacity for

31 Ibid., B125.

experiential knowledge.[32] According to Kant's argument, this is the only way to explain the possibility of a rational capacity for experiential knowledge. Now, to explain a rational capacity for experiential knowledge through an act of *a priori* knowledge of the capacity itself, does not explain the capacity in question through something that is different from what it explains. The act that explains how a rational capacity for experiential knowledge is possible already entails what it explains.

We might call a capacity that is explained through an act that already entails what it explains a self-constituting capacity. It is, as Kant argues, conceptually impossible to think of a rational capacity for experiential knowledge without conceiving it as a capacity that constitutes itself by employing concepts of objects that make objects of experiential knowledge possible in the first place and, hence, that constitutes itself through *a priori* knowledge of itself as a capacity for experiential knowledge.

---

[32] It is an advantage of our account of the Kantian position that we can allow ourselves to abstract from the specific Kantian distinction between the forms of sensibility and the forms of the understanding, because it allows us to liberate our account from the problems that affect the Kantian position due to this distinction. One of the deepest problems has been pointed out by McDowell in "Hegel's Idealism as Radicalization of Kant," where he brings out how the "brute fact" character of the forms of sensibility that go with the way in which Kant treats this distinction spoils the whole Kantian ambition to have succeeded in entitling himself to a position that is compatible with "empirical realism." This problem is due to his methodological starting point, which is to give an account of sensibility's contribution to knowledge in isolation from the understanding—which, as we discover at the end of the Transcendental Deduction, proves to be impossible. If one gives up this starting point, no such problem can even arise. However, to appreciate this problem does not entail that we have to ascribe to Kant a "two-capacity conception" of knowledge, according to which knowledge is the product of two capacities whose exercises can be conceived to be logically independent of one another. Although this is a widespread reading of Kant, it fails to do justice to what Kant actually achieves. I argue against such readings of Kant in "Spontaneity and Receptivity in Kant's Theory of Knowledge." That such a reading of Kant fails to appreciate the fundamental thought at which Kant arrives by the end of the Deduction is one of the crucial points of McDowell's *Mind and World* as well as of his criticism of Sellars's reading of Kant—see, e.g., McDowell, "Sellars on Perceptual Experience," "The Logical Form of an Intuition," and "Intentionality as a Relation."

# X

# Knowledge and Practice

## 1. Rational Capacities and Practice

The account of a rational capacity for knowledge as a self-constituting capacity that we have developed up to this point is abstract insofar as it abstracts from the idea of an empirical subject as the bearer of this capacity and thus from the idea that this capacity is, for example, my capacity, or yours, or Jim's. The insight that a rational capacity for knowledge of objects of experience is a self-constituting capacity responds to the question of how a rational capacity for knowledge of objects of experience is so much as intelligible. However, the answer to this question does not yet give us an answer to the question of how a self-constituting capacity, in the above sense, can belong to an individual, empirical subject. It does not explain how it is possible for an individual, empirical subject to possess the very concepts that make objects of experiential knowledge, as such, possible and hence to be in possession of a rational capacity for experiential knowledge. In fact, our insight into the self-constituting character of such a capacity makes this question all the more urgent. For it entails the negative idea that we cannot understand a rational capacity for knowledge as an "inborn capacity." However, if we cannot understand it in this way, how else are we to understand it?

---

This takes us back to a question that we raised in Part Three, although then we were not in a position to address it. To recall: In Chapter VI we worked with the preliminary Aristotelian claim that rational capacities are not "innate" but "come by practice."[33] Or, as Aristotle also puts it, rational capacities do not "come to us by nature," we instead get them "by first exercising them."[34] When we introduced the notion of rational capacities in this way, we were not yet able to say whether rational capacities essentially involve this specific form of acquisition or how precisely this specific form of acquisition would need to be understood in the case of a rational capacity for knowledge. Our aim now is to see why this anticipatory characterization is, in fact, correct. To that extent, we will be concerned to work out the sense of the idea of "practice" that Aristotle invokes in order to explain a subject's possession of rational capacities.

To this end, let us first clarify the import of Aristotle's distinction between capacities we have "by nature" and those we must acquire "by first exercising them." The distinction that Aristotle has in mind here is logical, not temporal. That is to say, it is not concerned to differentiate capacities one has from birth from those developed later on. The fact that one develops a particular capacity only after birth does not mean, for Aristotle, that one does not possess it "by nature." The distinction at issue is a distinction between two ways of explaining a subject's possession of a capacity. Aristotle formulates the distinction in the following way. On the one hand, there are capacities that are such that one cannot appeal to the acts that manifest them in order to explain one's possession of the capacity. Thus, we did not acquire our eyes by seeing various things. Rather, it is because we have eyes that we then "used them."[35] These capacities can be contrasted with those whose possession is explained by acts of precisely the sort the capacity itself explains. Aristotle famously expresses this point as follows: "but excellences we get by first exercising them, as also happens in the case of the arts as well. For the things we have to learn before we can do, we learn by doing,

[33] Aristotle, *Metaphysics*, IX.5, 1047b33–34.
[34] Aristotle, *Nicomachean Ethics*, 1103a26–31.
[35] Ibid., 1103a30.

e.g., men become builders by building and lyre-players by playing the lyre."[36] Rational capacities are capacities for doing things that one has to learn to do. We acquire these capacities, Aristotle argues, by doing the things we thereby learn to do. Their acquisition thus is a matter of learning—namely, learning by doing.

First off, it is not immediately clear how what Aristotle describes as "learning" is so much as possible. One is inclined to ask how it can be possible to acquire a capacity in a manner that Aristotle qualifies as "learning," if learning consists in performing acts of precisely the sort that the capacity in question is supposed to first enable one to perform. How are the acts that constitute learning—and on which the possession of rational capacities is supposed to rest—even intelligible, on Aristotle's account?

Let's look more closely at these acts that constitute learning. On the one hand, Aristotle characterizes them as acts of the very capacity that is supposed to be acquired through them. Now, in order to count as acts of the very capacity that is supposed to be acquired through them, they must be acts that agree with the capacity to be acquired through them. They might be, for example, acts of lyre playing, by means of which one acquires the capacity to play the lyre. Or they might be acts of building, by means of which one comes to be a builder. Or acts of reading, through which one acquires the capacity to read. And so on. On the other hand, however, Aristotle characterizes the subject who performs these acts as someone who does not (yet) possess the capacity with which these acts accord. How is it possible to combine both characterizations? How is it possible for a subject, who does not yet possess a certain capacity, to perform acts that are in agreement with that capacity?

Aristotle's answer is that we can explain such acts if we expand the scene of explanation to include not just a single subject but at least two subjects who stand in a particular relation to one another: namely, a relation that requires, on the one side, a subject who provides examples of exercises of the capacity and, on the other side, a subject who responds to the examples that are provided to her by repeating these examples. It is such a relation between two subjects that Aristotle

---

[36] Ibid. 1103a30–b1.

characterizes as a case of learning in the sense that is relevant to the acquisition of rational capacities. On one side of the relation there must be a subject who exercises the capacity in an exemplary manner, and on the other side there must be a subject who takes the exercises of the other as exemplary manifestations of a capacity to which she responds by repeating them. Learning in the sense that is relevant to the acquisition of rational capacities is learning from someone. For sure, such a relation of learning can take many different shapes. In many cases it will look like the competent subject is enjoining the other to repeat what she is doing. She might say: "Now, it's your turn! Do it yourself!" Yet there are many cases in which this relation of learning simply consists in one subject exercising the capacity in a paradigmatic fashion and the other subject's regardless of whether she is explicitly enjoined to do so or not, just striving to do precisely what the other subject is doing. What matters for Aristotle is not the specific shape of such a relation but its peculiar status. His argument is that such a relation of learning between two subjects, which is realized in their respective doings—the one providing examples of the capacity, the other responding to these examples—is constitutive for the explanation of the possession of a rational capacity. For it is precisely in virtue of referring to such a situation of learning that we can explain how it is possible for a subject's acts to agree with a certain capacity that the subject does not (yet) have prior to and independently of that situation of learning but acquires only in and through that situation of learning. For then we can explain such acts—acts of learning—through the very capacity with which they agree, in a mediated way: namely, by referring to the manifestations of that capacity in the acts of the competent subject as something on which the learning subject's possession of that capacity is dependent.

Let's look more closely at what is required in order for such a relation of learning to obtain. We first characterized it as a relation in which one subject takes the exercises of another as exemplary manifestations of a capacity to which she responds by repeating them. For then the acts of the learning subject are, indeed, related to the capacity in question in such a way that their agreement with the capacity can be explained through the capacity itself. This is what Aristotle implies when he characterizes these acts as exercises of the capacity in question, namely, that the acts through which one comes into possession of a capacity must themselves be explained by that very capacity. It is appropriate to say that such acts of learning are exercises of the capacity in question precisely because they are *responses to examples* of that capacity that are provided to the learning subject by the other, competent subject. Now for a subject's act to be a response to another subject's example of exercising a certain capacity, her act has to be guided by a representation of the other's act as a manifestation of that capacity, i.e., as a manifestation of something that can, in principle, also be manifested in other acts—such as her own. Thus, a subject who responds to examples provided by another subject in the manner that is characteristic for learning can do so only if she has a representation of the capacity that she is in the process of acquiring.

It is in this way that we can explain how a subject can perform acts that accord with a capacity that she does not possess prior to and independently of these acts—namely, by introducing into our framework a second subject who is distinguished from the former one in being competent with respect to the relevant capacity. For that enables us to explain the accord between the learner's acts and the relevant capacity through that very capacity in virtue of the fact that the capacity is available to the learning subject through the exemplary acts provided by the competent subject. Acquiring a rational capacity through practice in the sense we are inquiring about thus entails that one performs acts that are grounded in the relevant capacity in a particular way: namely, such that their actualization of the capacity is mediated by and dependent on the exercises of this very capacity by another subject.[37] Aristotle's claim is that a subject gradually comes to possess a capacity of the relevant sort precisely by repeatedly performing acts that agree with the capacity in this mediated manner. To come to possess a particular capacity in this manner thus means becoming capable

---

[37] On this reading, see Burnyeat, "Aristotle on Learning to Be Good," which discusses the general form of acquiring rational capacities by focusing on the specific case of acquiring ethical virtues.

of exercising it in a way that becomes more and more independent of its being manifested in the acts of another subject.

This account of what it means to acquire a capacity through practice explains why there is an intrinsic relation between a rational capacity and this manner of acquisition, just as Aristotle argues. For as we have seen, the idea of acquiring a capacity through practice is the idea of acquiring a capacity through acts—"acts of learning"—whose performance involves the learning subject's being guided by a representation of the relevant capacity that is in (either perfect or imperfect) accord with the relevant capacity that the subject thereby acquires. In performing such acts of learning, the subject comes to possess a capacity whose possession entails that she has an understanding of it precisely because and insofar as she has acquired that capacity in that manner, i.e., through acts of learning. That is to say, she has a capacity of which she has a representation that is in (either perfect or imperfect) accordance with the represented capacity just in virtue of the way in which she came to possess this capacity—namely, by performing acts that were guided by a representation of the capacity as something with which she brings her acts into accord, including her acts of representing this very capacity.

The idea of a rational capacity and the idea of acquisition through practice are thus intrinsically linked. Rational capacities can be acquired only through practice and cannot be possessed by nature, for it is only the former manner of acquisition that can explain why the capacity thus acquired is such as to contain an understanding of what it is to possess and to exercise the capacity in question. Conversely, we can also say that capacities acquired through practice are rational capacities. They are rational in the sense that possessing such a capacity entails having a representation of the capacity that can guide one's exercises of it and through which one can justify one's acts by representing them as being in agreement with the capacity. One can, for example, explain what one is doing on the slopes by saying, "I am lifting my left leg when I make a right turn because this is how one skis."

We have thus presented the acquisition of rational capacities as a process that builds on the learning subject's capacity to form a representation of the capacity that she is to acquire—a representation that is in non-accidental agreement with that capacity. For that is what all acts of learning are: acts that are in non-accidental agreement with the capacity in question in the sense that their agreement with the capacity is explained through the capacity in question. Yet having representations that are in non-accidental agreement with what they represent, we argued, means to be in possession of a rational capacity for knowledge. If that is so, however, then it seems to be impossible to explain the acquisition of a rational capacity for knowledge in the same manner as one explains rational capacities in general—namely, through practice. For it seems that the possibility of a subject's acquiring rational capacities through practice already presupposes the subject's possession of a rational capacity for knowledge. Hence, her possession of the latter capacity cannot be explained through practice.

The problem we encounter in our account of a capacity for knowledge is this: The thought that a rational capacity is acquired through practice seems to already presuppose the possession of precisely the rational capacity for knowledge that it is our chief aim to give an account of. It appears to follow from this that it is impossible to acquire a rational capacity for knowledge through practice, because the possibility of acquiring any rational capacity through practice already depends on just such a capacity. And this seems to force us to a thought that we already recognized as incompatible with the idea of a rational capacity for knowledge: namely, the thought that a rational capacity for knowledge must be a capacity that one has "by nature."[38] A rational capacity for knowledge cannot be a natural capacity, we followed Kant in arguing, because knowledge is a self-conscious end, which it could not be if it were a natural capacity. Yet now it appears that it cannot be

---

[38] A striking illustration of the sheer insolubility of this dilemma can be found in the discussion between Bakhurst and Luntley about the nature and presuppositions of learning. Bakhurst and Luntley are principally concerned with Wittgenstein and McDowell's idea of conceptual capacities as a matter of "second nature." Their debate is about whether the acquisition of conceptual capacities is something that occurs "through learning" or "by nature." See Bakhurst, *The Formation of Reason,* as well as his "Freedom and Second Nature in *The Formation of Reason.*" See also Luntley, "Training and Learning" and "Conceptual Development and the Paradox of Learning." A further intervention in this debate can be found in Stickney, "Training and Mastery of Techniques in Wittgenstein's Later Philosophy: A Response to Michael Luntley."

acquired through practice either, because every act of learning rests on just this capacity.

## 2. How Does One Acquire a Rational Capacity for Knowledge?

We seem to face a dilemma consisting of two equally impossible answers to the question of how an individual, empirical subject can acquire a rational capacity for knowledge—two answers that nevertheless seem to exhaust the spectrum of possibilities. The dilemma we have encountered is the following:

(1) A rational capacity for knowledge must be a capacity that we acquire through practice, because otherwise it could not be a self-conscious capacity.

(2) A rational capacity for knowledge cannot be a capacity that we acquire through practice, because the acquisition of a rational capacity through practice rests on that capacity. Hence, it must be a capacity we have by nature.

In what follows we will come to see that this dilemma rests on a false conception of what it means to explain the acquisition of rational capacities through "practice." It rests on the presupposition that the role of the idea of "practice" is to explain a subject's possession of a capacity through something that is logically more fundamental than the thing explained in the sense that it explains the subject's possession of the capacity in question through acts that do not yet, in a certain sense, manifest the capacity whose possession they explain. I will argue that this presupposition is a misunderstanding.

To this end, let us recall the principle governing the distinction between the sort of explanation we give when we represent a capacity as one that "comes to us by nature" as opposed to the sort of explanation we give when we represent it as a capacity that we acquire "by practice." The distinction lies in the fact that, in the one case, particular acts of a subject, which accord with the relevant capacity in a particular manner, have an explanatory role to play in accounting for the subject's possession of the capacity, whereas, in the other case, they do not. Now when Kant contends that a rational capacity for experiential knowledge can only be understood as a capacity that constitutes itself through *a priori* knowledge of the objects of experiential knowledge and hence through *a priori* knowledge of itself as a capacity for experiential knowledge, then this means that the question of how to understand an empirical, individual subject's possession of a rational capacity for experiential knowledge and the question of how to understand her possession of *a priori* knowledge of such a capacity is one and the same. There are not two things to be explained such that one might wonder which comes first. What is to be explained is the possession of a capacity that is constituted as what it is—namely, a rational capacity for experiential knowledge—through *a priori* knowledge of such a capacity. Now the Aristotelian answer to that question seems to be that a subject comes to be in possession of such a capacity "by practice." Just as one learns to ski by skiing and to dance by dancing, one learns to know by knowing. Yet, this answer, the above objection wants to say, is impossible because in order to be able to learn something one already needs to have a rational capacity for knowledge.

In order to see that this objection rests upon a misunderstanding of the relevant idea of "practice" we have to look, once again, at how one has to characterize the nature of those acts through which one acquires a rational capacity. For a learning subject to stand in a relation of learning to another subject, we argued above, she must perform acts whose agreement with the relevant capacity cannot be explained through a capacity the subject has prior to and independently of these acts. Nevertheless, such acts have to be explained through the relevant capacity in a particular manner—namely, in a manner that is dependent on the exercises of the relevant capacity of another subject to which the learning subject responds. Otherwise, the agreement of the acts of the incompetent subject with the capacity in question would be a mere coincidence, which would mean to deny that her act is an act of learning. If we apply this general thought to the case of knowledge, then it means that the learning subject acquires a capacity for knowledge by responding to the knowledgeable acts of another subject as examples of a capacity for knowledge. That is to say, the subject forms a representation of the capacity for knowledge that is exemplified in the latter's acts and guides her own acts by that representation. In the simplest case, she does this by simply responding to the knowledgeable act of the other with the same sort of knowledgeable act. Thus, a child might respond to her mother's judgment that there is a badger over there—which she might express by saying, "Look, there is a badger over there!"—simply by repeating that same judgment—which she might express by pointing at the badger and exclaiming, "Badger!" When the child is on the verge of acquiring a rational capacity for perceptual knowledge through the manner Aristotle describes—namely, through practice—then what she is doing when she exclaims "Badger!," while seeing a badger, is responding to her mother's perceptual judgment of a badger with a perceptual judgment that she represents to be an instance of the same capacity that she represents her mother's perceptual judgment to be an instance of.

We can thus affirm the Aristotelian thought that a rational capacity for experiential knowledge is acquired through practice. And that is to say it is acquired through acts of perceptual knowledge. For, just as in the case of any other rational capacity, what allows us to understand these acts as acts of perceptual knowledge is the fact that the subject stands in a relation of learning to another subject. For placing the subject into a relation of learning to another subject allows us to explain the acts of the learning subject through the capacity for perceptual knowledge, yet in a manner that is different from the manner in which we explain such an act in the case of an already competent knower. To explain perceptual knowledge in the case of an already competent knower would mean explaining it through a capacity for perceptual knowledge that the subject herself possesses and hence is available to the subject independently of another subject's exemplary exercises of that capacity. By contrast, when a subject is about to acquire a capacity for perceptual knowledge through practice, she performs acts of perceptual knowledge whose accord with the capacity for perceptual knowledge cannot be explained through a capacity that is available to the learning subject independently of the other subject's exemplary exercises of that capacity. Rather, a learning subject performs acts of perceptual knowledge whose accord with a capacity for perceptual knowledge is explained through a capacity that is available to her only through the exemplary acts of the competent subject.

The objection according to which the acquisition of a rational capacity for perceptual knowledge cannot be explained by practice because any such explanation already presupposes a subject's possession of such a capacity rests upon a misunderstanding about the relevant idea of practice that is employed in such an explanation. It must presuppose that explaining a subject's possession of a rational capacity through practice must mean explaining her possession of it through acts that are, logically, less than exercises of the capacity whose possession is thereby explained. What we have to realize instead is that possession of a rational capacity, whichever capacity it is, is to be explained through acts that already *manifest* the capacity in question, yet in a particular manner: namely, in a manner that is *mediated through and dependent on the exemplary acts of another subject.* We get caught up in the above dilemma only if we conceive of the acts through which one explains the possession of a rational capacity in terms of acts that do not yet depend, in the particular sense specified above, on the very capacity whose possession is explained. When it comes to the acquisition of rational capacities, however, the acts through which one acquires a rational capacity are acts of learning that do not precede and ground the possession of the capacity in the sense that one can perform them without thereby already manifesting the capacity in a particular, mediated, and dependent way.

This does not mean that possession of a rational capacity for knowledge is not subject to development. Quite the contrary. As with all rational capacities, their possession—as well as their mastery—is a matter of degree and, hence, is subject to development and perfection. Yet what explains their possession and mastery, on whatever level that might be, are acts that are already manifestations of the capacity in question—even if they are manifestations that are deficient, in whatever respect, and hence subject to further perfection. To be dependent on the exemplary exercises of another competent subject is just one among many ways of actualizing one's rational capacity for perceptual knowledge in a deficient manner.

## 3. Knowledge and Objectivity

Finite knowledge, we claimed at the outset of this investigation, is characterized by the fact that its content is objective. The minimal account we gave of objective content was that the truth (or falsity) of an objective content is fixed independently of whether or not someone believes it. It is therefore logically possible for a subject to err in forming a belief about an objective content. Davidson expresses this minimal account of objectivity by saying that it must be logically possible for any given one of our beliefs to be false.[39] This Davidsonian account of the objectivity of the content of our knowledge clearly makes no reference to the idea of a rational capacity for knowledge. Thus, if what we have said is correct and the fundamental employment of the concept of knowledge consists in describing a rational capacity, then the concept of objectivity we invoke in order to characterize the status of the content of beliefs must likewise receive its sense from the idea of a rational capacity for knowledge. This does not mean that the above account of objective content is false. But it does mean that the fundamental understanding of what it means to say that some content is objective comes into view with the idea of a rational capacity for knowledge. What does this more fundamental understanding of objectivity look like?

We can approach this understanding if we first make clear what sort of account of objectivity is incompatible with the idea of a rational capacity for knowledge. It is the account of objectivity that Michael Williams describes as "perhaps non-controversial."[40] Williams's thesis is that the concept of objectivity that characterizes the status of the contents of our perceptual knowledge about the world can be explained by saying that "our experience could be just what it is and *all our beliefs about the world could be false*."[41] Moreover, he wants to argue that such an account of the objectivity of the contents of our beliefs about the

---

[39] Davidson, "A Coherence Theory of Truth and Knowledge," 140.

[40] Williams, *Unnatural Doubts,* 73, see also 74–77, 248–249.

[41] Ibid., 74. It is worth noting that Williams does not commit himself to this account of the objectivity of the contents of our beliefs (nor to any other account). Rather, he wants to argue for the claim that this account of objectivity does not have the skeptical consequences the skeptic takes it to have.

world according to which it is logically possible for us to have precisely the same sense experiences that we presently enjoy, yet without possessing any perceptual knowledge about the world, does not have any skeptical consequences. Williams wants to suggest that this account of objectivity is independent of any particular conception of the nature of knowledge and therefore neutral with respect to the problem of skepticism. According to Williams, skeptical consequences follow from this account of objectivity only if we combine it with a particular conception of the nature of knowledge: namely, a conception of knowledge on which beliefs about the world can enjoy the status of knowledge only if they are grounded in such sensory experiences.[42]

Williams thinks that this thought about a "foundational" relation between *such* sensory experiences and beliefs about the world constitutes the deepest root of the skeptical problematic. However, as we have shown, the very question with which Williams is concerned, namely whether there must be a "foundational" relation between such sensory experiences and beliefs about the world or not, can be meaningfully posed only if one denies what we have established: namely, that perceptual knowledge is a rational capacity. The deepest root of skepticism is not the idea of a "foundational" relation between such sensory experiences and beliefs, but the very idea of a sensory experience that "could be just what it is and *all our beliefs about the world could be false.*"[43]

If perceptual knowledge is a rational capacity, then one cannot account for the objectivity of our knowledge about the world by claiming that it is logically possible for us to enjoy the very same sensory experiences we do, yet without enjoying knowledge through them. For on the capacity account of knowledge, someone who has perceptual knowledge about the world does not have the same sensory experience as someone who lacks it. Someone who enjoys a sensory experience without acquiring perceptual knowledge through it is hindered from exercising her capacity for perceptual knowledge perfectly, and hence her sensory experience is a deficient act of that capacity. By contrast, a sensory experience on the basis of which someone acquires perceptual knowledge is a

[42] Ibid.
[43] Ibid.

*Perceptual knowledge is a capacity?*

perfect act of that capacity. Instead of being "perhaps non-controversial," Williams's account of the objectivity of our knowledge about the world rests on a particular conception of the nature of perceptual knowledge: namely, one that denies from the very outset that perceptual knowledge is a rational capacity.

On the capacity account of knowledge, the objectivity of the content of perceptual knowledge is to be understood in the following way. The contents of perceptual knowledge are objective in the sense that they are facts that are, as such, perceptually know*able*. They are facts that are what they are independently of and prior to any particular act of perceptual knowledge of them. This not only means that such facts are independent of any particular actualization of a capacity for perceptual knowledge. It also means that such facts are independent of the particular shape this capacity for knowledge takes on when it is possessed by an individual, empirical subject. A rational capacity for perceptual knowledge always takes on a particular shape when we connect it with an individual empirical creature—e.g., Jim, or Denis, or Lisa.[44] When we characterize an individual creature by saying she possesses a rational capacity for perceptual knowledge, we are no longer talking about a rational capacity for perceptual knowledge in general; we are instead talking about a particular rational capacity for perceptual knowledge. The particularity of this capacity is, among others, a function of the particularity of the conceptual repertoire that the individual creature possesses. For a given individual creature always has a particular conceptual repertoire in the sense that she, as she is here and now, has acquired these particular concepts but not (yet) others. A given individual creature, for example Katharina, as she is here and now, might not (yet) have the concept 'refrigerator.' Someone who does not have this concept will be unable to perceptually know that there is still apple juice in the refrigerator. On the capacity account of knowledge, it might nevertheless be an objective fact that there is still apple juice in the refrigerator, though it is not perceptually knowable for someone who lacks the concept 'refrigerator.'

---

[44] McDowell makes an analogous point in reference to the Aristotelian concept of virtue in *Mind and World*, 78–84.

We must accordingly distinguish two levels on which we can articulate the concept of a rational capacity for perceptual knowledge: one level on which we describe what a rational capacity for perceptual knowledge, in general, is and another level on which we describe a rational capacity for perceptual knowledge as something that characterizes a particular individual subject. The description of what it means to have a rational capacity for perceptual knowledge, in general, is abstract insofar as it abstracts from the particularities that pertain to such a capacity when it is possessed by a particular individual subject. It is on this abstract level of description that the concept of objectivity that characterizes the status of the content of actualizations of this capacity has its home.

The facts that make up the content of perceptual knowledge are thus objective in the sense that they are independent of any individual act of perceptual knowledge as well as of the individual shape that a capacity for perceptual knowledge takes when it is possessed by a particular individual. Accordingly, the concept of the content of perceptual knowledge, on the capacity account of knowledge, is not the concept of that which is known by a particular individual (or all of us collectively). Nor is it the concept of that which is perceptually knowable for a particular individual (or for us all collectively) here and now, given the particular shape of the conceptual repertoire that an individual creature (or all of us) here and now has. It is instead the concept of that which is perceptually knowable, in general, that is deployed whenever a capacity for perceptual knowledge—regardless of the particular shape it has when it is actualized by a particular, individual creature—is actualized in an act of knowledge, whether perfectly or imperfectly.

In our account of the objectivity of knowledge we made use of the distinction between two levels of articulating the concept of a rational capacity for perceptual knowledge. To understand this distinction properly one has to see that it is connected with a thought that we exploited in Chapter IX when we argued that someone (e.g., a small child) can have a rational capacity for perceptual knowledge even though she is not yet able to form judgments in a manner that could find expression in a speech act of the form, "I know that there is a badger over there because I see one." That is to say, it can be true to say about a child who exclaims "Badger!," while seeing and pointing at a badger, that she exercises a rational capacity for perceptual knowledge without it being true to say that she is able to employ concepts in a form of explanation that is expressed in the above sentence. According to the capacity account of knowledge, the fact that she cannot yet employ concepts in such a form of explanation does not mean that she is not yet in possession of a rational capacity for perceptual knowledge. Rather, it means that her perception of the badger is not yet a powerful exercise of her rational capacity for perceptual knowledge because she does not yet possess that capacity perfectly.

When we say that our investigation is an investigation of the concept of a rational capacity for perceptual knowledge, in general, we want to say that we investigate the meaning of this concept as it is employed to describe a paradigmatic instance of it. A paradigmatic instance of a rational capacity for perceptual knowledge is an instance through which one understands the very concept of that capacity and without which one could not understand any other instance of it. A paradigmatic instance of a rational capacity for perceptual knowledge is one in which such a capacity yields perceptual knowledge. In unfolding the concept of a rational capacity for perceptual knowledge, we are thus describing the shape such a capacity assumes when it contains acts in which it is fully or perfectly actualized. This does not imply that one possesses a rational capacity for perceptual knowledge only if one is able to perfectly exercise it. Rather, as we argued above, to perfectly exercise a rational capacity is something one has to learn. And that implies that it is possible to possess the capacity in question without already being able to perfectly exercise it. Thus, the fact that a small child cannot (yet) manifest her rational capacity for perceptual knowledge in the manner in which it would be manifested in a case of its perfect actualization—for example, because she cannot (yet) employ forms of explanation she might express by saying, "I know that there is badger over there because I see one"—does not mean that the child does not yet possess a rational capacity for perceptual knowledge. It instead means that she is not yet in perfect possession of this capacity. In everyday speech, we register this point by speaking of "degrees of mastery" of a given capacity.

## 4. Skepticism and Philosophy

The capacity conception understands knowledge in a manner that dissolves skeptical doubt by showing that the very intelligibility of such doubt depends on the idea of a capacity for knowledge, which it seeks to deny at the same time. To finally bring to light the upshot of this response to the skeptic's doubt, we want to confront our conception with a final worry. The worry comes in the form of an objection that purports to grant that knowledge is an act of a rational and fallible capacity for knowledge but that seeks to maintain that this understanding of the nature of knowledge does not touch the skeptic's position. The objection is that the capacity account of knowledge can make sense of knowledge only by presupposing something that it cannot demonstrate is true. The presupposition is that precisely those circumstances on which the perfect actualization of a rational and fallible capacity for knowledge depends do sometimes obtain. Yet this presupposition, the objection runs, cannot be borne out. The capacity conception cannot rule out the possibility that such circumstances *never* obtain.

Let us consider this objection in more detail. The objection purports to grant that a subject can understand herself to be in possession of a rational capacity for knowledge while nevertheless taking herself to have always been prevented from perfectly exercising it. But under what conditions is such a self-understanding possible? Such a self-understanding is possible only if it is possible for one to understand oneself to possess a rational capacity for knowledge even though one has never exercised it (i.e., known something) even a single time in one's life. Now let us ask ourselves how someone could come to have such a self-understanding. Various possibilities come to mind. One might have been converted by a traveling preacher going from town to town convincing people that they possessed a rational capacity for knowledge. We might spin out this story further by supposing that this preacher inexplicably managed to convert everyone in the world and that they thenceforth understood themselves to possess rational capacities for knowledge. Or we might suppose that every human being, at some particular point in her natural development, is struck by the spontaneous intuition that she possesses a rational capacity for knowledge. Or it might be the result of a religious revelation, etc. We need not speculate any further. For what is crucial is that there is one particular explanation of this fact we specifically cannot give under the present presupposition. We cannot explain someone's understanding of herself as being in possession of a rational capacity for knowledge by representing her as exercising this capacity. For that is precisely what, on the possibility we are mooting, this subject is supposed to always be hindered from doing.

Let us contrast this case with one in which someone understands herself to possess a rational capacity for knowledge (e.g., perceptual knowledge), where we can explain this self-understanding by representing her as perfectly exercising the very capacity for knowledge she is self-ascribing. Such a subject would genuinely know that she possesses a rational capacity for knowledge. And it is absurd for someone who knows that she possesses a rational capacity for knowledge to entertain a skeptical doubt about that fact. She wouldn't be able to intelligibly formulate such a doubt. Moreover, it would be impossible for her to entertain the skeptical doubt we raised above, according to which one cannot rule out that the circumstances on which one's capacity for perceptual knowledge depend might never obtain and, hence, one cannot rule out that one might never have perceptual knowledge. For a subject who knows that she is in possession of a rational capacity for perceptual knowledge can rule out this possibility precisely through the kind of self-knowledge she has. Her knowledge that she is in possession of a rational capacity for perceptual knowledge rules it out that these circumstances might never obtain, for if they never did obtain, she would not have the kind of self-knowledge she has.

Yet it might still appear that this response to the skeptic fails to dissolve the skeptic's doubt. It only shows that the skeptic has to formulate her doubt more precisely. A more precise formulation would be that the capacity account of knowledge leaves open the following possibility. We can imagine a subject who doesn't know that she possesses a rational capacity for knowledge but who nevertheless hypothetically assumes that she does. Such a subject would not be able to rule out the possibility that she is always hindered from perfectly exercising the capacity she hypothetically supposes herself to possess. For such a subject, this situation would not be absurd, it would be quite conceivable. That is precisely right. And that is just how things have to stand if knowledge is an act of a rational capacity for knowledge. For if it is, that means that the only way to rule out the possibility this objection aims to raise is to perfectly exercise precisely the capacity that one is wondering might be constantly hindered from being perfectly exercised. To know that what one is presently doing is exercising a rational capacity for knowledge—and thus to know that it is false to believe that one is always hindered from exercising such a capacity—is not knowledge that one can have without precisely exercising the capacity in question. To demand that a subject must know that she is not hindered (either here and now or in principle) in exercising her rational capacity for knowledge independently of engaging in such an exercise is to fail to think through the thought that one is purporting to admit: namely, that knowledge is the act of a rational capacity for knowledge. One is not demanding something of such a subject that she is unable to fulfill. No, one is making a demand that one can only make if one denies that knowledge consists in the perfect exercise of a rational capacity for knowledge.

So what answer do we give to the skeptic? The answer is of the sort that Stanley Cavell formulates at one point as follows: "A formidable criticism of skepticism—as of any philosophy—will have to discover and alter its understanding of itself."[45] The debate with the skeptic cannot, on Cavell's view, merely have the aim of setting aside skeptical doubt. One must rather make skeptical doubt intelligible in a way that makes it clear that such doubt is not merely an error, a mistake, but also contains a "truth"—yet a "truth" that the skeptic herself does not properly understand. Our response to the skeptic is of this sort. It shows that the skeptic's doubt contains a genuine insight that we might describe as follows. The skeptic's insight is that grounds for belief that guarantee truth are not available for the subject independently of the truth of one's belief. She takes this insight to be an insight into a limitation on what we can do. She expresses this insight by saying that

[45] Cavell, *The Claim of Reason*, 38.

the best possible ground one can adduce in support of one's belief is one that cannot guarantee its truth. By contrast, if we realize that the concept of knowledge is the concept of a rational capacity, then we can reformulate what is correct in the skeptic's insight as follows: an individual act of knowing is dependent on a capacity that the knowing subject cannot guarantee she possesses except through an act that is (and must be) dependent on the very same capacity.

But this claim no longer has skeptical import. For if the concept of knowledge is the concept of a rational capacity, then this impossibility does not have the character of a limitation—it does not draw a limit between things we can do and those we cannot do. To point to this impossibility is a way of articulating what it means that knowledge is a rational capacity. That one cannot ensure one's possession of a rational capacity for knowledge except through an act that already depends on one's possession of it does not mean that there is something here that one can only wish for but not actually achieve. If the concept of knowledge is the concept of a rational capacity, then one cannot conceive of this way of ensuring one's possession of a capacity for knowledge as a limitation without thereby denying the very idea of the capacity the possession of which one wants to assure oneself. Hence, one cannot object that the capacity account fails to demonstrate what epistemology has sought since Descartes to show—namely, that we do actually have knowledge. One cannot object that the capacity account merely provides a conditional understanding of how knowledge would be possible if we were to have the requisite capacity for it.[46] The capacity account doesn't just leave it an open question whether we actually do have a capacity for knowledge. Indeed, it gives a certain answer to that question. For by showing what knowledge is, the capacity account shows what it means to answer this question. If knowledge is an act of a rational capacity for knowledge, then the question whether someone (e.g., oneself) possesses such a capacity can be, and can only be, answered by

---

[46] This objection can be found in Menke, "Die Dialektik der Ästhetik: Der neue Streit zwischen Kunst und Philosophie." The insuperable limitation of philosophy, on Menke's view, is that it cannot demonstrate the actual presence of the capacity it describes.

one's actually exercising that capacity. If knowledge is an act of a rational capacity, then it is nonsensical to demand that an answer to the question of whether someone possesses a capacity for knowledge should be available independently of any exercise of that capacity.

It is for this reason that Cavell is right to say that skeptical doubt is a form of "denial."[47] That of which we seek knowledge in epistemology—namely, our own capacity for knowledge—is something to which we stand in a quite peculiar cognitive relation. It is something of which we can fail to have knowledge only in a particular way: by denying our knowledge of it.

This description of the skeptic, as someone who denies something that she knows, presupposes that we have, for our own part, explicitly recognized what she denies. We have recognized our own capacity for knowledge; we have self-knowledge of it. How was this possible? How did we manage to recognize this?

Let's look back on the course our argument has taken. We recognized our own capacity for knowledge by questioning the skeptic's denial up to the point of asking how the beliefs that the skeptic must presuppose in order to so much as formulate her doubt are themselves possible. We thereby gained explicit knowledge of the fact that knowledge is an act of a rational capacity for knowledge by recognizing that it is impossible consistently to deny that this is the case. By thus driving the skeptic back to the point of self-refutation, we recognized that the concept of a rational capacity for knowledge is an indispensably necessary concept of all thought. This suggests that skepticism is not some avoidable epistemological confusion but rather an ineluctable stage in the course of epistemology. For it is only by means of the skeptic's denial of the concept of a rational capacity for knowledge that we were able to recognize the latter as a necessary concept of our self-understanding and to thereby make our ever-present understanding of knowledge as an act of a capacity for knowledge into the content of philosophical knowledge.

---

[47] See Cavell, *The Claim of Reason,* 154. See also Cavell, "Aesthetic Problems of Modern Philosophy," 96; Cavell, "Must We Mean What We Say?," 21. This is also how I understand Wittgenstein's interpretation of the skeptical problematic. I develop this reading in Kern, "Understanding Scepticism: Wittgenstein's Paradoxical Reinterpretation of Sceptical Doubt."

One can, of course, be in possession of a rational capacity for knowledge without knowing that the concept of a rational capacity for knowledge is a necessary concept of all thought. One can only recognize the necessity of this concept by confronting and engaging with attempts to deny it. Skepticism thus appears as an unavoidable form of philosophical reflection. Without the skeptic we would not develop a philosophical understanding of the kind of activity we engage in when we form beliefs about how things are in the world.

At the beginning of our inquiry, we thought it possible to understand ourselves as subjects who can form beliefs about how things are in the world while leaving it open whether any of our beliefs could ever amount to knowledge. We then came to realize that understanding of ourselves as subjects who have beliefs about how things are in the world already involves the exercise of a capacity for knowledge that one cannot have without exercising it. Hence, if nothing hinders us from perfectly exercising our rational capacity for knowledge, then to understand ourselves as subjects who can acquire knowledge about how things are in the world is actually to know that we are such subjects. Moreover, if nothing hinders us from perfectly actualizing our capacity for knowledge, we can even realize this kind of self-knowledge—a form of self-knowledge that we actualize in everything we think and do—in its most articulate form. We can realize it as philosophical knowledge.

BIBLIOGRAPHY

INDEX

# Bibliography

Almeder, Robert. "On Seeing the Truth: A Reply." *Philosophical Quarterly* 26 (1976): 163–165.

———. "Truth and Evidence." *Philosophical Quarterly* 24 (1974): 365–368.

Alston, William. "Concepts of Epistemic Justification." *Monist* 68, no. 1 (1985): 57–89.

Annas, Julia, and Jonathan Barnes, eds. *The Modes of Skepticism: Ancient Texts and Modern Interpretations.* Cambridge: Cambridge University Press, 1985.

Anscombe, G. E. M. "Causality and Determination." In *Metaphysics and the Philosophy of Mind,* 133–137. Oxford: Blackwell, 1981.

———. "The Causation of Action." In *Knowledge and Mind: Philosophical Essays,* ed. C. Ginet, 174–190. New York: Oxford University Press, 1983.

———. *Intention.* Cambridge, MA: Harvard University Press, 2000.

———. "The Intentionality of Sensation: A Grammatical Feature." In *Metaphysics and the Philosophy of Mind,* 3–20. Oxford: Blackwell, 1981.

———. "Memory, 'Experience,' and Causation." In *Metaphysics and the Philosophy of Mind,* 120–130. Oxford: Blackwell, 1981.

———. "Thought and Action in Aristotle: What Is Practical Truth?" In *From Parmenides to Wittgenstein: Collected Philosophical Papers,* 1:66–77. Oxford: Blackwell, 1981.

Aristotle. *Categories.* In *The Complete Works of Aristotle: The Revised Oxford Translation,* ed. J. Barnes. Princeton: Princeton University Press, 1984.

———. *Metaphysics.* In *The Complete Works of Aristotle: The Revised Oxford Translation,* ed. J. Barnes. Princeton: Princeton University Press, 1984.

———. *Nicomachean Ethics.* In *The Complete Works of Aristotle: The Revised Oxford Translation,* ed. J. Barnes. Princeton: Princeton University Press, 1984.

---

Audi, Robert. *Epistemology: A Contemporary Introduction to the Theory of Knowledge*. London: Routledge, 1998.

Austin, John L. "Other Minds." In *Philosophical Papers*, 76–116. Oxford: Oxford University Press, 1979.

———. *Sense and Sensibilia*. Oxford: Oxford University Press, 1962.

Ayer, A. J. *The Foundations of Empirical Knowledge*. London: Macmillan, 1964.

Ayers, Michael. *The Refutation of Determinism: An Essay in Philosophical Logic*. London: Methuen, 1968.

Bakhurst, David. *The Formation of Reason*. Oxford: Wiley-Blackwell, 2011.

———. "Freedom and Nature in *The Formation of Reason*." *Mind, Culture and Activity* 19, no. 2 (2012): 172–189.

Beckermann, Ansgar. "Wissen und wahre Meinung." In *Das weite Spektrum der analytischen Philosophie: Festschrift für Franz von Kutschera*, ed. W. Lenzen, 24–43. Berlin: de Gruyter 1997.

Beere, Jonathan. *Doing and Being: An Interpretation of Aristotle's* Metaphysics *Theta*. Oxford: Oxford University Press, 2009.

Blackburn, Simon. "Knowledge, Truth and Reliability." *Proceedings of the British Academy* 70 (1984): 167–187.

BonJour, Laurence. "Can Empirical Knowledge Have a Foundation?" In *Epistemology: An Anthology*, ed. E. Sosa and J. Kim, 261–273. Oxford: Blackwell, 2000.

———. "The Dialectic of Foundationalism and Coherentism." In *The Blackwell Guide to Epistemology*, ed. J. Greco and E. Sosa, 117–142. Oxford: Blackwell, 1999

———. *The Structure of Empirical Knowledge*. Cambridge, MA: Harvard University Press, 1985.

Boyle, Matthew. "Active Belief." *Canadian Journal of Philosophy*, supp. 35 (2009): 119–147.

———. "Die Spontaneität des Verstandes bei Kant und einigen Neokantianern." *Deutsche Zeitschrift für Philosophie* 63, no. 4 (2015): 705–726.

———. "'Making Up Your Mind' and the Activity of Reason." *Philosophers' Imprint* 11 (2011): 1–24.

Brandom, Robert B. "Knowledge and the Social Articulation of the Space of Reasons." *Philosophy and Phenomenological Research* 55, no. 4 (1995): 895–908.

———. *Making It Explicit: Reasoning, Representing and Discursive Commitment*. Cambridge, MA: Harvard University Press, 1994.

Brueckner, Anthony. "Brains in a Vat." *Journal of Philosophy* 83 (1986): 148–167.

———. "The Omniscient Interpreter Rides Again." *Analysis* 51 (1991): 199–204.

———. "Semantic Answers to Skepticism." *Pacific Philosophical Quarterly* 73 (1992): 200–19.

Burge, Tyler. "Cartesian Error and the Objectivity of Perception." In *Subject, Thought, and Context*, ed. J. McDowell and P. Pettit, 117–136. Oxford: Oxford University Press, 1986.

———. "Content Preservation." *Philosophical Review* 102, no. 4 (1993): 457–488.

———. "Interlocution, Perception and Memory." *Philosophical Studies* 86 (1997): 21–74.

———. "Other Bodies." In *Thought and Object: Essays on Intentionality,* ed. A. Woodfield, 97–119. Oxford: Oxford University Press, 1982.

Burnyeat, Myles. "Aristotle on Learning to Be Good." In *Essays on Aristotle's Ethics,* ed. A. Oksenberg Rorty, 69–92. Berkeley: University of California Press, 1980.

———. "Can the Skeptic Live His Skepticism?" In *The Skeptical Tradition,* ed. M. Burnyeat, 117–148. Berkeley: University of California Press, 1983.

———. *Notes on Eta and Theta of Aristotle's Metaphysics.* Oxford: Oxford University Press, 1984.

Cavell, Stanley. "Aesthetic Problems of Modern Philosophy." In *Must We Mean What We Say?,* 73–96. Cambridge: Cambridge University Press, 1976.

———. *The Claim of Reason: Wittgenstein, Skepticism, Morality, and Tragedy.* Oxford: Oxford University Press, 1979.

———. "Must We Mean What We Say?" In *Must We Mean What We Say?,* 1–43. Cambridge: Cambridge University Press, 1976.

Child, William. *Causality, Interpretation and the Mind.* Oxford: Oxford University Press, 1996.

———. "Vision and Experience: The Causal Theory and the Disjunctive Conception." *Philosophical Quarterly* 42 (1992): 297–316.

Chisholm, Roderick M. "The Myth of the Given." In *Epistemology: An Anthology,* ed. J. Kim, E. Sosa, 107–119. Oxford: Blackwell, 2000.

———. *Theory of Knowledge.* Englewood Cliffs, NJ: Prentice Hall, 1977.

Coady, C. A. J. *Testimony. A Philosophical Study.* Oxford: Oxford University Press, 1992.

Cohen, Stewart. "Contextualism and Skepticism." *Philosophical Issues* 10 (2000): 94–107.

———. "How to Be a Fallibilist." *Philosophical Perspectives* 2 (1988): 92–123.

———. "Knowledge, Context, and Social Standards." *Synthese* 73 (1987): 3–26.

Conant, James. "Varieties of Skepticism." In *Wittgenstein and Scepticism,* ed. D. McManus, 97–136. London: Routledge, 2004.

Craig, Edward. "Davidson and the Skeptic: The Thumbnail Version." *Analysis* 50 (1990): 213–214.

Crane, Tim. "The Nonconceptual Content of Experience." In *The Contents of Experience: Essays on Perception,* ed. T. Crane, 136–157. Cambridge: Cambridge University Press, 1992.

Dancy, Jonathan. "Arguments from Illusion." *Philosophical Quarterly* 45, no. 181 (1995): 421–138.

Davidson, Donald. "A Coherence Theory of Truth and Knowledge." In *Subjective, Intersubjective, Objective: Philosophical Essays,* 137–153. Oxford: Oxford University Press, 2001.

———. "Actions, Reasons and Causes." In *Essays on Actions and Events,* 3–19. Oxford: Oxford University Press, 2001.

———. "The Myth of the Subjective." In *Subjective, Intersubjective, Objective: Philosophical Essays,* 39–52. Oxford: Oxford University Press, 2001.

DeRose, Keith. "Solving the Skeptical Problem." In *Skepticism: A Contemporary Reader,* ed. K. DeRose and T. Warfield, 183–219. Oxford: Oxford University Press, 1999.

Descartes, René. *Meditations on First Philosophy.* In *The Philosophical Writings of Descartes,* ed. J. Cottingham, D. Murdoch, and R. Stoothoff. Cambridge: Cambridge University Press, 1984. Citations refer to volume and page number of the French edition: *Oeuvres de Descartes,* ed. C. Adam and P. Tannery, 12 vols. Rev. ed. Paris: J. Vrin, 1964–1974. [=AT]

Deutscher Verband für das Skilehrwesen e.V., ed. *Ski-Lehrplan,* vol. 1. Munich: BLV, 1994.

Diogenes Laertius. *Lives of the Philosophers,* trans. and ed. R. D. Hicks. London: Loeb Classical Library, 1925.

Dretske, Fred. "Conclusive Reasons." *Australasian Journal of Philosophy* 49, no. 1 (1971): 1–22.

———. "Epistemic Operators." *Journal of Philosophy* 67, no. 24 (1970): 1007–1023.

———. *Seeing and Knowing.* Chicago: University of Chicago Press, 1969.

Dreyfus, Hubert. "Overcoming the Myth of the Mental: How Philosophers Can Profit from the Phenomenology of Everyday Expertise." *Proceedings and Addresses of the American Philosophical Association* 79, no. 2 (2005): 47–65.

———. "The Return of the Myth of the Mental." *Inquiry* 50, no. 4 (2007): 352–365.

Evans, Gareth. *The Varieties of Reference.* Oxford: Oxford University Press, 1982.

Feldman, Richard, and Earl Conee. "Evidentialism." *Philosophical Studies* 48, no. 1 (1985): 15–34.

Firth, Roderick. "Are Epistemic Concepts Reducible to Ethical Concepts?" In *Values and Morals: Essays in Honor of William Frankena, Charles Stevenson, and Richard Brandt,* ed. A. Goldman and J. Kim, 215–229. Dordrecht: Kluwer, 1978.

Fogelin, Robert. *Pyrrhonian Reflections on Knowledge and Justification.* Oxford: Oxford University Press, 1994.

Foot, Philippa. "Morality as a System of Hypothetical Imperatives." *Philosophical Review* 81, no. 3 (1972): 305–316.

Freeland, Cynthia. "Aristotle on Possibilities and Capacities." *Ancient Philosophy* 6 (1986): 69–89.

Gettier, Edmund. "Is Justified True Belief Knowledge?" *Analysis* 23 (1963): 121–23.

Glendinning, Simon. *On Being with Others: Heidegger, Derrida, Wittgenstein.* London: Routledge, 1998.

Glüer, Kathrin. "Bedeutung zwischen Norm und Naturgesetz." *Deutsche Zeitschrift für Philosophie* 48, no. 3 (2000): 449–468.

Goldman, Alvin. "Discrimination and Perceptual Knowledge." *Journal of Philosophy* 73, no. 20 (1976): 771–791.

Goodman, Nelson. "The Passing of the Possible." In *Fact, Fiction and Forecast,* 4th ed., 31–58. Cambridge, MA: Harvard University Press, 1983.

———. "The Problem of Counterfactual Conditionals." In *Fact, Fiction and Forecast,* 4th ed., 3–27. Cambridge, MA: Harvard University Press, 1983.

Greco, John. *Achieving Knowledge.* Cambridge: Cambridge University Press 2010.

Grice, H. P. "The Causal Theory of Perception." *Aristotelian Society,* supp. 35 (1961): 121–152.

Haag, Johannes. "Faculties in Kant and German Idealism." In *Faculties: A History,* ed. D. Perler, 198–246. Oxford: Oxford University Press, 2015.

Haddock, Adrian. "Knowledge and Action." In D. Pritchard, A. Millar, and A. Haddock, *The Nature and Value of Knowledge: Three Investigations,*191–260. Oxford: Oxford University Press, 2010.

Hampshire, Stuart. *Freedom of the Individual.* Princeton: Princeton University Press, 1975.

Haugeland, John. *Having Thought: Essays in the Metaphysics of Mind.* Cambridge, MA: Harvard University Press, 1998.

Hegel, G. W. F. *Enzyklopädie der philosophischen Wissenschaften im Grundrisse (1830),* ed. F. Nicolin and O. Pöggeler. Hamburg: Meiner, 1991.

———. "Verhältnis des Skeptizismus zur Philosophie, Darstellung seiner verschiedenen Modifikationen, und Vergleichung des neuesten mit dem alten." In *Jenaer Kritische Schriften II,* ed. H. Brockard and H. Buchner, 34–89. Hamburg: Meiner, 1983.

Heidegger, Martin. *Aristoteles: Metaphysik IX, 1–3: Vom Wesen und Wirklichkeit der Kraft.* Frankfurt am Main: Klostermann, 1990.

———. *Die Grundbegriffe der Metaphysik: Welt, Endlichkeit, Einsamkeit.* Frankfurt am Main: Klostermann,1992 (1983).

Heil, John. "Doxastic Agency." *Philosophical Studies* 43, no. 3 (1983): 355–364.

Hinton, J. M. *Experiences.* Oxford: Oxford University Press, 1973.

———. "Visual Experiences." *Mind* 76 (1976): 217–227.

Hume, David. *An Enquiry concerning Human Understanding.* In *Enquiries concerning Human Understanding and concerning the Principles of Morals,* rev. P. H. Nidditch, ed. L. A. Selby-Bigge. Oxford: Oxford University Press, 1975.

———. *A Treatise of Human Nature,* rev. P. H. Nidditch, ed. L. A. Selby-Bigge. Oxford: Oxford University Press, 1978.

Hyman, John. "The Evidence of Our Senses." In *Strawson and Kant,* ed. H.-J. Glock, 235–254. Oxford: Oxford University Press, 2003.

———. "Vision and Power." *Journal of Philosophy* 91, no. 5 (1994): 236–256.

———. "Vision, Causation and Occlusion." *Philosophical Quarterly* 43, no. 171 (1993): 210–214.

Irwin, Terence. "Reason and Responsibility in Aristotle." In *Essays on Aristotle's Ethics,* ed. A. Oksenberg Rorty, 117–155. Berkeley: University of California Press, 1980.

Jansen, Ludger. *Tun und Können: Ein systematischer Kommentar zu Aristoteles' Theorie der Vermögen im neunten Buch der "Metaphysik."* Frankfurt am Main: Hänsel-Hohenhausen, 2002.

Kant, Immanuel. *Grundlegung zur Metaphysik der Sitten* [Groundwork of the Metaphysics of Morals]. In *Gesammelte Schriften,* vol. 4, ed. Königlich Preussische Akademie der Wissenschaften. Berlin: de Gruyter, 1911.

——. *Kritik der reinen Vernunft* [Critique of Pure Reason]. In *Gesammelte Schriften,* vol. 4, Berlin: de Gruyter, 1911.

——. *Kritik der Urteilskraft* [Power of Judgment]. In *Gesammelte Schriften,* vol. 5. Berlin: de Gruyter, 1913.

Kenny, Anthony. "The Argument from Illusion in Aristotle's Metaphysics." *Mind* 76 (1967): 184–297.

——. *The Metaphysics of Mind.* Oxford: Oxford University Press, 1989.

——. *Will, Freedom and Power.* Oxford: Blackwell, 1975.

Kern, Andrea. "Einsicht ohne Täuschung: McDowells hermeneutische Konzeption von Erkenntnis." *Deutsche Zeitschrift für Philosophie* 48, no. 5 (2000): 915–937.

———. "Knowledge as a Fallible Capacity." In *Conceptions of Knowledge,* ed. S. Tolksdorf, 215–242. Berlin: de Gruyter, 2011.

——. "Philosophie und Skepsis: Hume, Kant, Cavell." *Deutsche Zeitschrift für Philosophie* 48, no. 1 (2000): 17–35.

——. "Spontaneity and Receptivity in Kant's Theory of Knowledge." *Philosophical Topics: Analytical Kantianism* 34, nos. 1–2 (2006): 145–162.

——. "Understanding Scepticism: Wittgenstein's Paradoxical Reinterpretation of Sceptical Doubt." In *Wittgenstein and Scepticism,* ed. D. McManus, 200–217. London: Routledge, 2004.

——. "Why Do Our Reasons Come to an End?" In *Varieties of Skepticism: Essays after Kant, Wittgenstein, and Cavell,* ed. J. Conant and A. Kern, 83–103. Berlin: de Gruyter, 2014.

——. "Wissen vom Standpunkte eines Menschen." In *Philosophie der Dekonstruktion: Zum Verhältnis von Normativität und Praxis,* ed. A. Kern and C. Menke, 216–239. Frankfurt am Main: Suhrkamp, 2002.

Kornblith, Hilary. "Justified Belief and Epistemically Responsible Action." *Philosophical Review* 92, no. 1 (1983): 33–48.

Künne, Wolfgang. "Sehen: Eine sprachanalytische Betrachtung." *Logos* 2 (1995): 103–121.

Lear, Jonathan. *Aristotle: The Desire to Understand.* Cambridge: Cambridge University Press, 1988.

Lewis, David. "Elusive Knowledge." In *Skepticism: A Contemporary Reader,* ed. K. DeRose and T. Warfield, 220–239. Oxford: Oxford University Press, 1999.

Liske, Michael-Thomas. "Inwieweit sind Vermögen intrinsische, dispositionelle Eigenschaften?" In *Metaphysik: Die Substanzbücher,* ed. C. Rapp, 253–287. Berlin: Akademie Verlag, 1996.

Luntley, Michael. "Conceptual Development and the Paradox of Learning." *Journal of Philosophy of Education* 42, no. 1 (2008): 1–14.

———. "Training and Learning." *Educational Philosophy and Theory* 40, no. 5 (2008): 695–711.

Mackie, John M. *Truth, Probability and Paradox.* Oxford: Oxford University Press, 1973.

Makin, Stephen. "Aristotle on Modality." *Proceedings of the Aristotelian Society,* supp. 74 (2000): 143–161.

———. "Commentary." In Aristotle, *Metaphysics: Book Theta,* trans. Stephen Makin. Oxford: Clarendon Press, 2006.

Martin, C. B. "Dispositions and Conditionals." *Philosophical Quarterly* 44 (1994): 1–8.

Martin, M. G. F. "Perception, Concepts and Memory." *Philosophical Review* 101, no. 4 (1992): 745–763.

McDowell, John. "Aesthetic Value, Objectivity, and the Fabric of the World." In *Mind, Value, and Reality,* 112–130. Cambridge, MA: Harvard University Press, 1998.

———. "De Re Senses." In *Meaning, Knowledge and Reality,* 214–227. Cambridge, MA: Harvard University Press, 1998.

———. "The Disjunctive Conception of Experience as Material for a Transcendental Argument." In *Disjunctivism: Perception, Action, Knowledge,* ed. A. Haddock and F. Macpherson, 376–389. Oxford: Oxford University Press, 2008.

———. "Functionalism and Anomalous Monism." In *Mind, Value, and Reality,* 325–340. Cambridge, MA: Harvard University Press, 1998.

———. "Hegel's Idealism as Radicalization of Kant." In *Having the World in View,* 69–89. Cambridge, MA: Harvard University Press, 2009.

———. "Intentionality as a Relation." In *Having the World in View,* 44–65. Cambridge, MA: Harvard University Press, 2009.

———. "Knowledge and the Internal." In *Meaning, Knowledge and Reality,* 395–413. Cambridge, MA: Harvard University Press, 1998.

———. "Knowledge by Hearsay." In *Meaning, Knowledge, and Reality,* 414–443. Cambridge, MA: Harvard University Press, 1998.

———. "The Logical Form of an Intuition." In *Having the World in View,* 23–43. Cambridge, MA: Harvard University Press, 2009.

———. *Mind and World.* Cambridge MA: Harvard University Press, 1996.

———. *Perception as a Capacity for Knowledge.* Milwaukee: Marquette University Press, 2011.

——. "The Role of Eudaimonia in Aristotle's Ethics." In *Mind, Value, and Reality*, 3–22. Cambridge, MA: Harvard University Press, 1998.

——. "Sellars on Perceptual Experience." In *Having the World in View*, 2–22. Cambridge, MA: Harvard University Press, 2009.

——. "Virtue and Reason." In *Mind, Value and Reality*, 50–73. Cambridge, MA: Harvard University Press 1998.

——. "What Myth?" In *The Engaged Intellect: Philosophical Essays*. Cambridge, MA: Harvard University Press, 2009.

McGinn, Colin. "The Concept of Knowledge." In *Knowledge and Reality*, 7–35. Oxford: Oxford University Press, 1999.

Menke, Christoph. "Die Dialektik der Ästhetik: Der neue Streit zwischen Kunst und Philosophie." In *Ästhetik Erfahrung: Interventionen* 13, ed. J. Huber, 21–39. Vienna: Springer, 2004.

Millar, Alan. "Knowledge and Recognition." In D. Pritchard, A. Millar, and A. Haddock, *The Nature and Value of Knowledge: Three Investigations*, 91–188. Oxford: Oxford University Press, 2010.

——. "What Is It That Cognitive Abilities Are Abilities to Do?" *Acta Analytica* 24 (2009): 223–236.

Moline, Jon. "Provided Nothing External Interferes." *Mind* 84, no. 334 (1975): 244–254.

Moran, Richard. *Authority and Estrangement: An Essay of Self-Knowledge*. Princeton: Princeton University Press, 2001.

Nagel, Thomas. *The View from Nowhere*. Oxford: Oxford University Press, 1986.

Owens, David. *Reason without Freedom: The Problem of Epistemic Normativity*. London: Routledge, 2000.

Peacocke, Christopher. "Nonconceptual Content Defended." *Philosophy and Phenomenological Research* 58 (1998): 381–388.

——. *A Study of Concepts*. Cambridge, MA: MIT Press, 1992.

——. *Thoughts: An Essay on Content*. Oxford: Blackwell, 1986.

Pears, D. F. "The Causal Theory of Perception." *Synthese* 33 (1976): 41–74.

Perler, Dominik, ed. *Faculties: A History*. Oxford: Oxford University Press, 2015.

Pippin, Robert. "Kant on the Spontaneity of Mind." In *Idealism as Modernism: Hegelian Variations*, 29–55. Cambridge: Cambridge University Press, 1997.

Plato. *Theaetetus*. In *Complete Works*, ed. J. M. Cooper. Indianapolis: Hackett, 1997.

Pollock, John L. "Epistemic Norms." In *Contemporary Theories of Knowledge*, chap. 5. Lanham: Rowman and Littlefield, 1986.

Price, Henry H. *Belief: The Gifford Lectures*. London: Allen and Unwin, 1969.

Pritchard, Duncan. "Virtue Epistemology and Epistemic Luck." *Metaphilosophy* 34 (2003): 106–130.

Putnam, Hilary. *Reason, Truth, and History*. Cambridge: Cambridge University Press, 1981.

———. "Skepticism." In *Philosophie in synthetischer Absicht,* ed. M. Stamm, 239–258. Stuttgart: Klett-Cotta, 1998.

Quine, Willard V. O. "Epistemology Naturalized." In *Ontological Relativity and Other Essays,* 69–90. New York: Columbia University Press, 1969.

Rapp, Christoph. "Freiwilligkeit, Entscheidung, Verantwortlichkeit." In *Nikomachische Ethik,* ed. O. Höffe, 106–134. Berlin: Akademie Verlag, 1996.

Rawls, John. "Two Concepts of Rules." In *Collected Papers,* 20–46. Cambridge, MA: Harvard University Press, 1999.

Rorty, Richard. *Philosophy and the Mirror of Nature.* Princeton: Princeton University Press, 1979.

Ryle, Gilbert. *The Concept of Mind.* Chicago: University of Chicago Press, 1949.

Rödl, Sebastian. *Categories of the Temporal: An Inquiry into the Forms of the Finite Intellect.* Cambridge, MA: Harvard University Press, 2012.

———. "Interne Normen." In *Institutionen und Regelfolgen,* ed. U. Baltzer and G. Schönrich, 177–192. Paderborn: Mentis, 2002.

———. "Natur und Norm." *Deutsche Zeitschrift für Philosophie* 51, no. 1 (2003): 99–114.

———. *Self-Consciousness.* Cambridge, MA: Harvard University Press, 2007.

Schiffer, Stephen. "Contextualist Solutions to Scepticism." *Proceedings of the Aristotelian Society* 3 (1996): 317–333.

Schildknecht, Christiane. "Anschauungen ohne Begriffe? Zur Nichtbegrifflichkeitsthese von Erfahrung." *Deutsche Zeitschrift für Philosophie* 51, no. 3 (2003): 459–475.

———. *Aspekte des Nichtpropositionalen.* Bonn: Bouvier, 1999.

Schneider, Hans Julius. "Konstitutive Regeln und Normativität." *Deutsche Zeitschrift für Philosophie* 51, no. 1 (2003): 81–98.

Schnädelbach, Herbert. "Rationalität und Normativität." In *Zur Rehabilitierung des animal rationale: Vorträge und Abhandlungen,* 79–103. Frankfurt am Main: Suhrkamp, 1992.

Searle, John. *The Construction of Social Reality.* New York: Free Press, 1995.

———. *Speech Acts: An Essay in the Philosophy of Language.* Cambridge: Cambridge University Press, 1969.

Sellars, Wilfrid. "Counterfactuals, Dispositions and the Causal Modalities." In *Minnesota Studies in the Philosophy of Science,* ed. H. Feigl, M. Scriven, and G. Maxwell. Minneapolis: University of Minnesota Press, 1958.

———. *Empiricism and the Philosophy of Mind.* Cambridge, MA.: Harvard University Press, 1997.

Sextus Empiricus. *Outlines of Pyrrhonism,* trans. G. Bury. Cambridge, MA: Harvard University Press, 1976.

Shoemaker, Sydney. "Self-Intimation and Second Order Belief." *Erkenntnis* 71, no. 1 (2009): 35–51.

Shope, Robert K. *The Analysis of Knowing: A Decade of Research.* Princeton: Princeton University Press, 1983.

Snowdon, Paul. "The Objects of Perceptual Experience." *Proceedings of the Aristotelian Society,* supp. 64 (1990): 121–150.

———. "Perception, Vision and Causation." In *Perceptual Knowledge,* ed. J. Dancy, 192–208. Oxford: Oxford University Press, 1988.

Sosa, Ernest. *Knowing Full Well.* Princeton: Princeton University Press, 2011.

———. "Knowledge and Intellectual Virtue." *Monist* 68, no. 2 (1985): 226–245.

———. *A Virtue Epistemology: Apt Belief and Reflective Knowledge.* Oxford: Oxford University Press, 2007.

Stern, Robert. *Transcendental Arguments and Scepticism: Answering the Question of Justification.* Oxford: Oxford University Press, 2000.

Stickney, Jeff. "Training and Mastery of Techniques in Wittgenstein's Later Philosophy: A Response to Michael Luntley." *Educational Philosophy and Theory* 40, no. 5 (2008): 678–694.

Stine, Gail. "Skepticism, Relevant Alternatives, and Deductive Closure." *Philosophical Studies* 29 (1979): 249–261.

Stout, Rowland. *Things That Happen because They Should: A Teleological Approach to Action.* Oxford: Oxford University Press, 1996.

Strawson, Peter F. "Causation and Explanation." In *Essays on Davidson: Actions and Events,* ed. M. B. Hintikka and B. Vermazen, 115–135. Oxford: Oxford University Press, 1985.

———. "Causation in Perception." In *Freedom and Resentment and Other Essays,* 66–84. London: Methuen, 1974.

———. "Perception and Its Objects." In *Perception and Identity,* ed. G. F. Macdonald, 41–60. Ithaca, NY: Cornell University Press, 1979.

Stroud, Barry. "Kant and Scepticism." In *The Skeptical Tradition,* ed. M. Burnyeat, 413–434. (Berkeley: University of California Press, 1983.

———. "Kantian Argument, Conceptual Capacities, and Invulnerability." In *Understanding Human Knowledge,* 155–176. Oxford: Oxford University Press, 2000.

———. "Sense-Experience and the Grounding of Thought." In *Reading McDowell,* ed. N. Smith, 79–91. London: Routledge, 2002.

———. *The Significance of Philosophical Scepticism.* Oxford: Oxford University Press, 1984.

———. "Transcendental Arguments." In *Understanding Human Knowledge,* 71–82. Oxford: Oxford University Press, 2000.

———. "Understanding Human Knowledge in General." In *Knowledge and Skepticism,* ed. M. Clay and K. Lehrer, 31–50. Boulder, CO: Westview Press, 1989.

Thompson, Michael. *Life and Action: Elementary Structure of Practice and Practical Thought.* Cambridge, MA: Harvard University Press, 2008.

Tomasello, Michael. *The Cultural Origins of Human Cognition.* Cambridge, MA: Harvard University Press, 2000.

Tugendhat, Ernst. *Vorlesungen zur Einführung in die sprachanalytische Philosophie.* Frankfurt am Main: Suhrkamp, 1976.

Van Cleve, James. "Foundationalism, Epistemic Principles, and the Cartesian Circle." *Philosophical Review* 88 (1979): 55–91.

Vendler, Zeno. "Telling the Facts." In *Contemporary Perspectives in the Philosophy of Language,* ed. P. French, T. Uehling, and H. Wettstein, 220–232. Minneapolis: University of Minnesota Press, 1979.

Von Wright, Georg Henrik. "Laws of Nature." In *Truth, Knowledge and Modality,* 134–149. Oxford: Blackwell, 1984.

Wellmer, Albrecht. "Der Streit um die Wahrheit: Pragmatismus ohne regulative Ideen." In *Die Renaissance des Pragmatismus,* ed. M. Sandbothe, 253–269. Weilerswist: Velbrück, 2000.

Willaschek, Marcus. *Der mentale Zugang zur Welt: Realismus, Skeptizismus und Intentionalität.* Frankfurt am Main: Klostermann, 2003.

Williams, Bernard. "Deciding to Believe." In *Problems of the Self: Philosophical Papers, 1956–1972,* 136–151. Cambridge: Cambridge University Press, 1973.

——. *Descartes: The Project of Pure Inquiry.* Harmondsworth: Penguin, 1978.

Williams, Michael. "Epistemological Realism and the Basis of Scepticism." In *Scepticism,* ed. M. Williams, 416–439. Brookfield, VT: Dartmouth Publishing, 1993.

——. *Problems of Knowledge.* Oxford: Oxford University Press, 2001.

——. "Understanding Human Knowledge Philosophically." *Philosophy and Phenomenological Research* 56, no. 2 (1996): 359–378.

——. *Unnatural Doubts: Epistemological Realism and the Basis of Scepticism.* Oxford: Oxford University Press, 1992.

Williamson, Timothy. "Is Knowing a State of Mind?" *Mind* 104 (1995): 533–564.

——. *Knowledge and Its Limits.* Oxford: Oxford University Press, 2000.

Witt, Charlotte. *Ways of Being: Potentiality and Actuality in Aristotle's Metaphysics.* Ithaca, NY: Cornell University Press, 2003.

Wittgenstein, Ludwig. *The Blue and Brown Books.* Oxford: Blackwell, 1958.

——. *On Certainty.* Trans. G. E. M. Anscombe and D. Paul, ed. G. E. M. Anscombe and G. H. von Wright. Oxford: Blackwell, 1969.

——. *Philosophical Investigations.* 3rd ed., trans. G. E. M. Anscombe. Oxford: Blackwell, 2001.

——. *Remarks on Colour.* Trans. L. L. McAlister and M. Schättle, ed. G. E. M. Anscombe. Oxford: Blackwell, 1991.

——. *Remarks on the Foundations of Mathematics.* Trans. G. E. M. Anscombe, ed. G. E. M. Anscombe, R. Rhees, and G. H. von Wright. Oxford: Blackwell, 1978.

——. *Zettel.* Trans. G. E. M. Anscombe, ed. G. E. M. Anscombe and G. H. von Wright. Oxford: Blackwell, 1967.

Wolf, Ursula. *Möglichkeit und Notwendigkeit bei Aristoteles und heute.* Munich: Fink, 1979.

Wolff, Michael. *Das Körper-Seele-Problem: Kommentar zu Hegel, Enzyklopädie (1830), §389.* Frankfurt am Main: Klostermann, 1992.

Woolhouse, R. S. "Counterfactuals, Dispositions and Capacities." *Mind* 82, no. 328 (1973): 557–565.

Wright, Crispin. "(Anti-)Sceptics Simple and Subtle: G. E. Moore and John McDowell." *Philosophy and Phenomenological Research* 65, no. 2 (2002): 330–348.

———. "Facts and Certainty." *Proceedings of the British Academy* 71 (1985): 429–472.

———. "Scepticism and Dreaming: Imploding the Demon." *Mind* 100 (1991): 87–116.

Yourgau, Palle. "Knowledge and Relevant Alternatives." *Synthese* 55 (1983): 175–190.

Zagzebski, Linda. *Virtues of the Mind: An inquiry into the Nature of Virtue and the Ethical Foundation of Knowledge.* Cambridge: Cambridge University Press, 1996.

# Index

---

293